Knowledge Systems

for Business

Integrating Expert Systems & MIS

John P. Gallagher

PRENTICE HALL, *Englewood Cliffs, New Jersey 07632*

Library of Congress Cataloging-in-Publication Data

GALLAGHER, JOHN P. (date)
    Knowledge systems for business: integrating expert systems and
MIS / John P. Gallagher.
    p. cm.
      Includes index.
      ISBN 0-13-516551-2
      1. Management information systems. 2. Expert systems (Computer
science) I. Title.
T58.6.G336 1988
658.4'038—dc 19

The publisher offers discounts on this book when ordered in bulk quantities.
For more information, write:

> Special Sales/College Marketing
> Prentice-Hall, Inc.
> College Technical and Reference Division
> Englewood Cliffs, NJ 07632

Printed in the United States of America

10 9 8 7 6 5 4 3 2

ISBN   0-13-516551-2

Prentice-Hall International (UK) Limited, *London*
Prentice-Hall of Australia Pty. Limited, *Sydney*
Prentice-Hall Canada Inc., *Toronto*
Prentice-Hall Hispanoamericana, S.A., *Mexico*
Prentice-Hall of India Private Limited, *New Delhi*
Prentice-Hall of Japan, Inc., *Tokyo*
Simon & Schuster Asia Pte. Ltd., *Singapore*
Editora Prentice-Hall do Brasil, Ltda., *Rio de Janeiro*

To Robin

Contents

Preface   vii

1 Introduction   1

Using Information Technology to Gain a Strategic Competitive
   Advantage   6

2 Knowledge Systems Development Tools   15

Evolution from Techniques to Tools   17
Choosing Techniques and Tools for Knowledge Systems   19
The Nature and Impact of Available Tools   22
Separation of Knowledge and Reasoning   25
The Inference Process: Backward Chaining   29
Dealing with Uncertainty   33
The Inference Process: Forward Chaining   35
Frame-Based and Object-Oriented Systems   37

**3 Evaluating Knowledge Systems Development Tools
    As Mainstream Business Computing Systems**   41

Knowledge Systems and Mainstream Computing Hardware   44
Access to Data and Other Applications   47
Representing and Processing Information from Other Sources   50
The Support Environment for Applications Development   53

4 Some Sample Applications   57

A Load Control Advisor for the Small Electrical Utility Company   61
An Expert Data Analyst/Advisor for Consumer-Packaged-Goods
   Marketing   66
A Financial Statement Analysis Advisor   70

5 Knowledge Engineering: The Development of Intelligent Systems Applications   75

Traditional Structured Systems Development   77
Knowledge Engineering: Designing and Developing Expert
   Systems   78
The Holistic Approach to Systems Development   81
Representing the Structure of Knowledge   85
Automated Knowledge Acquisition: Rule-Induction Systems   89

6 A Review of Development Tools: M.1 from Teknowledge, Inc.   95

The Promotion Advisor Knowledge Bases   97
M.1 from Teknowledge, Inc.: An Overview   100
The Development Environment   101
Inferencing and Dealing with Uncertainty   104
Integration and Noninferential Processing   107
The Promotion Advisor in M.1   109
Summary   118

7 A Review of Development Tools: GURU from Micro Data Base Systems   119

Overview   121
The Development Environment   122
Inferencing and Dealing with Uncertainty   128
Integration and Noninferential Processing   130
The Promotion Advisor in GURU   133

8 A Review of Development Tools: The Expert System Environment from IBM   137

Overview   139
The Development Environment   140
Inferencing and Dealing with Uncertainty   144
Integration and Noninferential Processing   146
The Promotion Advisor in ESE   147

9 Forces Affecting the Future of Knowledge Systems in Business   153

The Need for Organizational Accommodation/Assimilation   157
The Need to Develop Supportive Technology   158
Uncertainty of the Application's Suitability for Knowledge Systems   159
Competitive Forces, the Acceptance of Risk, and the Future of
   Knowledge Systems   160

Appendix: Knowledge Bases for the Promotion Advisor Written in M.1, GURU, and Expert System Environment   163

Index   229

Preface

When the impact of knowledge systems on business practice is reduced to its simplest form, a relatively straightforward and simple phrase remains: *What is feasible has changed.*

There are many ways to marginally influence the efficiency, effectiveness, and profitability of any business unit. However, there are few opportunities to fundamentally alter the competitive structure or competitive scope within entire industries. In the past few years, information technology has increasingly brought about these types of changes. This history of impact, coupled with an impressive portfolio of success stories, has heightened management's interest in the strategic, competitive applications of information technology. Whenever what is feasible changes, significant business opportunities and problems follow. The theme of this book is the integration of knowledge systems, not only with existing information systems, but with the existing organization that influences, designs, supports, and applies them.

The origins of this work are easily traced. For the past five years, I have served as Director of Computing at the Fuqua School of Business, Duke University. In this capacity, my efforts have much in common with corporate organizations labeled variously as "Emerging Technologies" or "Strategic Information Systems" groups. That is, much of my time has been spent exploring new computing technologies and assessing their relevance for research, for the graduate curriculum in management education, and for executive education programs.

If there is one lesson I have learned through this experience, it is that in order for any computing technology to affect the practice of management, a constellation of factors must exist to create a receptive context. As an agent of change, technology is a catalyst. Technology stimulates change because of its interaction with multiple factors in a complex environment.

This book is an effort to define some of the characteristics of the technology of knowledge systems in terms of the environment of management computing. It attempts to create a broader perspective that incorporates the motivations of individual business units, the nature of their objectives, management's orientation toward computing, and the "installed base" of mainstream computing technology and professionals.

My involvement with artificial intelligence began with my doctoral studies at the University of California, Santa Barbara, in 1974. I was employed on a research project in the Computer Systems Laboratory to develop artificial intelligence applications for teaching mathematics problem solving skills with computers. That experience resulted in a strong vision of both the potential of this technology to support human intellectual activity, and the complexity of the problems inherent in its development.

In the past fifteen years, the technology has matured and come to be better understood by individuals outside of the closely connected world of academic research. Just a short time ago, the first knowledge systems development tools that were designed to be used by individuals unfamiliar with, and largely uninterested in, the technology's academic origins were commercially offered. Regardless of whatever significance might be attached to such an offering, it raised an important question: *Could the developer/user of a knowledge systems development tool be sufficiently isolated from the complexities of the technology to be productive in the creation of applications that exploit its unique capabilities?*

For the past three years I have been teaching executive audiences and graduate business students with these tools. I am convinced that the question raised above has been clearly answered. The next round of questions relate to the more complex issues that will determine the degree to which these technologies can be effective in their impact on management practice. This book is an attempt to articulate some of these issues.

JOHN P. GALLAGHER

1

Introduction

Increasingly, popular management literature has focused on the application of artificial intelligence technology to the solution of management problems. Most discussions in this area have addressed either the technology of various programming techniques or success stories of large-scale corporate profitmaking through their application.

Several interacting factors contribute to corporate interest in this technology. First, what were once remote, artificial intelligence programming techniques have been significantly redesigned and presented to the business computing market in the form of applications development tools. Recent advances in computing hardware have provided a suitable foundation for the delivery of these tools on new generations of "mainstream" business computers. These hardware and software technologies promise the kinds of power and ease-of-use that have been so successful in other applications development environments like spreadsheet modeling and data base management systems. The potential of such tools to open broad new territories to computing applications is very exciting and has captured management's attention.

Second, there is a developing perception of both information and knowledge as corporate assets. New computing technologies promise to make knowledge that has been implicit in the behavior of decision makers explicit in a machine-usable form. By codifying knowledge, managers make it a manageable asset, continuously available to their organization. The potential integration of machine-usable knowledge with machine-readable information promises to carry the information age into the era of "knowledge management."

Finally, the role of information technology is being redefined as a competitive weapon. This is in sharp contrast to internal applications of technology to gain increased efficiencies. As business planning looks to technology to help differentiate product offerings, new technologies like expert systems take on added significance. An interesting series of transitions has taken place in the perception of the role of computing as it has moved from data processing to information systems to management information systems and to strategic information systems.

The cumulative effect of these forces has created an atmosphere responsive to the promise of knowledge-oriented computing systems. The promise appears to be quite real, and the challenge, of course, is to exploit it to advantage. Just how this is to be accomplished depends on a number of factors including individual lines of business, competitive environments, existing attitudes toward information systems management, orientations toward risk, and so on, in addition to the technology itself.

Chapter 2 includes a more detailed discussion of the distinctions among artificial intelligence, expert systems, and knowledge systems. In general, however, artificial intelligence is the superordinate concept in this set. As a field, artificial intelligence is concerned with computing technologies that allow machines to accomplish tasks previously believed to be the exclusive domain of human intelligence. There are many smaller fields within artificial intelligence, such as natural language understanding, vision processing, speech generation, robotics, and the like. One of these areas, included in the larger field of artificial intelligence, is expert systems.

Expert systems, as a field, emerged fairly early in the development of artificial intelligence. It resulted from efforts to model human problem solving with computing technology. As a research paradigm, it became useful to model individual, exemplary human problem solvers within highly specific application areas. The modeling of these individuals resulted in the term "expert system." Since these early efforts, generalized techniques have evolved for representing human knowledge in a machine-usable form and applying it to solve a defined class of problems. Even though the techniques evolved from the early "expert system" research efforts, they are now being applied to modeling and using knowledge from sources other than individual "experts." Many applications are being based on composite sources of knowledge, such as more than one individual, books, manuals, regulations, reports, published procedures, and so forth. These systems employ the same underlying programming technologies as expert systems, but are based on a broader source of knowledge. As such, they are referred to by the more general term "knowledge systems." Chronologically, the emergence of knowledge systems followed expert systems. However, in terms of superordinate and subordinate relations, knowledge systems are a subordinate concept to artificial intelligence, and a superordinate concept to expert systems.

The argument made here is that although it does make sense under specific circumstances for management to initiate in-house artificial intelligence research and development efforts, the vast majority of this technology's impact will come from the growing number of tools designed for knowledge systems application development by end-users and information systems professionals. At present, the market has experienced the first wave of such tools. Although they range in flexibility and power, they share some common traits that are significant in determining their importance as a class. First of all, they run on the hardware systems familiar to the world of corporate computing. Second, they are designed to conform to the pattern of other, popular development tools: they require a minimum of ancillary study and knowledge for their effective application and use by end-users and/or systems professionals. Finally, whereas they represent only a subset of the techniques that define the broader field of artificial intelligence, these techniques have been proven to be robust and appropriate for a broad range of applications that typify managerial decision making.

The challenge is to integrate these tools with the mainstream of business computing to achieve management's objectives. With this perspective, this book is about practical matters in the selection, development, management, and maintenance of knowledge-based systems with this new generation of development tools. A minimum of space is allotted to the more esoteric issues from the field of artificial intelligence. Discussed in their place will be the more germane issues of how knowledge systems technology fits within the context of corporate computing, how the nature of managerial computing is changing, and how to plan for, prototype, implement, and manage new generations of knowledge systems for management. In short, this book is about "getting on with it."

There is, and will continue to be, a considerable variance in available knowledge systems application development tools. Vendors have provided a wide range of functions and features in their attempts to distinguish their products. However, the underlying technologies are relatively straightforward. The common technological base for these products will be discussed in a generic fashion. Later, however, specific tools will be discussed in some detail to better describe the value and applicability of some of the more important distinguishing characteristics of present offerings.

In most instances, organizations with an interest in applying knowledge systems find themselves faced with a number of questions, only some of which are directly related to the technology itself. Examples include

Who will provide project leadership?

That is, to what extent is the development of knowledge systems fundamentally different from existing applications? Under what circumstances will current information systems professionals be able to provide support and leadership in systems development? Is the very nature of the technology sufficiently distinct to require new approaches to development? Or are the applications themselves different enough to thwart existing procedures for systems development? Who is best able to identify and evaluate potential application areas?

Who will implement and maintain systems as they are developed?

Regardless of the source of leadership in project identification and orientation, there are questions as to whether or not knowledge-oriented computer systems are sufficiently similar to other computer applications to be written and maintained by the same professionals who coded the payroll systems. That is, is it necessary to compete for and hire highly trained graduates of artificial intelligence departments to investigate these technologies and develop and maintain applications? Or can existing organizational units learn to apply these techniques and develop and maintain knowledge systems? Will knowledge systems follow the pattern of other end-user, workstation-oriented development tools because of the close ties of potential applications to the knowledge of functional area workers? Or might we also see efforts to centralize and explicitly manage corporate knowledge systems in a fashion similar to centralized data processing and information systems development?

What hardware and software systems should be purchased?

Most of the business applications of knowledge systems that are widely discussed have been developed with hardware and software systems specifically created to support artificial intelligence research. Is it important to invest the time and capital to introduce a new computing technology? If so, how substantial a commitment is required? Can these highly specialized technologies be integrated with existing information systems? Or is there a danger in supporting parallel technologies? One of the reasons for the increasing interest in knowledge systems is the emergence of applications development tools. Their promise is to reduce the development cycle and operate in the computing mainstream alongside familiar hardware systems. Are these empty promises, or has a significant transition in systems development technology taken place?

Another characteristic of the approach taken here is a strong belief that these questions should be addressed in the larger context of corporate computing as it currently exists, and as it appears to be evolving. Each of the general questions raised above, and the multitude of smaller, related questions that emerge like layers of an onion, cannot be answered by understanding only the nature of these new tools. The apparently alien nature of the technology should not detract from the fact that its management is a management issue that must be understood in the larger context of the corporate computing mix.

USING INFORMATION TECHNOLOGY TO GAIN A STRATEGIC COMPETITIVE ADVANTAGE

Many of the issues related to knowledge systems development and management are closely tied to the changing nature of corporate computing itself. Recently, a high level of attention has been paid to the larger issues of strategic corporate computing and changes in the nature and role of information management.

Recent discussions of the nature of corporate computing have resulted in a variety of related conceptual models of the use of information technology as a strategic competitive force. Although several of these exist, one of the more general and useful, described by James Cash, is the "three era model." This model creates an image of overlapping categories, or types of corporate computing. These types of computing applications are distinct, have appeared sequentially, and have, therefore, been designated as "eras." The primary characteristics of each era, including its administrative framework, primary clients, and sources for justifying systems development, are depicted in Figures 1-1 through 1-3.

Era I, beginning in the early 1960s, focused on the dominant, transaction-oriented, backbone corporate information systems like those for order entry, personnel records, payroll, and sales data. Because of the time frame for their development, they were generally written in-house by emerging data processing departments in COBOL or some other third-generation language.

Large data processing departments have developed over the past 25 years to oversee the creation and maintenance of such systems. The resulting administrative framework has been characterized as a "regulated monopoly," in that the data processing department, in concert with other organizational units, has determined priorities for which systems are developed, modified, or placed in the ever-lengthening queues. The primary clients for Era I systems are either the corporate organization as a whole, or large administrative units. Justification for prioritizing Era I

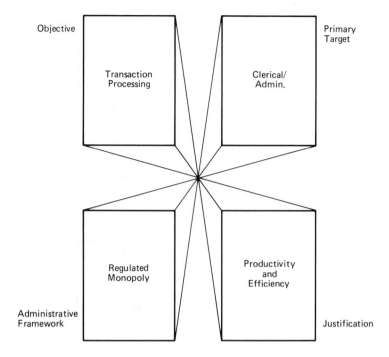

Figure 1–1   Era I

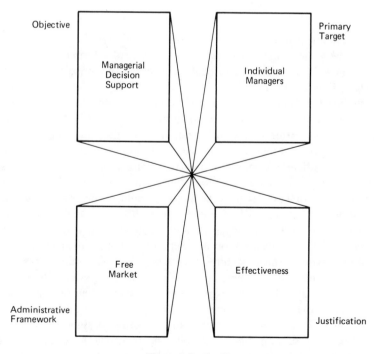

Figure 1–2   Era II

7

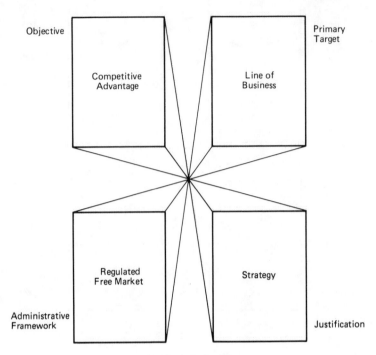

Figure 1-3 Era III

systems development has been based on the productivity-efficiency, cost-benefit model. Just how the management of these centralized information systems has evolved in many corporations is a critical factor in the enterprise's response to the challenges of Eras II and III.

With the advent of the early, stand-alone personal computer, beginning about 1980, Era II corporate computing was introduced. Whereas Era I computing focused on the processing of the organization's records, Era II has as its client individual managers and their needs for decision support. Numerous accounts are available of sophisticated information management and decision support systems developed either by, or under the close supervision of, the end-user. In many cases, these end-user systems have been comparable or superior in function to systems for which corporate MIS/DP departments had projected multiyear development cycles. For most of these applications the result is not a system of the type that the professional would develop and support, but individual managers have been willing to sacrifice these features for quick prototyping, rapid development, and the sense of self-control characteristic of personal computing solutions.

One result of Era II computing has been the development of small-scale Era I-type systems that have been waiting with a low priority in the MIS queue. More importantly, however, entirely new forms of computing, designed specifically for managerial decision support, have emerged. These include the variety of spreadsheets and other modeling tools that had no real counterpart in the mainframe MIS environment. Era II applications have had a powerful impact on managerial views of computing applications, creating a climate of high expectation for the competitive applications of computing in general, and for new computing technologies in particular.

If one were to take a marketing perspective, what occurred in the transition from Era I to Era II has a lot to do with the concept of "sampling" or the use of "trial size containers." Management, for relatively low cost, has now sampled a new style of support. A very competitive industry has developed to supply this lucrative market with even more effective and promising technology. The offerings of this industry have created a new market that spends significant amounts of time anticipating upcoming products. In a sense, the success of the current generation of personal computing products has created high expectations for future products and a predisposition to believe that new technology will continue to enhance managerial effectiveness. This attitude on the part of the managerial computing market has a great deal to do with the enthusiasm currently expressed toward knowledge systems technology.

Era II applications, for the most part, have not been under the control of a central information systems organization. It seems fair to characterize the administrative framework for Era I transaction-oriented systems as monopolistic, whereas Era II applications have been more akin to free market structures. The means of justifying Era II expenditures has largely been defined as managerial effectiveness as opposed to the administrative efficiency arguments used to justify Era I systems. This shift in the basis for the justification of systems development has been a contributing factor to the interest in knowledge systems technology as well.

Management has experienced a great deal of benefit from its introduction to Era II computing, owing to its unique attention to managerial decision support applications. This has resulted in a newly perceived relevance for the application of computing to general management. The apparent utility of knowledge systems applications for managerial decision making place them in this same context, as tools intended to extend and leverage managerial activity.

The third era of computing is closely tied to the concept of strategic competitive analysis. In its briefest form, this application of computing is concerned not with the general objective of making the internal, organizational operations of a business unit more efficient, nor with making the individual managers and/or management teams more effective. Rather, the focus is on using information technology to gain a competitive advantage.

Figure 1-4 describes some of the fundamental concepts of the competitive forces model as presented by Michael Porter. The competitive forces model is a popular and appropriate conceptual framework for clarifying the unique characteristics of Era III computing. In this model, such forces as potential new entrants, the bargaining power of buyers, the threat of substitute products/services, and the bargaining power of suppliers join with traditional intra-industry rivalry to act on any strategic business unit. Figure 1-5 adds to the model several approaches to reducing the impact of these competitive forces. For example, to reduce the force of potential new entrants to the market, the business unit in question can produce

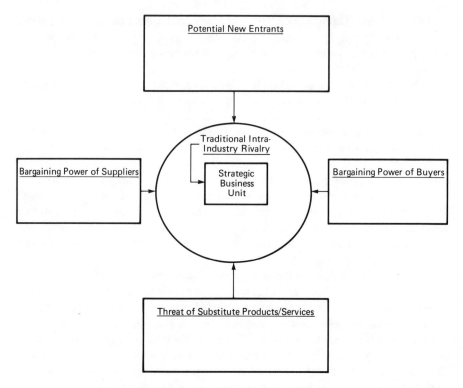

Figure 1–4 The Competitive Forces Model

new entry barriers through such factors as economies of scale, increasing customer switching costs, product differentiation, and restricting distribution channel access. The application of techniques such as these to the reduction of competitive forces is the subject of a well-developed literature on competitive analysis and competitive strategy. The thrust behind Era III computing efforts is to find ways in which information processing technologies can provide the basis for these efforts to gain a competitive advantage.

Michael Porter's concept of the "value-added stream" provides another model for structuring this type of analysis. It describes six stages of an organization's interaction with its product or service. These begin with research and development and end with product servicing. This model is briefly summarized in Figure 1–6. Porter describes each of these stages in the service/product flow as opportunities for corporations to add value and gain a competitive advantage by differentiating their service or product, or lowering costs. Booz, Allen, and Hamilton have added to this model relating specific categories and methods for applying information technology to add value to products and services.

One example of Era III applications that is frequently described is that of American Hospital Supply. Briefly, American Hospital Supply offered to install

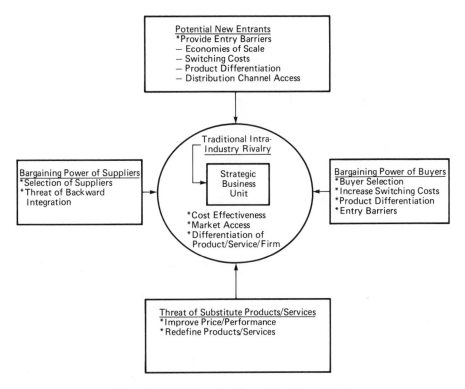

Figure 1-5　The Expanded Competitive Forces Model

terminals within the purchasing offices of major hospitals. These terminals were directly linked to American Hospital Supply's order entry system. This innovation allowed hospitals to speed order processing, check on delivery schedules, and so forth. One result was a reduction in the average hospital inventory from approximately 90 to 30 days.

In the sense of competitive strategies, this innovation increased switching costs for American Hospital Supply customers. It also increased the cost for new competitors entering this market by creating entry barriers. The "value added" to the hospital supplies by this order entry system is significant. These effects reduce the competitive forces from both the potential for new entrants and the bargaining power of buyers. Although the means by which this innovation was accomplished was information systems related, by nature the approach is more closely related to strategic competitive analysis than information technology.

The extreme nature of the distinctions between Era III objectives and those of traditional Era I information systems is becoming an increasingly important issue for management. The implications of this style of information systems application are sometimes hard to grasp, as it deviates significantly from the general role of corporate computing. For some industries the potential to gain competitive

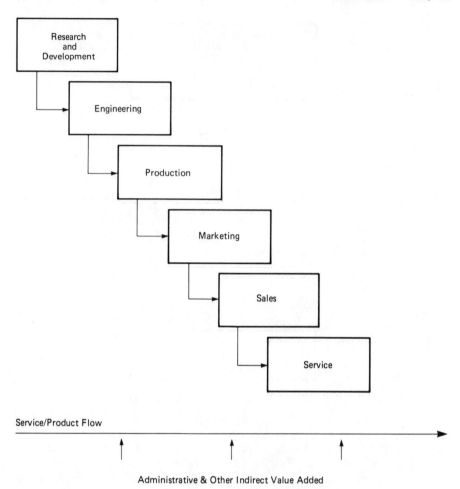

Figure 1-6 Value-Added Stream

advantage through the integration of information processing technology with products and services is of central importance. The financial services industry provides an obvious example. In other industries competitive applications of information systems are less obvious, and there is little history of this perspective on technology.

When upper management embraces the message of Era III computing applications, a number of issues arise quickly. Generally, these fall into two categories, strategic and tactical. The strategic question, "Given our line of business, and the competitive forces that define our environment, how can we apply information technology to gain competitive advantage?", is usually followed by the more tactical, "To whom do we turn in our information systems group for help?" The issue here is whether or not the existing systems organization is capable of providing support for these types of objectives.

Most information systems departments have strong roots in Era I applications. And most information systems professionals are much more firmly grounded in data processing than in the nature of the business they support. Upper management is becoming aware that the organization most responsible for information management and information technology is largely ill-informed regarding the firm's line of business. In most cases, the systems organization has not been included in the strategic planning process, and is poorly equipped to assume such a role. This lack of information systems leadership, as a function of overlapping and evolving eras of computing applications, occurs at a time when there is a perceived critical need for alignment of information systems and strategic planning.

As described earlier, all three eras continue to exist simultaneously, each in its own growth cycle. Many Era I backbone systems were written in the late 1960s and early 1970s using some third-generation language such as COBOL. These older payroll, accounts receivable, and inventory systems have been modified and maintained by data processing professionals for many years. However, this certainly does not imply that data storage and retrieval systems are not being developed currently. Changes in data management techniques and tools are continuing to impact the effectiveness and contribution of Era I applications.

Many new systems are being developed using sophisticated data management hardware and software. Mainframe relational data base tools like Structural Query Language (SQL) can vastly improve managerial access to transaction-oriented data. Although mainframe data management and query languages have evolved, other technical innovations promise widespread access to corporate-level backbone data by Era II managerial decision support systems developed on personal computers.

The rapid proliferation of local area networks, the developing connections between mainframe and personal computing, tremendous increases in personal computer power, and the potential of distributed processing and distributed data bases are changing the nature of Era II computing applications quickly and promising some technical, not managerial, solutions to the problem of two parallel technologies—one comprised of a central information systems organization, and another made up of personal, managerial computing systems. Indeed, there appears to be what might become an overreliance on the technology of communication systems to solve a problem that is equally managerial in nature.

Technologies for all eras of computing are in a state of change. As each era develops and takes on new importance, management becomes increasingly sensitive to the enterprisewide nature of information systems issues. This has led to changing styles of information systems management and organizational structures. All these changes are in response to an increasing awareness that the innovative and cost-effective application of information systems may well be a major force in determining the winners and losers in the competitive arena of the 1980s and 1990s.

As management becomes increasingly aware of the potential impact of information systems as a competitive weapon, its interest in knowledge systems is enhanced. In many ways, it may appear that these new technologies represent opportunities to extend the power and role of information systems at a critical time. The point here is that significant attention is being paid to the role of this technology by influential members of the corporate community for a variety of reasons. This opportunity may extend beyond the technology itself, as it provides a catalyst to efforts at aligning information systems and strategic business planning.

It is in this larger context that the role of knowledge systems should be explored and managed. These technologies will have to exist in a complex organizational environment defined by the nature of specific industries, management styles, organizational structures, corporate cultures, and historic decisions about the role of information systems in the running of the business.

In the chapters that follow, the nature of knowledge systems technologies is discussed, as is the variety of hardware and software forms in which they are available. However, the managerial and organizational contexts that surround their application are also addressed as a basis for recommending appropriate procedures for exploring, developing, and implementing knowledge-based computing systems.

2

Knowledge Systems Development Tools

Artificial intelligence (AI) is a relatively young field. Most accounts of its history place early, distinguishable attempts to develop machine intelligence in the early 1960s. Until recently, these efforts have been in the form of basic research. That is, AI researchers have concentrated on constructing theories and models for machine intelligence, understanding the basic human intelligence being emulated, and developing programming environments and techniques to support these activities.

There is a strong parallel between the stages of development in the field of artificial intelligence and other technologies. Even though the objectives and programming techniques that make up the field are quite distinct, the evolution from highly specific research paradigms and esoteric development environments to more generally understood and useful tools is a familiar one. The distinction between techniques and tools and the evolution from one to the other is central to better understanding the growth of interest in artificial intelligence in general and knowledge systems in particular. This understanding is also critical in planning, organizing, and implementing knowledge systems in the context of management.

EVOLUTION FROM TECHNIQUES TO TOOLS

For a number of years graduate schools of business have included courses in their curricula under the generic titles of "quantitative methods," "operations research," and "decision analysis." In each course, students are introduced to techniques, usually mathematical in nature, for solving specific classes of management problems. These courses generally stress the underlying assumptions and mathematical qualities of the techniques being taught, and then provide opportunities for students to apply these techniques to textbook problems.

For many years, students have criticized these courses from the perspective of their practicality. The techniques have been difficult to apply under "real-world" circumstances. In addition, the algorithms that underlie these techniques have alienated practitioners of general management. The techniques have always been good ones; they have just not been practical to apply.

One of the primary contributions of Era II managerial computing has been the provision of user-friendly access to these and other techniques. Most of the difficulty involved in applying complex mathematical models has been eliminated by creative software developers, who have recognized that applying complex techniques is often a multistage, hierarchical process that involves

1. Recognizing individual problems as members of a more general class
2. Identifying the relevant components of a problem in terms of the applicable techniques
3. Placing the components in the correct relationships to one another
4. Applying complex algorithms for their solution

The continuing effect of Era II computing has been profound in bringing about a transition in American management toward a new emphasis on analytical techniques by simplifying these procedures and making complex problem-solving techniques more accessible. These are the same techniques that have been prescribed for many years; however, they have now matured to the stage that they can be called tools.

An example of this transition from techniques to tools is the use of simulation modeling for decision support. Until the advent of spreadsheet programs like VisiCalc and Lotus 1-2-3, mathematical simulation modeling was a complex process restricted to situations in which a considerable amount of risk was involved in some specific decision. Under these conditions, intricate mathematical models representing the relevant components of the decision were constructed using third-generation programming languages like FORTRAN. The development of the model required a team of professionals. Team members took responsibility for a division of tasks including assuring the conceptual accuracy of the model from the business perspective, assuring the mathematical accuracy of the algorithms being applied, generating and documenting the computer code itself, and interpreting results.

Once the generalizable components of the simulation technique became obvious, and the sophistication of personal computing technology developed sufficiently, spreadsheet tools made the same complex underlying techniques accessible to general management. This evolution from techniques to tools within any field depends on several factors:

1. A "shakeout" must occur in the marketplace of techniques. In the early development of any field, there is competition among techniques and models for solving problems. Some of these come to be identified as robust and powerful. Others, which at first may appear promising, prove to be too demanding in terms of assumptions, limited in real-world opportunities for applications, or unnecessarily complex to apply. Over time and through experience, the "shakeout" results in the equivalent of a portfolio of techniques that have demonstrated generalizable utility. In a sense, the field converges on a set of useful techniques from the larger set of early contenders.

2. There must be a sufficient market for the tools to be developed, which may precede or follow the development of the tools themselves. Before general

management sampled the power of "what if" simulation in the form of spread-sheets, there was little practical attention paid to these techniques. Once the techniques had become well understood and general management had "sampled" their utility with a low-cost, trial-sized personal computer, the tool created the market for widespread application. The effort required to bring about such a transition from esoteric, isolated techniques to generally available tools must be motivated by a perceived market for the tools, or a faith on the part of the developer that the market will emerge.

3. The technology to make the tools cost-effective and deliverable must exist or be feasible for development. If the technology of the spreadsheet were developed on large mainframe computers during the early stages of Era I computing, the tool would have had little impact. The technology to deliver the tool to the manager's desk was simply not cost-effective in a mainframe format. The availability of relatively low-cost, accessible personal computing greatly facilitated the development of this tool's market.

CHOOSING TECHNIQUES AND TOOLS FOR KNOWLEDGE SYSTEMS

One of the important factors in the increasing interest in knowledge systems as a practical technology has been this evolution of early techniques to tools. It appears that some robust, generalizable techniques have been identified, and software developers are quickly bringing them to market in the familiar vehicles of personal computers and corporate-style mainframe machines. However, a great deal of laboratory research is still ongoing. This research employs technologies still alien to corporate computing. These include specialized artificial intelligence languages like LISP and PROLOG, as well as unique hardware in the form of artificial intelligence workstations. In some cases the hardware and software have been wedded in the form of complete development systems like LISP Machines.

A significant decision for any management group interested in the technology is whether to invest in this specialized hardware and software and the highly trained personnel required to operate it, or to begin exploring knowledge systems technology using the numerous end-user development tools that have been created in the mold of other Era II tools. The tradeoffs inherent in each approach are important.

The advantages of tools vs. emerging techniques described above are very real, but they come at a price. That price is in the absolute amount of flexibility available in systems development. Again, spreadsheet programs provide an example of familiar tools. They are very appropriate for the specific types of problems for which their designers intended them. That is, if your problem is one of the types for which the tool is designed, then many advantages become available to you. If, on the other hand, your problem area does not fit well, the tool itself may not provide sufficient flexibility. The tool is based on specific assumptions regarding its use. Sometimes these assumptions include the need for great flexibility through end-user modifications of basic features, and this ability is provided. Sometimes it does not. Later, specific end-user tools for knowledge systems development will be described, and the flexibility vs. ease-of-use of each will be discussed. For now, however, let it just be said that this is an inherent tradeoff in the use of tools.

The disadvantages of descending from the level of tools to the level of developmental techniques obviously follow. Few people within the existing organization have the background to effectively develop techniques in a field with alien concepts and technologies. The learning curve in this area is a very steep one, and should be approached with extreme caution. Not only is a commitment required of "time to learn" but also of "time to develop" and carry out the necessary "shakeout" of those techniques that are developed and explored.

The decision to purchase and employ the technologies of artificial intelligence researchers (LISP, PROLOG, artificial intelligence workstations, and the like) is a decision to engage in artificial intelligence research and development. For this to be justifiable, the results of those efforts must be critical success factors for the survival and growth of a line of business, and be unavailable in the form of commercial tools.

The choice, however, is not limited to considerations of flexibility and ease-of-use. In many cases, the system under development must be integrated with existing information systems. Although a prototype may be a "stand-alone" system used to demonstrate the underlying role of the technology, the finished system may be severely limited by this isolation. So even in the prototyping stages of systems development, the choice between environments can be critical.

In the robotics industry, the rapid development and integration of vision processing systems with robotics systems is clearly critical. Whereas the field of visual information processing has been one of basic research in the larger arena of artificial intelligence, end-user tools have not yet emerged from any set of generalizable, robust techniques. However, when we examine the field of robotics from the perspective of Era III computing applications, we see that any improvements in the ability of robots to intelligently process visual information is critical in terms of value-added. The ability of robots to see things, understand what they are seeing, and make decisions about what to do next based on that understanding is likely to be a necessary factor in the survival of any producer of this technology.

In terms of the competitive forces model of Figures 1–4 and 1–5, the ability to develop and deliver vision processing systems as components of other robotic products would reduce the impact of competitive forces from such sources as potential new entrants, as well as the bargaining power of buyers, threats of substitute products, and traditional intra-industry rivalries. The effect of these competitive forces would be reduced by the production of entry barriers, reduction of buyer selection, product differentiation, and so on. In this example, where the use of the technology is both critical to success and not available in an applications development tool format, the incentive to invest heavily in the growth of in-house specialization in artificial intelligence research and development technologies is strong.

A contrasting set of circumstances may be constructed for the furniture manufacturing industry. Here, the use of robotics in some aspects of manufacturing may become an important factor in any one company's success. Over the long run, those mass producers who do not orient their manufacturing techniques to the use of robotics may find themselves at a significant disadvantage. However, the incentive to get involved in the artificial intelligence research and development industry, as it relates to vision processing systems for robotics, is much less strong than for the robotics industry itself.

"Getting a jump" on the rest of the furniture manufacturing industry by being the first with vision processing robotics systems, as opposed to "off-the-shelf" robotics, is unlikely to provide a sufficient competitive advantage to justify the costs involved in such a development effort. This argument does not preclude the fact that there may well be other components of the "product/service flow" of the value-added stream in the furniture manufacturing industry for which it would be reasonable to invest in artificial intelligence research and development. However, in the context of the robotics example, the robotics manufacturer has far greater incentives to become involved in such activity than does the furniture manufacturer.

In the area of financial services, information technology has been an important factor for success, and will continue to be so for the foreseeable future. An institution in this line of business may come to the conclusion that they could gain a competitive advantage if they could, through some knowledge systems technology, model and disseminate the underlying rules and decision-making processes of some of their top financial analysts throughout their firm. These experienced and knowledgeable individuals are in short supply, and they are always in demand. After some analysis of their pattern of work, it may be determined that much of their time is spent in providing advice to managers lower in the organization on matters that do not fully employ the analysts' skill and knowledge. If it were possible to provide this advice via a knowledge system, and thereby off-load this responsibility, several organizational advantages could be realized. Perhaps the more knowledgeable, senior manager would be freed for more effective activities. Perhaps the readily available knowledge of this individual could significantly increase the decision-making power of lower-level managers. It is conceivable that investors themselves could directly access advice from such a knowledge system, resulting in a new service in the industry.

In any number of ways, the modeling and dissemination of senior managers' knowledge could be just as critical in the financial services industry as vision processing systems in the robotics industry. In contrast to the case of vision processing, the applications development tools to model and disseminate the knowledge of the senior manager in the financial services industry exist. They have been generalized from numerous research and development efforts through the use of specialized artificial intelligence languages and hardware. Their robust characteristics are well known, and have been packaged for the developer in the form of rule-based knowledge systems development tools.

Strong incentives exist for both the financial services industry and the robotics industry to develop in-house expertise in the use of artificial intelligence. This technology may be equally important from the Era III computing perspective of gaining strategic competitive advantage. However, the nature of the needs in the financial services example leads to a very different choice among available technologies. This is a result of the current state of the art in terms of available tools.

THE NATURE AND IMPACT OF AVAILABLE TOOLS

Restating some of the discussion above, we see that several factors have combined to create a market for artificial intelligence in business. These include

1. The success of Era II computing efforts, and the resulting belief that managerial effectiveness can be enhanced by means of information technology. This has resulted in a market that is highly anticipatory of new developments in managerial support tools.

2. The current emphasis on Era III applications of information technology to gain competitive advantage. This has resulted in increased sensitivity of upper management to the need to consider advanced information technology as a competitive weapon in a strategic sense.

3. The demonstrated ability of artificial intelligence technologies to provide added value and competitive advantages for early developers.

It is time to add more factors to this group.

4. Techniques that have evolved from the artificial intelligence development arena to the end-user tool format are in the general class known as knowledge systems. These tools are particularly well suited for modeling the sort of reasoning and decision-making processes that characterize an important management function.

5. The types of problems to which the tools are applicable are numerous, and represent opportunities across industries. The problem-solving tasks that the tools model well are not industry-specific, but generalizable. Therefore, applications developed in one setting transfer to others quickly. This speeds the spread of applications through examples in a broad set of industries.

6. It is becoming increasingly clear that with the use of these tools in numerous settings, groups that ignore this class of application are likely to find themselves at a disadvantage. That is, the ante has been raised in the management computing game. Simply in the context of Era II computing, there is a new tool in town. The impact of relatively simple personal support levels of knowledge systems development tools may equal and surpass the impact of spreadsheet and other quantitative modeling tools. Ignoring these tools may result in loss of effectiveness for the individual manager at the Era II level. The greater threat is that Era III applications will be developed that create increased competition for business units that sit on the sidelines.

In short, the first tools are on the shelf, and they appear to be important ones from various corporate computing perspectives. It is also apparent that they represent a first wave in a series of knowledge-based development tools. The task is to identify applications that result in the greatest advantage and choose the most appropriate tools for those applications. The remainder of this book focuses on the classes of tools currently available and those coming onto the market soon. These tools are differentiated in terms of function and features. Finally, these functions and features are discussed in terms of the resulting classes of applications for which they are appropriate, their integration with existing information systems, and the personnel and training considerations for each. We hope the result will be some clarification of the process for selecting tools and techniques, carrying out the project development cycle, and managing the resulting knowledge systems.

One of the earliest artificial intelligence techniques for creating machine models of intelligent behavior is the expert systems approach. As the name implies, its early applications were in the creation of techniques for modeling expert reasoning, or problem-solving behavior. Later, as the techniques became recognized as more generalizable, the label "expert" became problematic because of its seemingly restrictive application to true "expertise." When these same programming technologies are applied to model reasoning of a less rare and lofty status, they are referred to as "knowledge" systems. The technologies are the same; the "quality" or "rarity" of the knowledge being modeled provides the distinction. The label "knowledge" system is somewhat more general and useful than "expert" system; however, the early establishment of the term "expert" system makes it a resistant incumbent. As discussed earlier, the more general term, knowledge system, is used throughout this book.

As basic research progresses in any field of science, there are generally examples of "top-down," or deductive approaches to building theories and models, and "bottom-up," or inductive approaches, being carried forward at any one time. In the deductive approach, theorists attempt to formulate general, high-level principles or laws as a starting point. From that position, various implications of these principles are deduced, and their validity is tested via some experimentation. The inductive approach focuses on trying to formulate lower-level principles and models based on research findings. The attempt here is to work from the bottom up, by trying to generalize the lower-level models and seeing if they can be expanded to cover ever larger sets of circumstances. Their generalizability is then tested in additional experimental settings. In most fields of scientific endeavor, these two approaches occur simultaneously and interact to a large extent.

In developing expert systems, early artificial intelligence researchers employed a bottom-up approach. The efforts were to begin somewhere in trying to accomplish two tasks of primary importance to the field:

1. Find effective, generalizable methods for representing knowledge in a form consistent with machine applications.

2. Develop effective, generalizable methods for reasoning with this knowledge in a way that can be carried out by a machine.

In both cases, the effort was driven by exploring the ways in which humans appear to store and reason with knowledge. In this manner, there have continued to be strong ties between artificial intelligence research and the psychology of cognition and learning.

These early efforts proceeded by modeling individual "experts," by looking at what they knew and how they reasoned about what they knew when solving problems. For these efforts to progress, it was necessary to start with relatively small, well-defined areas of expertise. When one is learning how to model something, it is easier to start with a well-constrained domain in order to concentrate on the development of modeling techniques without being distracted by unnecessary complexities in what is being modeled.

These attempts resulted in some successful, and promising, methodologies. However, these techniques were found to have some limitations from the perspective of basic research. The methods for representing knowledge, although useful in very well-defined problem areas, suffered when attempts were made to expand their range to include more general, or "common-sense" knowledge. Also, the methods for reasoning worked well with particular types of problems but have not proven useful for problems outside these specific classes. What is of interest in this context is that several of the programming techniques developed during early research efforts are generalizable and very useful in applied research.

The strengths and weaknesses of the knowledge representation and reasoning methodologies that constitute the knowledge systems development field are well understood. The good news is that many areas of application are an excellent match for these techniques. In their current form, these approaches are capable of solving numerous problems that resist traditional, quantitative modeling techniques. And these application areas can yield real benefits in the context of corporate computing applications.

The detractors of artificial intelligence technologies have focused on weaknesses in the field from the perspective of progress in basic research paradigms. That is, they criticize AI as science. On the other hand, advocates for these techniques have pointed to the growing number of successful applications and the resulting benefits to the developers. As one might expect, an evaluation of AI depends on the criteria by which the results are measured. From the perspective of new tools for corporate computing applications, something of very real significance has occurred.

The result has been a class of approaches to modeling knowledge and reasoning that do not require the developer to be versed in the underlying theories and concepts that generated the methods. In a simple analogy, one does not have to be a mathematical theoretician to learn to apply algebra to solve problems, though it is certainly important to be well versed in the mathematical sciences to create such a complex mathematical approach to representing and reasoning with quantitative information. Algebra has weaknesses that give rise to more complex schemes for representing the world, such as calculus. This does not preclude the utility of algebra, however. Similarly, the limitations of the techniques developed in the domain of knowledge systems do not preclude their utility. As stated before, in the context in which users wish to apply these techniques, the limitations are not prohibitively restricting at all. They simply define the set of problem areas to which the techniques can be applied.

The requirements for applying these techniques are very similar to those for learning to use other applications development tools. It is far easier for a management team of individuals with expertise in the applications area to successfully apply these technologies to solve real business problems than it would be for scientists from the field of artificial intelligence who have neither experience in corporate information systems development nor knowledge of the applications area.

SEPARATION OF KNOWLEDGE AND REASONING

As stated above, one of the features of knowledge systems is the separation of knowledge from the methods for reasoning with that knowledge. One of the characteristics of presently available knowledge systems development tools is that, with varying degrees of user control, they provide the methods for reasoning with knowledge. The user supplies the knowledge with which the system will reason, which must conform to the tool's knowledge representation scheme.

Two knowledge representation schemes have dominated knowledge systems development tools: rule-based systems and frame-based systems. Of these, rule-based systems are the more common, have proven to be easy for end-users to learn, and have been dominant in early commercial tools.

The rules in rule-based systems are, in most instances, very similar to the IF . . . THEN form of rules appearing as conditional statements in procedural programming languages. The role they play and the way they are processed are quite different; but the structure is highly similar. Each rule is a modular element of knowledge; that is, each rule can be thought of as a ''chunk'' of knowledge. For example, a marketing manager may believe the following ''chunk'' of knowledge to be true:

> ''If the product I am trying to market is one for which multiple purchases will lock consumers out of the market, and one for which consumers will use more if they have more in their pantries, then I should try to promote the product by providing an incentive for consumers to purchase several units at one time.''

The phrase ''multiple purchases will lock consumers out of the market'' simply means that if someone buys a lot of the product, he or she will not buy more of it until the first purchase is consumed. This "locking out" of the market makes the consumer resistant to incentives to buy similar products from another supplier who may offer a promotional scheme of their own.

An example of a product for which "consumers will use more if they have more in their pantry" would be soft drinks. A product that does not have this characteristic is toothpaste. If you have several tubes, you still brush your teeth the same amount. This relationship between the amount of a product on hand and its rate of consumption is called "inventory and use correlation."

When this "chunk" of marketing knowledge is represented in a rule-based knowledge system, it could be translated into the following form:

```
If multiple-purchase-lock-out = true
and inventory-usage-correlation = true
then promotion-strategy = convenience-purchasing.
```

The process of transforming knowledge that exists in the first, narrative form into the proper rule syntax of a particular knowledge-based development tool is an important part of the larger skill of "knowledge engineering."

When several chunks of knowledge relevant to solving a particular class of problems have been converted to rules of the proper syntax, and these rules are combined with some other components discussed later, they form a rule-based "knowledge base."

Figure 2–1 contains a small, intentionally trivial knowledge base for deciding among various places to advertise a product or event. The purpose of this example is simply to provide a specific point of discussion as a context for describing just how rule-based systems reason with these chunks of knowledge. Each element of this knowledge base is labeled for easy reference as kb__1 through kb__10 (knowledge base entry 1 through knowledge base entry 10). The knowledge base in Figure 2–1 conforms to the conventions of a particular knowledge system development tool, M.1, from Teknowledge, Inc. Although this knowledge base is written in the syntax of that specific tool, the fundamental qualities of rule-based systems described below are generic to that entire class of development environments. It is important to note at this point that what is depicted in Figure 2–1 is actually what the developer must supply (although in this trivial example, the quality of the knowledge is questionable and hardly complete).

In Figure 2–2, two sample "runs" of this knowledge base with the M.1 system are provided to give a flavor of a typical user-system interaction. In fairness to the developers of M.1, it should be noted that a completed knowledge base would contain additional instructions for the system to further enhance screen formats and generally "pretty up" the interaction. In the context of this discussion, it would confuse the issue to add the additional formatting instructions to the knowledge base.

```
kb_1: goal = where-to-advertise.

kb_2: if product-category = liquor
      or product-category = tobacco
      then media = print.

kb_3: if product-category = automobile
      then media = television.

kb_4: if product-category = local-event
      then media = radio.

kb_5: if media = print and
      status-of-target-market = upscale
      then where-to-advertise = 'Gourmet Magazine'.

kb_6: if media = print and
      status-of-target-market = middle-income
      then where-to-advertise = 'Time Magazine'.

kb_7: if media = television and
      age-of-target-market = children
      then where-to-advertise = 'Saturday Morning Cartoons'.

kb_8: if media = television and
      age-of-target-market = middle-aged
      then where-to-advertise = 'The Johnny Carson Show'.

kb_9: if media = radio and
      age-of-target-market = youth
      then where-to-advertise = 'Rock Radio Stations'.

kb_10: if media = radio and
       age-of-target-market = senior-citizens
       then where-to-advertise = 'Easy Listening Radio
Stations'.
```

Figure 2-1 Sample Knowledge Base for Deciding Among Specific Outlets for an Advertising Campaign

Again, the analogy to the well-understood spreadsheet development tools may be helpful. Figure 2–3 contains an equally trivial spreadsheet model that could actually be entered in Lotus 1-2-3. The knowledge base in Figure 2–1 and the spreadsheet in Figure 2–3 are analogous in that the end-user is not supplying information about how the model is to be processed. The processing of the user-supplied material is part of the tool itself. Although it is possible in Lotus 1-2-3 to alter the order in which functions and formulas are computed, this capability is infrequently

Dialog 1

```
> go

  What is the value of: product-category?

> local-event

  What is the value of: age-of-target-market?

> senior-citizen

  where-to-advertise = Easy Listening Radio Stations (100%)

                 because kb_10.
```

Dialog 2

```
> go

  What is the value of: product-category?

> tobacco

  What is the value of: ses-of-target-market?

> upscale

  where-to-advertise = Gourmet Magazine (100%) because kb_5.
```

Figure 2-2   Sample Dialogs with the Knowledge Base in Figure 2-1

	January	February	March	Total
Sales:				
Product 1	75	250	300	@sum(B5..D5)
Product 2	75	150	250	@sum(B6..D6)
Product 3	150	200	350	@sum(B7..D7)
Total Product Sales: ==>	@sum(B5..B7)	@sum(C5..C7)	@sum(D5..D7)	@sum(B11..D11)
Average Product Sales: ==>	@avg(B5..B7)	@avg(C5..C7)	@avg(D5..D7)	@avg(B5..D7)

Figure 2-3   Sample Lotus 1-2-3 Spreadsheet

used in practice. Similarly, it is possible to alter the process by which the knowledge base in Figure 2-1 is processed by the M.1 tool, but it is not necessary to do any more than type the word ''go'' for the default processing methods to be applied.

In this way, the representation and processing of the knowledge are separated. This leads to a division of labor, so to speak. The developer primarily focuses on the nature of the knowledge and the way in which it is to be represented. The tool developer has, to a large degree, provided the methodology for processing and applying this knowledge in solving specific problems. In more complex problem areas, it is desirable to have more flexibility and control over the processing of knowledge. Tools with this increased power come at the price of lower ease-of-use.

THE INFERENCE PROCESS: BACKWARD CHAINING

Rule-based knowledge systems can be generally categorized as "backward" or "forward" chaining in the ways that they process knowledge bases. The more popular have been backward-chaining inference systems. These have evolved from the famous MYCIN system for medical diagnosis of infectious blood diseases and its spin-off, one of the first attempts at a generalized knowledge systems development tool, EMYCIN. EMYCIN stands for Empty MYCIN in that the separation of the rules and methods for processing the rules that appeared in the original MYCIN program allowed the developer simply to remove the rules for medical diagnosis and insert rules appropriate for different applications.

This evolution to generalizable methods from MYCIN to EMYCIN was an important development in the field of expert systems research and has been a major factor in the spread of development tools. However, one of the primary characteristics of the original MYCIN program remains a characteristic of backward-chaining, rule-based knowledge systems in general: They are primarily useful in solving problems that are diagnostic in nature. Some of the literature refers to this type of problem as a "structured selection" problem. In essence, these problems are characterized by a set of solutions (diagnoses) that are enumerable and specifiable in advance. The objective of the system is to determine which of these prespecified choices is the correct one under the prevailing circumstances.

In the trivial example of Figure 2–1, the problem is to select "where-to-advertise" from the choices provided. Although the "diagnostic" nature of backward-chaining systems is a built-in limitation to their application, numerous management problems fit well within these boundaries.

Again, the example knowledge base in Figure 2–1 is intentionally trivial in order to illustrate the fundamental operating characteristics of the backward-chaining inference technique. Normally, a knowledge base would also contain other types of information that controls the flow of processing and formats the interaction with the user. Regardless of the presence or absence of these additional features, the basic process of drawing inferences is simple and straightforward.

At all times, the system's activity in processing a knowledge base is driven by a "goal." In Figure 2–1, kb__1 states "goal = where-to-advertise." The system will process the knowledge base until it achieves a value for this goal, or has tried every means at its disposal to do so and fails to conclude such a value.

By just examining the rules in Figure 2–1, readers could apply them to achieve a value for the goal of "where-to-advertise." In so doing, however, they would find that other information (values of key expressions) is needed. For example, there is no way to use the rules in Figure 2–1 to conclude a value for "where-to-advertise" without first concluding a value for "media." In turn, a value for media cannot be found without first determining a value for "product-category." It can also be seen that, depending on the value found for "media," values must be found for either "status-of-target-market" or "age-of-target-market." It is important that the reader confirm these statements by examining the knowledge base in Figure 2–1.

The concept here is simply that in finding the value of one expression, in this case "where-to-advertise," the system will generally have also to seek the value of other expressions (e.g., "media," "product-category," and either "status-of-target-market" or "age-of-target-market"). During the process of finding a value for the goal of "where-to-advertise," that goal can be made dormant, or temporarily suspended, while the system seeks one of the subgoals (e.g., "media"). In an iterative fashion, each of these subgoals can also be suspended while the system seeks another subgoal (e.g., "product-category"). The setting of subgoals for other subgoals is an important capability of backward-chaining rule-based systems.

When seeking the value for an expression, the system has several methods to apply in a particular sequence. This sequence can be modified under user control, and to varying degrees with different tools; however, in their simplest form, backward-chaining systems follow this sequence of methods to find the value for a goal or subgoal:

Method 1:

Check the system's "temporary" or "working" memory to see if a value for the goal has already been found by some previous operation.

Method 2:

Try to find a rule in the knowledge base that would be useful in determining a value for the goal or subgoal. Such a rule is called a "relevant" rule. The nature of "relevant" rules is described below.

Method 3:

Ask the user for a value for the goal or subgoal.

If either Method 2 or 3 results in a value for a goal or subgoal, that value is noted in working memory in case it is needed later in processing the knowledge base.

The finding of "relevant" rules is critical to understanding the nature of backward chaining. All rules are in the

    IF premise THEN conclusion

format. A relevant rule is one for which the conclusion results in a value for the current goal or subgoal being sought.

To clarify the nature of backward chaining, it will be helpful to examine the knowledge base in Figure 2–1 to see how Dialog 1 of Figure 2–2 was generated. Readers should follow this description closely and verify the processing by referring to the relevant figures. This will provide a fundamentally greater understanding of the inferencing process than would a casual review. To begin, the system must establish a goal. This goal is supplied by kb__1, which states "goal = where-to-advertise."

Method 1 is tried and, of course, fails, because no value for the expression "where-to-advertise" has been found by a previous operation and is not to be found in working memory. In fact, as the session has just begun, working memory is completely empty.

In applying Method 2, the system begins looking for a "relevant" rule and finds kb__ 5:

    if media = print and
    status-of-target-market = upscale
    then where-to-advertise = 'Gourmet Magazine'.

This rule is relevant because it concludes a value for the present goal. Only after identifying a rule as relevant is the premise of the rule examined. Kb__5 has as its premise

    if media = print and status-of-target-market = upscale

The first clause, if media = print, forces the system to establish a subgoal. The previous goal of "where-to-advertise" is made dormant, and "media" becomes the active subgoal. At this point, the process begins anew, and the system applies Methods 1–3, in sequence, for the newly established subgoal, "media."

Again, Method 1 fails. Method 2 results in a new relevant rule, kb__2:

    if product-category = liquor
    or product-category = tobacco
    then media = print.

It is relevant because it concludes a value for "media," the currently active subgoal.

Again, the premise of kb__2 is now, and only now, examined. Its premise:

```
if product-category = liquor or product-category = tobacco
```

results in the establishment of a new subgoal, "product-category," and the current subgoal of "media" is made dormant.

With a new subgoal, the system begins again by applying Methods 1–3. Method 1 fails again. Method 2 also fails as there are no rules that conclude a value for "product-category." Method 3 is applied and, as can be seen in Dialog 1 of Figure 2–2, the system asks the user for the value of "product-category." The user responds that the value is "local-event."

At this point, the value of "product-category" is noted in working memory, and the current subgoal of "product-category" is eliminated, as its value has been found.

The last-made dormant subgoal, "media," reawakens and becomes the system's active subgoal. Rule kb__2, which the system was working on when "media" became dormant, now can be tested. It fails because the required value of "product-category" is known to be inconsistent with the rule's premise.

The system continues applying Method 2 in finding a value for "media" and finds another relevant rule in kb__3. Readers can see why this rule will fail and, subsequently, why rule kb__4 will succeed. Rule kb__4 is successful and "fires." Its success results in a value for "media" placed in working memory. The long-dormant goal of "where-to-advertise" reawakens. When it does, rule kb__5 is retried, as the system was busy applying Method 2, and looking at rule kb__5, when the goal was made dormant. The premise of kb__5 requires that the value of "media" be "radio," so kb__5 fails.

The process continues with "where-to-advertise" as the goal. Rules kb__6, kb__7, and kb__8 fail, in sequence, as the first clauses of their premises are false. However, when kb__9 is examined, it is also relevant. The first part of its premise is true; however, the second clause, " and age-of-target-market = youth," includes a new, and unknown, expression.

The user should be able to see why Dialog 1 in Figure 2–2 proceeds as it does, and how the final value of "where-to-advertise" is derived from the success of kb__10.

The important point to be made in this "walk through" the knowledge base is that the system works backwards from conclusions to test premises and does so in a recursive fashion through a simple algorithm. In short, the system applies simple methods, in a particular order, to draw inferences. The means by which inferences are drawn is called the system's "inference engine." In this case, the inference engine is of the backward-chaining type.

The processing required to create the simple, very short interaction of Dialog 1 in Figure 2–2 is considerable. However, the perseverance and consistency of the system in applying these inferencing methods is one of its significant strengths. Inference engines once were hand-coded for each knowledge system. However, this is an example of an "off-the-shelf" inference engine. The nature of the inference engine, its flexibility, and details of its operation are important characteristics of any knowledge systems development tool.

DEALING WITH UNCERTAINTY

One of the often discussed capabilities of knowledge systems is reasoning with uncertainty. Two concepts underlie this ability. The first is that of certainty factors, and the second is the set of algorithms for combining certainty factors. Figure 2–4 displays an identical knowledge base to that found in Figure 2–1, with the exception that certainty factors have been added to the conclusions of several of the rules in the form "cf 70," where 70 indicates the level of certainty, or "certainty factor," the developer has in the conclusion, on a scale of 0 to 100.

That is, the conclusion of kb__3, that the proper media for advertising automobiles is television, has been "hedged" by the statement "cf 90," which follows the conclusion. This indicates that the developer is 90 percent certain that this conclusion would be correct. Similarly, kb__4 has been amended to draw two conclusions for the value of "media" under the conditions of its premise. Under these conditions, the system would conclude that both "radio" and "print" would be appropriate media for advertising, with certainty factors of 70 and 60, respectively. Because one could be confident of both these conclusions simultaneously, there is no need for them to "add" to 100, as with probabilities.

These simple "hedges" may appear straightforward at first glance; however, it can soon be seen that there are many opportunities for them to be combined, or accounted for, as the system gathers information from one rule and uses it to test the premises for later rules. For example, in Figure 2–4, if kb__4 were to "fire" and the two conclusions for the value of media were stored in working memory, along with their certainty factors, how would this affect the processing of rules kb__5, kb__6, kb__9, and kb__10? Would their premises be found to be true? If so, how does this affect the system's confidence in the conclusions of these rules?

The ability to work with uncertainty varies somewhat from tool to tool, but generally follows methods that have been handed down from the original MYCIN and EMYCIN systems. Without going into the details required to explain these algorithms completely, we can say that the methodology for combining and/or weighting confidence in various sources of information does not come from either probability theory or from Bayesian statistics. In some systems, the user has some control over the ways in which evidence for conclusions is combined and interpreted; in others, the user has no such control. In some systems, users can apply negative certainty, that is, confidence that something cannot be true. In others, this capability is not provided. However, all rule-based systems development tools

```
kb_1: goal = where-to-advertise.

kb_2: if product-category = liquor
      or product-category = tobacco
      then media = print.

kb_3: if product-category = automobile
      then media = television cf 90..

kb_4: if product-category = local-event
      then media = radio cf 70 and
           media = print cf 60.

kb_5: if media = print and
      ses-of-target-market = upscale
      then where-to-advertise = 'Gourmet Magazine' cf 60.

kb_6: if media = print and
      ses-of-target-market = middle-income
      then where-to-advertise = 'Time Magazine' cf 80.

kb_7: if media = television and
      age-of-target-market = children
      then where-to-advertise = 'Saturday Morning Cartoons'.

kb_8: if media = television and
      age-of-target-market = middle-aged
      then where-to-advertise = 'The Johnny Carson Show' cf 50.

kb_9: if media = radio and
      age-of-target-market = youth
      then where-to-advertise = 'Rock Radio Stations' cf 60.

kb_10: if media = radio and
       age-of-target-market = senior-citizens
       then where-to-advertise = 'Easy Listening Radio Stations'.
```

Figure 2-4 Sample Knowledge Base for Deciding Among Specific Outlets for an Advertising Campaign with Certainty Factors Added to Conclusions

provide some methodology for reasoning with uncertain or completely absent information.

Backward-chaining systems, with their search for "relevant" chunks of knowledge, are very effective in processing the modular rules that act as components of the knowledge base. It should be evident why this approach is so applicable to the broad class of "diagnostic," or "structured selection," problems.

Backward-chaining systems have been the most popular design for the first group of knowledge systems development tools, for several reasons. First, the technique has proven to be successful in numerous applications. Second, many applications fit the approach very well and form an attractive set of application areas. Third, inference engines that are rule-based and backward chaining are relatively easy to code and deliver on mainstream hardware. Finally, the approach seems to be quite intuitive. Users who are unfamiliar with knowledge systems seem to grasp rather quickly just how their knowledge bases are being used by the inferencing system. This is a substantial factor in the "demystification" and acceptance of this technology.

THE INFERENCE PROCESS: FORWARD CHAINING

Rule-based systems can also use an inference technique known as "forward chaining" in place of, or in addition to, the backward-chaining inference engine described above. This approach also has been generalized from several individually developed and proven applications. The most notable and most often discussed forward-chaining knowledge systems application is the R1, or XCON system, developed for the Digital Equipment Corporation. This system, an eXpert CONfiguration system, creates specific configurations of computer components from a large inventory of available parts to meet specific customer needs. As in any manufacturing technology, when a producer like Digital provides a large number of interactive components assembled to produce a specific, unique system for an individual customer, the problem of identifying the proper components and assuring that their interaction will result in a working system is a difficult one. Like most other computer manufacturers, they had encountered problems as sales representatives in the field, working with individual customers, specified system components that would sometimes turn out to be unworkable in combination, redundant in function, unnecessary, or would fail to identify necessary components as part of the total configuration. As each order was entered, system engineers had to begin the process of analyzing the order, and then "refining" it, or "working out the bugs" with the sales representative and customer. This process was time-consuming, required highly trained and highly paid employees, and formed a bottleneck in the flow of products and services.

The XCON system was developed to operate from constraints in the form of performance standards, and to create or design the proper combination of components to do the job. It is most important to note that the problem for this system is not a diagnostic or structured selection problem. This is, it is not possible in advance to enumerate all possible configurations that could be constructed from the available components and then choose from this set. The combinatorial aspects of the problem simply make such an approach infeasible. The problem is a design as opposed to a diagnosis issue.

Forward-chaining inference procedures appear to be the most applicable in this design mode. The distinction between forward and backward chaining is a relatively simple one in terms of how the inferencing is done. The knowledge bases for the two approaches need not be structurally different. They both are rule-based, composed of IF . . . THEN type units, and have a goal.

In the forward-chaining mode, the premise of each rule is sequentially examined. If information exists in working memory that allows the premise to be true, then the conclusion of the rule can be drawn and added to working memory.

As might be imagined, rules further down in the knowledge base may fire, adding information to working memory that will allow for the firing of a rule further up in the knowledge base. Because this is the case, the procedure is an iterative one. The inference engine begins with the first rule and works its way down through the entire knowledge base, firing each rule for which the premise can be confirmed as true. After this first pass through the knowledge base, the system begins anew with the first rule. This process continues until either the goal is met, or until a pass through the knowledge base results in no new rules being able to fire.

The reader should be able to use the knowledge base in Figure 2–1 to illustrate how a forward-chaining inference system would use these knowledge chunks. If the system were first supplied with key values of expressions like "product-category," "status-of-target-market," and "age-of-target-market," the system would begin with kb__2 and examine each rule's premise to see if the conclusion could be noted.

The system would continue to run through the knowledge base until either a value for "where-to-advertise" were found, or a complete pass through the knowledge base resulted in no rules firing. If the system were provided with the same information that the user supplied in Dialogs 1 and 2 of Figure 2–2, the forward-chaining system should arrive at the same conclusions for the value of "where-to-advertise." It would do it using a different inferencing technology, however.

Forward-chaining systems have not been as popular in the first group of available development tools as have been backward-chaining systems. Generally, to add value to backward-chaining approaches, some tool vendors have also allowed the user option of forward chaining. This means that the user can request that a knowledge base be processed in a forward or backward manner. The popularity of strictly backward-chaining compared with forward-chaining systems may result from the more intuitive nature of the former, and, perhaps most important, the rather obvious nature of a wealth of backward-chaining applications. In some sense, forward-chaining applications may be more difficult for a new system designer to identify. This phenomenon may turn out to be a function of the market's sophistication, and could change as industry gains experience with the use of knowledge systems development.

FRAME-BASED AND OBJECT-ORIENTED SYSTEMS

Another method of knowledge representation and inference is found in the frame-based and object-oriented technologies. These have evolved from attempts to implement the "semantic network" class of models for human memory that emerged from cognitive psychology in the early 1970s. Object-oriented programming technologies emphasize the underlying concepts (objects) in an application area and the linkages between them. This is somewhat distinct from a strictly rule-based approach to representing knowledge. As an example, one might model a marketing manager's knowledge regarding product promotion and advertising in the rule-based format demonstrated above. An alternative method, however, is not to emphasize the "rules" that a manager might have regarding product promotion, but the "structural relationships" among the relevant concepts that may be in the manager's memory. In the area of product promotion, one might hypothesize that an important, high-level concept is that of a promotion device. A promotion device might be a trial-size container, a coupon, a rebate, a free sample, and so on.

In an object-oriented system the developer could begin by specifying the attributes that the concept of a promotion device might have. These attributes might be target markets, cost to the company, historical effectiveness, appropriate product categories, speed of market impact, effectiveness for new product introduction, and so on. Some of these attributes may be owned by every promotion device; others may or may not be present for specific types of promotion devices.

Taking the example further, we note that coupons are a promotion device and have some of the attributes of promotion devices in general. However, they have their own unique characteristics as well. The media for their distribution, the subtypes of coupons (e.g., cents-off or progressive purchase refunds), the size of the coupon, how it is redeemed, and so forth are all attributes of coupons that make them unique promotion devices.

Finally, we may go even one level lower and discuss cents-off coupons as a subcategory of coupons in general. They will have some unique attributes, and some that are shared, by their very nature, with the larger class of coupons, and the even larger class of promotion devices.

Object-oriented systems allow the developer to specify the hierarchical relationships among concepts like these, the attributes general to all, and those that are specific to each level or concept in the hierarchy. The developer can also specify those attributes that must be present and those that are optional. The structure for describing these and other qualities of a concept-object is called a "frame." Because frame-oriented development and "object-oriented" programming environments are closely related, they are frequently discussed in the same context.

Also associated with each object may be rules or procedures that specify what to do to obtain the value for an attribute, or what to do when a value for an attribute is found. These rules or procedures are sometimes referred to as methods owned by the object, and are specified in the object's frame structure. The purpose of such systems is usually to find the values for the attributes of a particular object. In the example above, the values for a cents-off coupon may need to be found to design a specific promotion device.

In the process of finding the values for attributes, the "what to do when you need to get a value for this attribute" type of rule or procedure comes into play. These sometimes are "inheritance" rules that tell the system how to look to objects higher in the hierarchy to derive default values; they may require asking the user for information or require that backward chaining be applied. When values for some attributes are found, the system may encounter "go and do this when you find that this attribute has one of these values" types of rules or procedures. Systems like this can be thought of as having both forward and backward styles of inference built into their approach to resolving problems.

In addition to this highly structured, concept-oriented environment, the more powerful of this class of system provide for something called "truth maintenance." With such a feature, whenever the value of a key parameter changes, all the implications of that change are computed and updated. This is the knowledge systems equivalent of a spreadsheet recalculation.

Such systems seem to be harder for developers unfamiliar with AI techniques to learn than are simpler rule-based systems. The method of knowledge representation seems to be less intuitive than the structure of IF . . . THEN rules. However, with the assistance of increasingly sophisticated development support tools and user interfaces for systems like these, this objection may be overcome. Those who argue for the strengths of object-oriented vs. rule-based development systems point to the potential for such systems to provide a better environment for large, complex systems. They also argue that many problems are defined in terms of objects and their relations, and that attempts to represent such domains entirely as sets of IF . . . THEN rules are unnatural and inefficient.

Because the natures of forward- and backward-chaining rule-based systems and object-oriented systems overlap and are not clearly defined, many producers of end-user development tools claim they have a "backward-chaining" system with "some forward-chaining" capabilities and/or "some limited ability to provide object-oriented reasoning," and so forth. In fact, the first group of development tools has tended to fall within one category or the other; however, the direction is clearly to increase the integration of these methodologies to provide the optimum combination of power, flexibility, and ease-of-use. This mix, as with other end-user tools, will likely turn out to be a different one for different classes of applications and users.

In the next chapter, we discuss some of the distinctions between tools in terms of their power and the important ability to be integrated with other, established information processing technologies. It is important to note here, however, that whereas these tools are new and still evolving, the ability of the applications developer with no formal training in artificial intelligence to take advantage of these approaches to modeling and problem solving is very real.

The trivial knowledge base provided in Figure 2–1 is a running example of what the developer would have to produce to achieve the interaction in Figure 2–2 with a backward-chaining inference system. This does not mean that the skills for applying the tools are trivial or insignificant. Spreadsheets are easy to use, but users who learn the use of those tools in depth, and understand how to create, verify, document, and interpret the results of their use, have developed important skills distinct from a formal understanding of the workings of a spreadsheet. Similarly, skills in systems development in the knowledge-based arena are not trivial, and no tool will nullify the value of a fundamental understanding of the material being modeled. The purpose of the tool is to allow the developer to concentrate on these issues.

3

Evaluating Knowledge Systems Development Tools As Mainstream Business Computing Systems

The technology of knowledge systems is new to the business computing environment. Because it requires a new perspective on the role of computing, most discussions of the tools focus on its unique characteristics. That is, the questions "How is this different?" and "What can it do that other tools cannot do?" have dominated most discussions. This has led to the publication of checklists and comparison charts that clarify the knowledge systems functions and features of various tools. Owing to the lack of convergence in the market on clear classes of function and features, this style of discussion is very appropriate. There is no denying that the internal knowledge systems characteristics of specific tools will be highly influential in creating the right match of technologies and applications. However, another, more general perspective needs to be applied when exploring the utility of this technology. That perspective does not focus on the unique characteristics of specific tools but on evaluating these new tools as business-oriented information processing tools.

Because the focus of this work is the application of tools in the larger context of management, the most important and distinguishing features of these tools are those affecting their ability to serve the needs of the business computing community. This ability corresponds to the degree to which tools can operate on the mainstream hardware of business computing, take advantage of existing business-oriented computing tools and data, and be used successfully by the appropriate business-oriented applications development and support personnel. In some cases these developers and users may be general managers writing small, stand-alone systems; in other cases they may be information systems professionals developing and maintaining large-scale projects.

As has already been discussed, the fundamental technologies for both representing and reasoning with knowledge in knowledge systems have not changed significantly since they were first developed. The relatively recent interest in this technology is due to its packaging in ways that eliminate the need for learning highly specialized artificial intelligence techniques, and promise integration with the mainstream of corporate information systems. One part of this packaging involves the transfer of the tools of business-oriented hardware. Another is newly developed user interfaces and support environments for applications development and delivery. The final component of this technology is its integration with other applications development tools and systems.

KNOWLEDGE SYSTEMS AND MAINSTREAM COMPUTING HARDWARE

Interest in knowledge systems applications in business is, to some degree, a result of the willingness of management to consider new information processing technologies as a means to achieve its objectives. This willingness is stimulated by recent, positive experiences with personal computing, more sophisticated mainframe-oriented decision support systems, and the currency of the competitive analysis model described earlier. To be successful, knowledge systems development tools must look and behave, from the development and delivery perspective, very much like other computing applications with which the relevant development community has had success. There is a multimillion dollar market in bringing knowledge systems technology across the border from AI research to mainstream business computing. The suppliers of this new technology have been awakened to this market, and have every incentive to produce products for it. To better understand the distinctions among the currently and soon-to-be available products, it will be helpful to briefly review their origins.

Developments in AI have come from basic research efforts in the computer science community. Later, contributions were made by computer-oriented researchers in psychology and other cognitive sciences interested in human problem solving, language understanding, and perception. Researchers in these domains commonly worked on centralized, time-sharing systems via terminals. Early program development in AI looked very much like program development in scientific and engineering departments. At that time, the mainframe computing environment of university research was primarily based on Digital Equipment Corporation (DEC) machines. These were the DEC-10s, DEC-20s, and later, the DEC VAX machines for large-systems development, and DEC PDP-11 machines for smaller efforts. Artificial intelligence programming was done almost exclusively in the LISP language. As is often the case when a computing language becomes the favorite of academic research communities, there quickly arose a number of institutional variants of the language, as there were no existing standards.

The early LISP development environments in academic research centers were not entirely unlike those for FORTRAN or other languages. Researchers used terminals, edited their code in conventional line-oriented text editors, and ran their programs in a time-sharing mode. As some of the results of early research in AI became more generalizable within the community, more custom AI development environments became available. This tailoring of the tools first took the form of special editors for LISP code. In terms of its structure and flow of control, LISP has little in common with other languages. It has no line numbers, and is function-rather than line-oriented in its underlying structure. Special editors were developed to allow programmers to deal with the unique structure of LISP code. During this same period, various tracing and debugging features became available. LISP was originally a very lean language in that it provided only a small library of basic functions. All other functions had to be developed by programmers from these basic building blocks. As the results of AI research provided more and more generalizable approaches to representing and reasoning with knowledge, libraries of higher-level routines become available to perform these increasingly universal AI tasks. The AI community had begun to develop a highly dedicated and unique development environment.

Soon thereafter, researchers at Xerox's PARC facility in Palo Alto, California, and others began to advance the AI research development environment to a very high level. These efforts focused on the development of AI workstations. These workstations were characterized by large, high-resolution black-and-white screens, the use of the first "mice" as screen pointing devices, the use of "windows" to access and monitor several aspects of the programming environment at one time, "pop-up" and "pull-down" menus of commands, and icon-based representation schemes.

As efforts like those at the PARC facility progressed, it became obvious that the amount of system overhead required for the machine to maintain the interface and development environment, combined with the high computational demands of the LISP language itself, required more and more memory and faster central processors. Soon, the LISP Machine emerged. This specially designed hardware was optimized for running LISP code and maintaining this complex development environment. The basic processor itself was microcoded to optimize the running of LISP programs. The combination of this hardware and the complex and rich interface and development environment resulted in a powerful technology for programming AI applications. The result was a significant increase in research productivity. A generation of AI researchers was raised in this world of highly specialized hardware and software.

These environments were the stimulus behind the revolutionary Macintosh computer interface introduced to the personal computing world by Apple Computers. This intuitively appealing work environment began to challenge the existing form of personal computing, as well as mainframe computing, for dominance as a standard style of user interface. Recently the use of the mouse, pull-down and pop-up menus, windowing, high-resolution graphics, and multi-tasking development environments have become highly desirable components in most personal and managerial computing interfaces.

Although these advances served well the development of AI and provided the model for other, more general-purpose tools, their legacy causes problems for the effort to transport AI applications to more general hardware. Some of these problems are technical, and relate to the speed of developing and running large AI applications on standard hardware. Another set of problems, however, comes from the perception that real AI work is done on exotic hardware. A community of vendors and consultants benefits from the mystique created by the "strange and exotic" technology of AI's roots. But keep in mind that these environments are designed to support research in AI.

Several recent developments are providing a rapid and promising shift in the ability of more mainstream computing tools to support knowledge systems development. These include the availability of increasingly powerful workstation processors, the rewriting of LISP-oriented development environments in more generally available languages like C and PASCAL, the incorporation of many of the attractive characteristics of AI development tools in more conventional operating systems, and the development of new LISP languages designed specifically for mainstream hardware. The nature of these developments and their implications for business applications of knowledge systems are discussed below.

As a language, LISP has provided a rich and unqiue environment for AI research. Its ability to perform symbolic as opposed to numeric computation was explored early as researchers developed the first theorem provers and other symbolic applications. This genuine advantage of the language was quickly coupled with the huge investment that took place in creating support environments for LISP program development. Although it is true that essentially anything written in one language can be written in another, in many cases such translations are simply infeasible. The use of LISP in AI research is analogous to the application of such languages as FORTRAN for scientific and engineering work, and COBOL for business-oriented data processing. Some LISP advocates will argue that performance suffers when LISP-based applications are rewritten in other languages, and that the finished products may lack some elegance. However, the increasing power of mainstream business processors is quickly making the speed argument less relevant, except for the largest applications.

The very first applications to make it across the border from the AI labs to the world of business applications were those that required the least of LISP's unique power. These are the rule-based applications. There are many other reasons for their relatively rapid appearance, such as their intuitive appeal, the clarity of their underlying concepts, and their broad range of applicable problem domains; however, they were also easy to rewrite for conventional computing languages and hardware. The next group of technologies to be translated is the more technically complex frame- or object-oriented systems. As discussed earlier, these offer some significant enhancements compared with strictly rule-based development environments; but they come at a higher price in terms of systems complexity and portability to conventional hardware.

There are two reasons for this emphasis on the transporting of knowledge systems development tools to mainstream business computing hardware. First, the corporate world is much more likely to adopt the technology if it can be made more familiar. Second, there is a critical need to *integrate* this technology with existing and future business information processing technologies for the applications to have any significant impact on the practice of management.

There is another issue that results from the translation of knowledge systems environments from LISP to specialized applications development tools. When programming even the simplest backward-chaining inference system in a native language like LISP, the developer has the option of abandoning the backward-chaining mode and performing complex procedures at will. That is, if a list of departments needs to be sorted by annual sales, or if a standard deviation needs to be computed, the developer has full access to the native language to carry out these noninference processing needs. When a tool is provided for the development of knowledge systems, the capability to handle noninference or procedural processing is often required as well. The need to alternate between inference-oriented and procedural programming can be very great. Just how much procedural processing and what type is required for any one application can be a strong factor in choosing among application development tools. There is wide variation among tools in how this function is provided to the systems developer.

Still another issue is the access of a tool to data that already exist in some machine-readable form. If the information required for a knowledge system to advise someone is currently in a file stored by another program, how can it be found and understood by the knowledge system? These are not issues of interface with users but interface with other applications.

ACCESS TO DATA AND OTHER APPLICATIONS

The appearance of personal computing in the corporate environment had, and is continuing to have, widespread effects. The most obvious are those specifically related to the Era II-style computing, enhancing the effectiveness of general management. But personal computing also brought to center stage a number of issues that had long been present but not prominent. These are the issues of communications, connectivity, shared data, distributed processing, and the like. The shift from Era I to Era II and Era III computing applications has moved these issues squarely onto the critical path. All players in the computer industry, both hardware and software vendors, have had to develop both short- and long-range plans to solve these types of problems, which cut across types of applications, sizes of machines, and communities of users. There is a need to integrate applications packages and data bases within any one computing environment and across environments. The same forces driving the need for integration of all other aspects of computing systems are driving a significant amount of effort in the development of new generations of knowledge systems development tools.

The computer industry as a whole is dedicating enormous amounts of resources to the development of standards and techniques for solving these problems of integration. The potential of increased market share for vendors who help solve the larger integration problems is a substantial incentive. The potential increase in total market size for the industry that would result from a significant increase in integration is also important. These two forces are driving mainstream business computing hardware and software down an exciting and promising path. The resource represented by this focused industry effort is of great value to knowledge systems tool developers. This is another reason for the "porting" of these technologies to the mainstream. When knowledge systems product developers succeed in placing their products in this context by conforming to emerging standards, the solutions provided by the industry are available to them as members of the community. That is, as the industry creates standards and techniques for solving communications and integration problems, these are available to any producer that adheres to those standards. By joining with this effort, these developers will leverage their own contribution with that of the industry as a whole.

Many of the early knowledge systems development tools available on conventional hardware and software systems can be characterized as largely stand-alone. From the simple example of the backward-chaining, rule-based inference system described in Chapter 2, a knowledge system can make certain deductions from available information using a set of rules in a knowledge base. The problem with stand-alone systems is that any required information is explicitly supplied by the user at the keyboard. In the following chapter, a prototype knowledge system called the Peak Load Advisor is described. This system is intended to serve a small electric utility company by advising managers when to institute load control measures for customers in order to reduce electricity consumption during periods of peak use. The system needs to know the month, day of the month, day of the week, historical information about peak loads for this period, the peak load for the current month, and a number of factors related to current and predicted weather conditions. With a stand-alone system, the inference process would identify the need for this information in its attempt to come to a conclusion. The knowledge base would be searched for rules that would help conclude values for these parameters. When no rules are found to make these conclusions, the system user is asked for the data. Even though the information may exist within files in the system, there is no way in a stand-alone system to access that information. This is a serious limitation in the development of any substantial business application of knowledge systems with stand-alone tools. Below are discussed various levels or degrees of access to other sources of computerized information that are now, or are becoming, available as features of knowledge systems development tools. The degree to which any set of knowledge systems applications depends on access to machine-readable information brings these features into focus as critical considerations in the selection of appropriate tools.

In the lowest level of systems integration, the systems developer or end-user must manually enter information, originally stored in another format, in a new format that can be read by the knowledge system. Such a manual conversion would require requesting that one program, perhaps a data base management application, print the data first. At this time the user would enter the information anew in a fashion consistent with the representation of information within the knowledge systems environment; for example:

```
IF month = March
THEN average cases shipped = 1272.
```

This reentering of data was typical of many early personal computing applications. As long as the data being entered are relatively static and of low volume, this task can be regarded as a one-time expense, and may be tolerable. If, however, there is a need for data to be updated, or for new data to be entered on a regular basis, this type of system can become an unacceptable bottleneck for users. It also effectively eliminates applications that require real-time monitoring of conditions.

A slightly more advanced form of integration comes about when the knowledge systems tool can access data in the most common format, an ASCII-based or straight text-oriented computer file. In this scenario, data stored in one format for one applications package need to be specially converted via translation programs to a common, text-oriented format before being read by the knowledge systems application. Most applications programs for data bases, spreadsheets, and the like store data in highly specialized formats for their own use. If, for example, the historic data were maintained by a personal computer data base management package, such as dBASE, a mainframe relational data base management package such as SQL, or a spreadsheet format such as that of Lotus 1-2-3, the user would have to run translation programs provided by those individual packages to convert the information to a more common file structure. Once converted, the knowledge system could read information from the converted file.

This style of integration is suitable when the data being accessed are, again, fairly static. If, however, the data were regularly updated, the conversion process would have to take place each time new data were to be accessed. This approach is not appropriate for data-intensive applications, or ones in which very timely data are required.

Even when data are available in this form, the knowledge system must be told specifically where information resides in the file. Nothing in the file itself says to the knowledge systems environment, "this is what you are looking for." For example, if some relevant information were contained as a part of a larger aggregation of data, there is no way for the knowledge system to know which numbers in the file to attend to. The exact location of the data in the file must be supplied to the knowledge system along with the file itself.

This problem is exacerbated when the knowledge systems development tool has weak or missing procedural capabilities. In the above example, even if the knowledge system knew where in the file the information resides, the system still needs to be instructed, in some procedural fashion, to find it. In some way, the knowledge system must be told to sequentially search the file, line by line, until some key word is found, and then to read some information. Although this is a trivial task in any procedural language, it can be very difficult to implement in a development environment that provides only inference-based processing. In such limited environments, developers end up writing awkward backward- or forward-chaining rule systems to achieve relatively straightforward procedural objectives.

In a still more sophisticated level of integration, the knowledge system is able to read data directly from existing files that were created in other formats. This is, some tools allow the knowledge system to go directly into the file created by a data base management application and read information without any previous conversion having been carried out. In this mode, the knowledge of file structures of several major application packages is a part of the knowledge systems development environment. By telling the knowledge system that the data are stored by a specific application package, the system knows how to read the data from the file itself. This can be a great advantage in that data stored by one program, for one application, become accessible without additional processing or reformatting.

In a significantly greater level of integration, the knowledge system can request data from another application. In this scenario, the knowledge system could directly request that a data management system, such as dBASE, extract data from its files and return it to the calling system. In the most primitive version of this style of integration, the knowledge system would send a command to another program requesting that some action be taken and the result of the request be written to a file. The knowledge system, after receiving the message that processing was complete, would read the result from that file. In this mode, the knowledge systems environment is beginning to act as an agent of the user in that it makes requests for data given its specific needs. In the most advanced integration scenario, the knowledge system and the programs it needs to access communicate directly with one another and exchange information and data in a peer-to-peer relationship. In such an environment, the knowledge system can become a callable process for other applications as well. For example, a quantitative modeling process could request that a knowledge system review data and estimate values for parameters required in the evaluation of a model.

The solutions requiring knowledge systems development environments to read data from files are achievable by the developers of the tools themselves. These approaches are fairly common components of other applications packages, and can be incorporated into knowledge systems development tools as well. Moving data from one format to another requires breaking no new ground, technically. The ability of one applications program to read data from files created in another format by another application is also a familiar method of integration. The ability of one program to directly call another and pass information and requests between themselves is an announced goal of the computer industry. This ability requires significant increases in sophistication in computer operating systems, as well as the willingness of applications developers to adhere to new guidelines in the construction of their products. As of this writing, this level of integration is technically possible, though it is not widely available.

REPRESENTING AND PROCESSING INFORMATION FROM OTHER SOURCES

The ability to access data is only one component of the larger integration issue. Other components of the issue are somewhat more complex, but can be critical in data-intensive applications. These have to do with the knowledge system's internal representation of information, its ability to engage in noninference processing, and the bandwidth of the communication channel with other sources of data.

Addressing the first of these, we consider for a moment the differences in the way a spreadsheet, a data base management system, and a word processor store and process information. In a spreadsheet the key structural elements are the individual cells that make up the larger matrix of the spreadsheet. The resulting spreadsheet operates on cells through an addressing structure defined by the cell's location in the spreadsheet. The spreadsheet model is constructed by a complex network defining the interrelationships of cells. Each cell can contain text, numerical information, or procedural information for computing the value of a cell. Because of the very nature of spreadsheet applications, this structure is central to efficient processing of models developed in this environment.

In contrast, data base management systems, in their simplest form, rely on such underlying concepts as records and fields. The structure of information in data base files is defined by the nature of each field and its location in a record. Each record is another instance of the general data model contained in the individual fields. In some data base systems, the value of individual fields can be computed as a function of other fields for each record.

In a word processor, information is stored in the form of text using constructs like individual letters, words, paragraphs, and documents. Each of these elements may be associated with a particular format like print font, justification, spacing, and so on. Each of these applications—spreadsheets, data bases, and word processors—can represent information in limited and specific ways because of the very nature of their function and the type of information they are designed to process.

Most knowledge systems, or artificial intelligence systems in general, are designed to work with their own particular structures for information. These structures reflect the way in which information, usually knowledge applied to solving certain classes of problems, is stored and processed. Although a knowledge system may be able to call and retrieve data from another source, it may be very limited in the way it can store and represent those data. For example, in the simplest rule-based knowledge systems development environments, the key elements in the structure of information are rules and facts. Facts may be similar to assignments of variable names to values in other computer languages. In some instances, even this analogy is inappropriate, however. For this argument, let us assume that a simple knowledge systems development tool can represent facts in this way. Given this set of circumstances, such a system would represent the information stored in a data base as a series of variable names and assignments of values. If such a system were to read a record from a data base, it might have to construct statements of fact similar to the following:

```
Last Name = "Smith"
First Name = "John"
Middle Name = "Edward"
Street = "901 Clearview Lane"
City = "Atlanta", etc.
```

These variables like "Last Name" would have to receive new assignments as each record of a data base was examined. This is very different from the array, or record-oriented structure, of a simple data base system. Because the knowledge system may not have the ability to represent the data in tabular form and might be unable to effectively process tabular data, the fact that it can get access to the data is only part of the solution. The same principle holds true for data stored for processing via spreadsheets or other applications packages. The processing of the data may be very inefficient and very clumsy if the tool does not have the ability to work with it in an efficient representation format.

There are different approaches to solving this problem. One is to provide the ability to represent and process data in a variety of common formats, such as tabular data, text (or string) data, or procedural data, within the knowledge systems environment itself. This requires a substantial redesign of the original function of most knowledge systems development environments for AI research applications. These requirements were not a part of that environment. The need to access and process substantial amounts of data necessitates much more than transporting inferencing systems written in LISP to more general languages.

Another solution to the problem requires the knowledge system to request processing of data by other programs that were designed to accomplish these tasks. That is, ask the data base management system to search data bases and summarize data, and ask the spreadsheet modeling package to do sensitivity analyses on key parameters. This ability requires that the knowledge system have knowledge of other packages and be able to communicate efficiently with them. Again, this is a substantial new requirement that goes well beyond the basic functions of knowledge systems. These requirements are for integration of function, not simply integration of data.

This is an important requirement for many business-oriented applications, though certainly not for all. There are many applications for which substantial amounts of data processing in a real-time environment are not required. However, the novice with an introductory familiarity with knowledge systems applications should be aware of the significant increase in sophistication required for these types of applications, and recognize the value they represent.

Another issue regarding access to data relates to the bandwidth of the channel for its communication. Bandwidth is a concept that describes the amount of data that can be simultaneously transmitted over some channel. In the example above—a knowledge system having to represent tabular data in the form of individual variables and their values—the fact that the data cannot be represented in tabular form indicates that they probably cannot be passed from one program to another as a table, but rather as a series of individual values, one at a time. In some knowledge systems packages, this is the only way that data can be transmitted, as single values. And in the most extreme cases, each request for data is restricted to a single value being passed from a file to the system. In this case, the need to read a series of 100 values would require 100 separate requests to read data from a file, instead of one request to read 100 values from a file, or one request for a single table. The difference in processing efficiency can be very significant under these different conditions. In other systems, numerical data must be passed as either integers, or real numbers, but cannot be passed as both, or must be passed as text strings to be converted to numerical form inside the knowledge system. All these issues regarding access to data, and how to work with the data when they have been accessed, are important for data-related applications.

Some tools with strengths in these areas are available, and more are becoming available. It is important to assess the need for this type of integration when identifying tools for specific classes of applications. There is a tendency to select tools based on their capabilities defined in terms of knowledge representation and other knowledge-systems-specific characteristics, and to downplay the need to integrate them with existing applications. As applications move from the proof-of-concept and stand-alone prototype stage into the production of working systems, these aspects of design and implementation begin to take on increasing importance. More attention will be focused later in this book on the personnel and support issues raised by the integration of knowledge systems development tools with mainstream business computing.

THE SUPPORT ENVIRONMENT FOR APPLICATIONS DEVELOPMENT

One of the characteristics of the artificial intelligence research and development environments described earlier is the highly specialized hardware and software support for working in the LISP language. This environment is defined by special tools, utility programs, methods of screen presentation, and other technologies specifically designed to assist in working with a particular development tool, and for a specific class of applications. Most well-received end-user development tools are characterized by this type of support. Several examples of familiar personal computer development environments will serve to make this point.

Most personal computer users take advantage of word processing and spreadsheets. When well implemented, each of these tools is complete with a support environment specifically designed for its kind of tasks. For example, in the task of editing, quality examples of both these types of applications environments provide specialized editing facilities. In a word processor, the elements, or units that have meaning to the user, are individual characters, individual words, paragraphs, and entire documents. When editing a document, the tool provides the ability to "search and replace." That is, it is possible to search the document for every instance of a particular word—say, "enough"—and replace it with another word—say, "sufficient." It is also generally possible to move the screen's cursor through the text word by word, sentence by sentence, and so forth. With such commands as "delete," it is easy to use the tool to delete individual words, sentences, or paragraphs, for example.

Spreadsheet programs are designed to work with the units of cells, rows, columns, and rectangular arrangements of cells. Even though spreadsheet models frequently contain text, there is no ability to "search and replace," as is generally possible in word processing. Similarly, when deleting material in a spreadsheet, one usually has the option of deleting entire rows or columns. This capability would be useless in a word processor, where the concepts of rows and columns are meaningless.

The support environment has other important characteristics besides editing features. For example, most spreadsheet programs follow the interface model presented by Lotus 1-2-3, with its hierarchical menu of commands occupying a small portion of the screen, and its familiar row-and-column display of the spreadsheet itself. This screen can be divided into windows so the user can examine different areas of the spreadsheet simultaneously, even though these two areas may be widely separated in terms of cell locations. This ability to view two areas of the spreadsheet at the same time is very valuable in the development and use of large models. This feature of the development and delivery environment is specific to the world of spreadsheet modeling, and constitutes another element of support for user and developer.

Similarly, many word processors have developed methods for specially displaying text that is formatted as bold, underlined, or italicized. The more sophisticated word processors also have the ability to display two documents at one time and to allow for the movement of text from one to the other. This is an important feature for document preparation and management. Features like these would be less useful in a spreadsheet environment, however, owing to the anchoring of information in each spreadsheet in terms of specific cell addresses.

The point of this discussion is that each applications development tool, to some degree or another, has a support environment, and that environment is a very important aspect of the tool's utility. Consider for a moment a system in which spreadsheet modelers were forced to develop models in a word processing package. In some way, they would have to manually enter the cell location for each entry, and then the cell's contents. Once the model was built in this fashion, the resulting word processing file would be read by the spreadsheet program. Testing the model would undoubtedly result in the identification of areas that needed changing or expanding. To accomplish this modification, they would have to leave the spreadsheet environment and once again call on the word processor. Once the file was read, the modifications would have to be entered as text, resaved, reloaded into the spreadsheet, and so on. There would be no way to skip through the cells within the word processor, as the unit of cells has no meaning. The information would all be stored as letters, words, sentences, paragraphs, and documents. These units and structure have very little correspondence to the underlying concepts of the spreadsheet modeler.

Also, most development environments provide the ability to document the model under construction. (Here, the term "model" can be interpreted very loosely, and applies to documents prepared with word processors.) Many of the more sophisticated word processors have the ability to display the special instructions that format the text along with the text. This display may take place on the printed page, on the screen, or on both. Most word processors use "invisible" control characters imbedded in the text itself to control such formatting instructions as margins, line spacing, boldfacing, underlining, and the like. The processor uses this mechanism to change these display or formatting characteristics within a document. Although it is usually undesirable to display these control characters in the finished document, it is often most desirable to have the option of displaying them during document development. This allows the writer to view and edit the formatting instructions. In a sense, the model of the document can be accessed and is documented by the system as it is being created. The developer does not have to provide documentation as a separate task.

Similarly, in a spreadsheet model, documentation is provided as a part of the development environment. In most spreadsheet development environments, a cell can contain some form of text label, a numeric value, a formula, or a function. Each cell that contains numeric information of some form also has associated with it instructions for the formatting or display of the value. For example, the value may be displayed as a percentage or in currency format. Similarly, the text labels in cells may be centered, left-, or right-justified. When the model is displayed on the screen or printed to the printer, it may be presented in its final format, much like a final display of a word processing document, or its underlying structure and formatting information may be displayed or printed. Along with formatting information, the actual formulas and/or functions that have been entered into the cells may be displayed in place of their computed values. This documents the spreadsheet model to some degree, freeing the modeler from the task of maintaining separate records of the contents of individual cells. This component of the development environment for spreadsheets is a significant contribution to their value as an applications development tool.

These examples are from the personal computing arena. However, the need for support environments has also been well recognized for mainframe-oriented systems development. Early examples of editors and compilers exhibited a line orientation because most languages being used were line-oriented themselves. As mainframe computing tools have evolved from third-generation languages to fourth-generation tools, development environments increasingly have taken on characteristics first introduced in the personal computing arena. Modern tools for developing mainframe decision support systems provide editing and documenting facilities similar to those found in personal computer modeling environments.

The underlying structure of any knowledge systems development tool, with its concepts or units, should be reflected in the support environment, as in any other development tool. The self-documenting features and special, structurally oriented editors that enhance other applications development tools are at least as useful in this applications development arena. The following characteristics are important considerations in the match of the tool to the application:

1. Access to externally maintained data
2. Internal representation and processing of data
3. Development and support environment

In fact, it is likely that for many applications these characteristics are at least equal

in importance to the underlying knowledge representation and inferencing procedures of any one tool in determining the success of an application. Because the
field of knowledge systems development is relatively new to business computing
and there is little understanding of the novel concepts of knowledge engineering
and inferencing, it is these unique aspects of the technology that seem to be
highlighted in the assessment of new tools. In the longer run, however, it will be
their ability to stand as members of the applications tool community that is likely
to define the winners and losers in the fight for market recognition.

It is clear that no one tool will be right for all types of applications development projects. The software features that define an appropriate environment for
a stand-alone, proof-of-concept prototype to be developed by an end-user manager
will of necessity be inappropriate for use in a project defined by extensive "front
ending" and "back ending" of existing mainframe transaction processing systems.
It is, of course, the match of the tool's characteristics to the nature of the problem
at hand and the skills of developers that will have the greatest influence on success.

4

Some Sample Applications

Although the technology described in the previous chapter is relatively straight-forward, it results in numerous issues that are not. Only the simplest applications of knowledge-based systems are destined to be "stand-alone." That is, whereas the tools themselves are appropriate to model a range of managerial decision making, that decision making very often requires some support in the form of information. Unless the application is integrated with other components of the supporting organization's information processing and retrieval systems, it will be constantly asking some system user for data. The same problems that plagued initial Era II applications will reemerge: The need to access information is as important for knowledge-based applications as for any other. Decision support systems are not often effective without access to supporting data.

As indicated by the discussion in Chapter 1, corporate computing is becoming increasingly a strategic planning issue. Because of the potential for computing applications to contribute significantly to competitive advantage, and because of the history of information systems development, there is a need to align corporate strategy and corporate information systems.

The emergence of artificial intelligence has caught the attention of upper management at a potentially critical time, given this newly recognized role for information systems. In this context, it may be appropriate to examine four management issues that surround the implementation of knowledge systems technologies. These issues could provide an opportunity to address some of the more comprehensive aspects of corporate computing discussed in Chapter 1.

1. There is a need to examine the impact of this technology from a strategic, enterprisewide perspective, using the concepts of the three-era model. For some business units, at some points in time, these tools may represent an opportunity for significant development of competitive advantage. For others, it may represent an opportunity to enhance the effectiveness of individual managers and small work groups. For others still, it may represent no opportunity at all.

2. Knowledge systems development tools very likely will need to be integrated with other components of the larger information systems architecture. It is unlikely that effective knowledge systems applications will exist as "stand-alone" entities any more than have other decision support and modeling tools.

3. In some corporations the information systems group has been well aligned with general management. In others, this alignment has been less complete. To the extent that the application of knowledge systems represents a strategic direction and would benefit from integration with existing systems, this technology may provide a catalyst to initiate or strengthen any efforts at organizational realignment.

4. Some sensitivity to the impact of knowledge systems on the nature of managerial work must be developed. Although it is not presently possible to predict the nature of this impact, it is clear that the opportunity to formally "own" a commodity like knowledge is emerging. That is, the knowledge being modeled in knowledge systems becomes a capital good that is available to be managed, leveraged, and applied as any other asset. There will be, necessarily, some effort applied to developing, validating, updating, and otherwise managing the knowledge that a corporation has in machine-usable form. The nature of the impact and the dimensions of the management task will vary as the applications vary in nature, scope, and size; however, it is not at all clear that the present style of managing information systems will endure intact. In some ways, the forerunner of this issue has been the use of sophisticated quantitative modeling for managerial decision support. These types of modeling efforts often require the assembling of a team of managers and systems personnel. The resulting model may be highly "reusable" in that it supports some recurring corporate decision-making process. Its assumptions and underlying operations must be carefully documented and available for modification in light of new information. However, whereas some of the organizational responses to sophisticated decision support modeling are similar to any such modeling task in the knowledge systems domain, the explicit nature of the knowledge represented in the system, its modular and modifiable nature, and its potential strategic value seem to set it in a class apart in terms of potential organizational impact. Although the organizational changes will vary considerably within and across industries and specific applications, there will be instances in which these changes will be significant. Management must monitor and respond to them as they occur. They will be largely unpredictable, but sensitivity and the ability to respond to them as their character becomes clearer will likely be important assets in being able to respond to change.

To the degree that any strategic business unit is desirous of a more comprehensive organizational perspective regarding information systems, the introduction of artificial intelligence technologies may provide an opportunity to focus enterprisewide attention on this larger issue. This could prove to be a critical factor in drawing attention to the lack of such a perspective, and creating awareness of the need. Fundamentally, the effective use of this technology requires management and technology to become aligned. Therefore, it requires the alignment of their organizational counterparts.

As is illustrated below, many worthwhile applications will require management working in teams composed of "domain experts," "knowledge engineers," and "applications programmers." Just who assumes these roles and how they are managed could provide an opportunity to examine and redefine other components of the organization's management of information systems.

In order to clarify some of these issues, it may be helpful to describe some examples of knowledge systems applications. Each of these brief examples will serve to differentiate types of applications in terms of who is doing the development, how the systems are developed, and why the application is appropriate in its specific context.

A LOAD CONTROL ADVISOR FOR THE SMALL ELECTRICAL UTILITY COMPANY

The Small Electrical Utility Company (SEUC) is a supplier of electrical power to residential and small industrial users. SEUC is capable of producing some, but certainly not all, of the electricity that it sells. The difference between what it can produce and what it needs to meet customer demand is purchased from a larger supplier of electricity, the Large Electrical Utility Company (LEUC). The SEUC must pay for this commodity on a monthly basis.

As is common in the utilities industry, any supplier must have the capacity to meet the peak levels of demand for its product, even though this peak may far exceed the average demand. This means that capital expenditures must be made for equipment to meet that peak demand. One problem for this industry is that the marginal return on investment for the additional equipment to meet the peak demand is quite low. This equipment, needed only to meet peak demand, is not in use at other times. There is a strong incentive, therefore, to "flatten" the peaks in order to reduce the expenditure needed to address this excess capacity requirement.

The LEUC has a common method for reducing its peak levels. It simply charges its customers more for power supplied during this time. More specifically, during each month there is one hour when demand is at a peak. The rate the SEUC is charged for the electricity it consumes during the entire month is based on its level of use during that one peak hour. It would be beneficial to the SEUC, and therefore to the LEUC, to be able to predict the peak hour of use for the LEUC, and to control (lower) its use during that period of time.

To predict the peak hour for each month, the SEUC has been provided with a real-time system to monitor levels of use for the LEUC. That is, at any time, the SEUC can see just how much power the LEUC is having to supply. Because the SEUC is not the only customer of the LEUC, the peak period of use for the SEUC is not generally the same as that for the LEUC.

If the SEUC could predict precisely the peak period for any month, it still would need some way of controlling the level of its own customers' use. A mechanism is in place for this in the form of a voluntary "load control program." This program provides incentives (in the form of lower rates) to residential customers to allow the SEUC to place radio-controlled switches on two appliances within each participating home: the air conditioner and the hot-water heater. During those periods in which the SEUC wishes to reduce customer demand, it can send out a radio signal that is received by these controlling switches. "Hitting the switch" shuts down the air conditioners and hot-water heaters until the switch is "hit" again, to turn them back on.

The effectiveness of this system is confounded by several factors. First and foremost, it is difficult to predict the exact hour of peak load for the LEUC for any month. There are many problems associated with the detection of false peaks and with "close misses." For example, if the actual peak for a month occurs at 6:00 P.M. on the tenth day of the month, and the SEUC mistakenly predicts that it will occur at 5:00 P.M., the SEUC will "hit the switch" an hour early. This results in power being denied to air conditioners and hot-water heaters at that time, which in turn results in hotter houses and cooler water. Under radio control, the appliances are turned on at the end of the mistakenly predicted hour. As they are controlled by their own thermostats, they will cycle on to cool the houses that have warmed during the hour, and warm the cooling water. This results in an arbitrary, sudden rise in electricity consumption for the customers of the SEUC at that very hour when its monthly rate is being determined! This will result in a much inflated rate compared with that which would have occurred if no attempt to control the peak were applied.

Also, as the program is supported through residents' voluntary participation, it is important to maintain their cooperation by reducing inconvenience to a level at which they feel they are being fairly treated in exchange for the rate reduction they receive. This requires careful judgment so as not to overuse the switch in order to "catch the peak." "Chasing the peak" is another problem. This refers to "hitting the switch" on one hour, only to see the peak load rising, and having to hit it again in the subsequent hour, and so on. The effect of two or more consecutive hours of nonservice is more damaging to customer relations than are two or more unconsecutive hours. In fact, it would be helpful if the SEUC could promise its customers that there would be a limit on total service disruption, in order to secure more volunteers. This is a promise it currently cannot make. This inability is seen as a detriment to selling the voluntary program. Finally, hitting the switch at incorrect times unnecessarily reduces the amount of electricity sold at that time, and yields no advantage to the SEUC. This simply results in lost revenue.

The information available to the SEUC for predicting the month's peak is varied. First of all, there are weather data provided by a computer service in electronic form. It is possible to acquire daily, and hourly, current and predicted information on precipitation, temperature, humidity, cloud cover, wind speed, wind direction, and so on. Second, real-time data are available regarding the current load for both the LEUC and the SEUC.

In addition to these sources of data, however, there is a set of heuristics, or rules-of-thumb, that have been developed over the years by the managers responsible for load control. These managers possess knowledge relating such factors as the following:

1. *The time of day and day of the week.* What drives the loads is the pattern of electricity use within a population. The behavior of the population is affected by weather, to be sure; however, it is also influenced by other patterns, as when people rise in the morning and turn on electric heaters, take showers, and so on, and when they come home in the evening and adjust thermostats, do laundry, and the like. These factors are greatly influenced by the day of the week, the presence of holidays, and so forth.

2. *The specific season of the year.* The patterns of power use shift through changing seasons. In winter, for example, peak loads tend to occur in the morning, as people heat their homes at the same time that they being other daily chores. In summer, the peaks tend to come late in the day, as people return home from work and cool their homes. Transition seasons present other, more difficult patterns of use.

3. *Local events and other intervening circumstances.* For example, the ways certain holidays are celebrated influence patterns of energy use in determining which groups within the community are enjoying time off from work, when people tend to get together in the day to celebrate, and so forth.

Factors of this type result in a great deal of personal judgment being applicable, all supported by data. The managers responsible for these decisions, using judgment, requesting data when needed on an hourly basis, discussing the currently appropriate factors, and monitoring load levels, are correct in "hitting the peak" about 50 to 70 percent of the time. This results in very real savings. However, this activity is only one component of their responsibilities. The time they spend on this work takes them away from other tasks. On days when it is highly unlikely that a peak will occur, they are free to fulfill other responsibilities. However, on days when a peak might occur, they spend most of their time in a monitoring and decision-making mode. There is a strong incentive to accomplish improvement in any combination of three performance areas:

1. Accurately predict the peak hour with greater frequency
2. Minimize the number of incorrect or unnecessary attempts to reduce load
3. Reduce the time spent managing this activity

The importance of these issues arose as a critical factor during management meetings. It was decided to hire a consulting firm to complete a feasibility study of building a regression-based statistical model to help with the accuracy of the predictions and partially automate the process. This approach had been applied by other, larger utility firms, and was thought to be of sufficient promise to warrant a study. The SEUC did not possess a large MIS group, and did not have a history of development in this type of decision support. It was evident that the model would have to be created by an outside firm, and that this firm would have to train the in-house staff in the use of the system.

One of the members of the management team had an interest in expert systems, having seen some demonstrations and participated in discussions at a recent conference. Although she had little experience in the technology, it did appear that the heuristic, rule-of-thumb nature of the decisions being made, the need to reason with uncertain information, and the "structured selection" nature of the problem (choose to "hit the switch" or "not hit the switch") appeared to be a good fit for the technology. It was decided to pursue both paths simultaneously. The consulting firm would be called in to help in the study of statistically based approaches, and the knowledge systems proponent manager would pursue the feasibility of applying a new approach.

Several features of this problem led to the development of a small-scale system prototype using a PC-based, stand-alone knowledge systems development tool:

1. The project was clearly prototypical in nature. A finished system was not the objective. Rather, the feasibility of applying knowledge systems technology was being explored. A correlated objective was to develop some in-house experience with this style of development tool so that its application to other areas might be evaluated.

2. The SEUC did not possess a large-scale MIS department. It was unlikely that there would be sufficient system support to provide the integration of the weather and real-time load-monitoring systems. If the integration of the systems was critical, then the project was unlikely to succeed, owing to the lack of internal support personnel.

3. There appeared to be a very close match between the nature of the project and the contribution of the tool. That is, the match between the tool's rule-based capabilities and the project's requirements was very close. This meant that little sacrifice of the finished system's features was involved in using an off-the-shelf development tool.

4. The individual manager in charge of conducting this study did not have a large amount of time to spend with a hard-to-learn system. If the system were not relatively quick and easy to learn and use, it could not be attempted.

With "proof-of-concept" as the objective, the approach taken was to break the problem into two parts. First, create a system that would decide whether or not the current day was likely to be one on which the use of the switch should be considered. Then, if it were such a day, develop a second system to help identify the appropriate hour to administer the load control. It was thought that the approaches to solving the first and the second problems were very similar, and that if the technology were appropriate for one, it could likely be generalized to the other.

The problem was further simplified by including only a subset of the factors that were usually considered in the decision-making process. The decision regarding which subset of factors to employ came from an analysis of which factors were likely to be the most difficult for the tool. That is, a critical set of factors that needed to be in the final set but seemed the most questionable in terms of the tool's ability was chosen as a starting point. This kept the prototype manageable but allowed the effort to yield nontrivial results. If only the relatively easy and obvious elements of the problem were modeled, the success of a prototype might erroneously encourage the development of a larger system.

The factors included in the model were those that required reasoning with certainty factors about numerical information. This required some skills that did not seem trivial from the initial examination of the tool's capabilities and the sample applications provided. A sample dialog with the prototype system is included in Figure 4–1.

This example is one in which a very small group (essentially one full-time person with occasional assistance) was responsible for doing a feasibility study of a new technology, the technology was likely to be applied in a stand-alone mode, and the problem could be seen from the beginning to fit the tool well. A small-scale, PC-based prototyping tool was selected, and the prototype was completed with relative speed; however, the result of the study indicated that the technology was applicable, and that a larger-scale model should be developed.

An interesting outgrowth of this effort, one that seems to be somewhat common to prototyping efforts in expert systems, was the modeling process itself, quite apart from its intended result. The two people primarily responsible for

```
> go.

What has been the peak for the month-to-date?

Please enter an integer number.

>> 12689

What is the predicted peak for the next 24 hours?

Please enter an integer number.

>> 12890

What is the peak predicted for the NEXT 24 hour period.   That is,
the period of the day after next?

Please enter an integer number.

>> 12790

What has been the average monthly peak for this month from
historic data?

Please enter an integer number.

>> 11896

What is the current day of the month?

Please enter an integer number from 1-30.

>> 24
     hit-the-switch-today = yes (80%) because kb-26.
```

Figure 4–1 Sample Dialog with the Peak Load Manager Prototype

making these decisions over many previous months had to achieve a consensus regarding just how those decisions were made. This resulted in a clarity of relevant factors and the subjective importance of each. When complete, the existence of a formal model of just how the decisions were made resulted in a much more clearly defined, manageable problem, independent of the application itself. The result of focusing attention on previously unclear issues and requiring their resolution has always been an important outcome of quantitative modeling. The application of knowledge systems development tools seems to yield similar benefits in the area of qualitative modeling.

AN EXPERT DATA ANALYST/ADVISOR FOR CONSUMER-PACKAGED-GOODS MARKETING

In a recent book, *The Marketing Workbench*, John McCann surveys the use of information systems by marketing managers in the consumer-packaged-goods industry. In support of this discussion, he provides an overview of the nature of marketing management in this industry. Typically, individual marketing managers have responsibility for a single brand. For example, there are likely to be national brand managers for Crest® brand toothpaste and Cheerios® brand breakfast cereal. Figure 4–2 presents a simplified model of the brand manager's responsibilities and activity. As discussed in *The Marketing Workbench*, there are two major inter-acting forces destined to alter the practice of brand management in this industry: (1) a rapid increase in both the quality and quantity of marketing data available to the manager in assessing the performance of the marketing plan, and (2) a strong move from a single, national marketing plan to a portfolio of regional marketing plans.

As presently practiced, the cycle of activity described in Figure 4–2 is essentially an annual one. Much of the reason for the length of this cycle is the quality and quantity of data available to assess the effectiveness of the marketing plan. Brand managers have access to measures of product movement in the form of warehouse shipment data, reported for several regions of the country along with other data on various advertising and product promotion activities in the market-place. These data are generally reported either quarterly, monthy, or bimonthly depending on the data supplier. When these data are provided, they often lag behind actual product movement considerably, and are aggregated at such a level that the impact of specific product promotion activities is difficult to discern. This means that the manager is often "flying blind" in regard to the real-time impact of a particular marketing plan. It is often not until well into the year's cycle that the impact of a particular marketing plan can be quantified and evaluated. Even then, it is difficult to identify the impact of any individual component of the plan.

The introduction of a variety of microelectronic-based data-gathering instru-ments is quickly providing an opportunity to access much more timely and "actionable" information. One of the major sources of these new data is in-store,

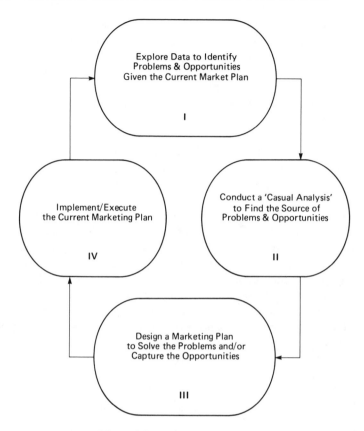

Figure 4–2 Brand Management Cycle

point-of-sale product-scanning equipment. Machines of this type are capable of recording every purchase at over 15,000 retail outlets across the United States. These check-out counter scanners read the Uniform Price Code, printed in a bar-code format, on each item purchased. Each transaction is recorded on magnetic tape and can be made available to monitor product movement at a high level of resolution.

In addition to these point-of-sale data, other relevant information regarding specific advertising campaigns, product promotion activities, and in-store variables like allocated shelf space and display information is becoming available. The potential is emerging to engage in ''real-time marketing,'' and abandon the annual marketing plan in favor of a more responsive strategy based on accurate and timely information reflecting the success of promotion devices as they are introduced.

The availability of timely data of high quality also supports another major force in the consumer-packaged-goods industry, the movement away from a single national marketing plan to a portfolio of regional plans. It has become evident that particular approaches to marketing types of products have an impact that varies for different regions of the country. It is generally believed that if it were possible to create a portfolio of marketing plans, each one more or less appropriate for varying regions of the country, aggregated sales would benefit. As it is now possible to obtain data from individual stores and the demographic data describing the customers generally served by each store, it is even possible to think of designing and implementing marketing plans at the store level.

Given these forces and an understanding of the model of activity provided in Figure 4–2, a national consumer-packaged-goods manufacturer began to explore the potential of knowledge systems technology to take strategic advantage of opportunities in this new, data-intensive environment. Several possibilities were identified.

In Phase I of the cycle in Figure 4–2, exploring data for problems and opportunities, several potential applications were discussed. First, it appeared obvious that with vastly increasing quantities of data available for analysis, and with the need to explore the data both at highly aggregated and regional levels, the existing staff of analysts would not be sufficient to fully exploit the information contained in these data. In the new, adaptive environment the importance of and need for analysis is greatly increased. It seemed promising to develop an expert system that would be able to guide the analysis process and employ rules for indentifying key indicators of deviation from market plan. Such a system would have to be able to interact with the existing mainframe analytical and data management programs, and in a sense, operate as an "intelligent front end" to these existing tools. Such a system could operate as an "agent" of the brand manager by "trolling" through the data, following up promising leads, and pointing out situations that may require intervention.

Phase II in the cycle in Figure 4–2 (conducting a "causal analysis" of the problems and opportunities identified in Phase I) is highly dependent on an iterative process of constructing statistical models, and then examining key indicators reflecting the performance of the model. Analysts engaged in this type of activity are trying to construct a "best" statistical model in some sense. During this activity, many attempts are tried and discarded. It was thought that the rules the analyst uses in evaluating the performance of a model, and subsequently modifying the model, might be amenable to representation in a knowledge system. If so, individuals with less formal training could receive expert advice in obtaining a proper model of the data and create more accurate analyses of the causes of problems and opportunities. In this sense, a knowledge system would operate as an "advisor" to the novice or less trained analyst. This would make the expertise of some of the company's most valuable senior analysts available to a wide base of individual managers, greatly leveraging their skill.

In Phase III, another type of knowledge systems support was explored. In this phase, the brand manager takes information about the brand itself, its performance in the market, and the nature of the market to construct a strategy for the brand's promotion. Under certain circumstances, for example, it may be appropriate to promote a brand by providing opportunities for new customers to sample the product more easily. Under other circumstances, it may be best to promote the product by providing an incentive for the customer to purchase large quantities of it at one time.

Once a particular product promotion strategy has been determined, it is necessary to identify a specific promotion device, like a coupon, a low-price trial-size container, a sweepstakes, a contest, a rebate, or a special price on a large-quantity purchase. This process of assessing a particular brand's "situation," determining the proper strategy for promoting the brand in that situation, and then selecting the appropriate, specific promotion device also seemed promising for knowledge systems support. If such a system could be developed, advice in developing an approach to promoting products could be made available to managers in regional offices. Again, this would leverage the knowledge of the existing, senior brand managers, making it readily available to less experienced members of an expanding brand management force.

Finally, in Phase IV, the marketing plan must be implemented by a sales force at the local level. Members of this force call on individual customers and offer "trade promotions" or incentives for distributors and retailers to participate in promotion activities. Often the success of a marketing plan has much to do with the ability of the sales force to respond to an individual customer's needs by providing options that are specifically tailored to that customer's circumstances. Again, it was seen that the availability of an "advisor" style of system to help the sales force develop alternative approaches to promoting products at the customer level would allow the marketing decision-making process to be passed further down the chain and into the field. This would increase the adaptiveness of the sales force, and support the further regionalization of the marketing process.

The analysis identified a number of potential applications of knowledge systems. Characteristic of them all is a need for any resulting system to be firmly integrated with the mainstream of existing information systems. They all require access to significant amounts of existing data that are currently recalled and manipulated by existing data management software. In most cases, the potential applications involve either assuming some responsibility of an existing manager whose activity very much depends on the availability of data in an interactive mode. That is, in many of the cases above, a resulting system would request some information, apply certain rules to the interpretation of that information, and based upon the result, request some other information. This interactive, iterative approach to existing data systems requires something very much apart from the stand-alone type of system described in the utility company example first cited.

Also of importance is that this organization has a large, supporting information systems group. The availability of this technical expertise would be a vital resource if any of the endeavors described above were to be undertaken. Clearly, the "systems" aspects of these potential applications are as much critical factors as are the knowledge representation and modeling tasks.

Because of the potential for these applications to have Era III types of impact on the nature of the consumer-packaged-goods business itself and the competitive forces at play in this marketplace, capturing opportunities like these has a high strategic value. Therefore, the resources required to initiate projects of this type may be justified.

Because of the scale and nature of these applications, it was decided to begin exploring development systems that were highly ''integratable'' with existing data management and analysis technologies. These would include software systems that could run either in the mainframe data processing environment common to existing systems or on separate, dedicated machines having access to data from the mainframe processor. Some development systems appeared to meet the requirements of this group of related projects.

A FINANCIAL STATEMENT ANALYSIS ADVISOR

Financial institutions, as a matter of daily operations, evaluate the financial strength of other organizations. They may need to value a company's stock, assess the attractiveness of a business merger or acquisition, evaluate the risk involved in lending money, and so on. The primary source of information regarding a business's financial position is its financial statement. There are strict principles and rules regarding the way in which a company reports its status in a financial statement. These are referred to as Generally Accepted Accounting Principles. However, even within this structure, companies have options in the way they choose to report their status. Most often, when these options are exercised, they are documented in the form of footnotes to the financial statement.

Depending on the impression that a company may wish to create, it can exercise some discretion in its reporting. With differing objectives in mind, the same set of ''facts'' may be presented in different ways to create different impressions for different readers. Financial institutions need to interpret financial reports in order to make lending or investment decisions. Generally, highly trained and experienced mangement engages in careful analyses and reviews of financial statements to make these decisions. There is no one way of completing such an analysis, because there is strong interaction among such factors as the intent of the reporting company, the methods of accounting employed, and the objectives of the financial institution evaluating the report. If one were analyzing a financial report with an eye toward acquiring a company, the questions asked and analyses conducted would generally be different than if one were trying to determine the risk involved in lending the company money for capacity expansion.

Within one such institution, it was recognized that the time-consuming ability to analyze financial reports to support specific types of decisions formed a bottleneck for many operations. The lack of skilled analysts restricted the number of options that could be assessed at any one time. When several opportunities were available for investment, the set of opportunities necessarily had to be restricted, owing to the time involved in conducting an analysis of each. It was thought that any leverage of managerial expertise in this area would expand the ability to consider alternatives, and increase the profitability of decisions by providing a wider range of choice, and possibly more accurate analyses.

The first possibility considered was to "clone" a senior analyst in the form of a knowledge system. Upon more detailed investigation of this approach, it became clear that several distinct domains of knowledge were employed by financial statement analysts. One such area is knowledge of accounting practice and reporting. Another is related to the criteria for comparing one company with another, given a specific set of investment objectives. There is also a need for knowledge of the nature of the business being evaluated. For example, some factors might be important in evaluating an aerospace company but would be relatively unimportant in the health care industry. Finally, knowledge of trends within the industry and the general economy is required. These sources of knowledge are, of course, interdependent.

This analysis led to the conclusion that any attempt to substantially duplicate the activity of a financial statement analyst was a very complex one involving a great deal of general knowledge. The complexity of the task made it appear too complex, risky, and resource-intensive to attack at one time. Instead, it was decided to apply knowledge systems techniques to one aspect of the problem. The objective was to provide an expert assistant to the financial statement analyst to support the more technical aspects of the process.

The preliminary exploration of the nature of financial statement analysis revealed a component of the larger task that seemed to be sufficiently well bounded to be modeled, and worthwhile in and of itself. The decision was made to model specific knowledge guiding the analysis and interpretation of spreadsheet-based information in support of very specific types of decisions within a specific industry.

An analyst typically changes quantitative values in some model. For example, the modeler may vary the value of the discount rate or the cost of goods sold over some range of values in order to assess the impact of various scenarios on other components of the model like net present value or internal rate of return. In this way, sensitivity analyses are conducted to identify areas of risk in a decision by systematically varying some key quantitative elements in the model.

The type of "what if" analysis generally carried out in the process of financial statement analysis could be characterized by questions of the form, "What if they reported these lease payments as short-term debt, rather than near-term debt?" That is, the "what if" generally relates to "what if the model were constructed somewhat differently." In this way, financial statement analysis may involve a considerable amount of "remodeling" the financial statement, each time trying to gain another insight into some aspect of the company's financial health from some new perspective. The process involves modifying the structure of the model, as well as modifying the values of specific variables within each model.

It was decided that constructing an expert "modeling assistant" to support the financial statement analyst in making a restricted class of decisions within a specific industry would be a tractable task, one that would yield some benefits in and of itself, and could be a component in a larger system that might be developed as the firm gained experience with knowledge systems technology. Such a system would provide summaries in the form of reports based on preliminary reviews of financial statements. If the user desired, the knowledge system could vary some components of the spreadsheet model to better identify critical information and report the findings.

As before, an important component in deciding on a tool and an approach to managing systems development has to do with the extent to which the new system will interact with existing applications, and the availability of support and expertise. The computing environment for this application may be best thought of as "work group" computing. Work group computing may be positioned as an intermediate point on the scale from individual, personal support computing to centralized information systems. Here, members of the work group engage in a considerable amount of individual, personal support computing on desktop workstations. However, because of the nature of the group's work, there is a great need for information exchange by sharing both data and models. Because members of the work group will serve as participants in group efforts, and conduct similar types of analyses in the solution of similar types of problems, it is necessary for their individual systems to be connected to some type of network in order to have access to file transfer and communication facilities and common sets of tools. Typically, the software support for this type of effort includes some type of data base management facility, some quantitative modeling capability (like spreadsheets and/or statistical modeling), word processing, report generation, graphics, electronic mail, and calendar/scheduling support. The similarity of the work being performed, the professional nature of the activity, and the need to form small groups of cooperative co-workers around specific projects defines these information systems needs. The networking capabilities for such systems may be provided by a local area network or some departmental-level minicomputer. Only rarely do the data needs of such a group require real-time access to centrally located, corporately maintained transaction-oriented data. When centrally maintained data are required, they are generally of a historical nature and are used in forecasting to support other modeling efforts. Real-time updates and sophisticated connectivity to centrally maintained data sources are rarely required.

The level of technical sophistication required to support this type of system is significantly higher than that required for any individual professional to care for his or her own computing effort. The amount of "system" knowledge is simply greater because there is a "system" to be managed. This burden is sometimes sufficient to warrant the hiring of a full-time systems support person. In less demanding circumstances, the gap between individual and work group support has been filled by one or two members of the work group who have an interest in the system itself. This person (or persons) provides the primary level of support for the rest of the group, and may be able to call on other, more highly trained systems support personnel from the MIS department or the information center when the need arises. However, it is the knowledge that this individual (or individuals) has of the applications and profession that makes his or her support most valuable. Such an individual can make systems decisions with full knowledge of the implications for practice. In this way, one of the benefits of the personal computer—the closeness of the user to the system—is maintained as the technology becomes somewhat more sophisticated in meeting work group processing needs.

This form of computing, with its emphasis on personal and small-group support and fourth-generation computing applications development tools, was an important factor in deciding on a tool for the knowledge systems development project. Another important factor was the data needs of the project. This system requires data, to be sure, but it is neither voluminous nor centrally maintained; there is no need to integrate the new system with existing, centrally maintained sources of information.

The requirements of this task and the nature of the computing environment led to this group's choice of an "integrated" as opposed to an "integratable" system. A critical feature for this application is the integration of knowledge systems with the types of analytical functions ordinarily associated with this class of task. The individual components of the system must access one another. In such an environment, knowledge systems routines must have easy access to numerical analysis functions, modeling tools, and data.

In each of these examples, the application areas have been described in terms of their systems and personnel requirements. This is not to downplay the relevance of any particular tool's knowledge representation or inferencing capability. These factors are most certainly important in selecting a development environment. The emphasis here is intended to sharpen the perspective that the issues of noninferential processing, access to data, and support personnel are also critical.

5
—

Knowledge Engineering: The Development of Intelligent Systems Applications

One theme developed throughout this book has been that of using knowledge systems development tools run on mainstream business computing hardware. The discussions of tools in general, and the emphasis on the compatibility and integration of knowledge systems development tools with other applications environments, may lead to the conclusion that knowledge systems development is highly analogous to existing methodologies for traditional systems design, coding, delivery, and maintenance. There are several reasons why this is not the case. Developing knowledge systems applications in business is a fundamentally different process from the development of algorithmically based applications. Some of this distinction arises from the current level of maturity among available tools, as well as the general lack of familiarity among systems developers with artificial intelligence techniques in general. However, still other distinctions arise from the very nature of knowledge systems. These distinctions are the topics of this chapter.

TRADITIONAL STRUCTURED SYSTEMS DEVELOPMENT

Techniques generally applied in systems design and development have evolved from Era I computing applications. These origins have resulted in an emphasis on the efficient design, development, documentation, and maintenance of algorithms. Design and development techniques for this style of application focus on the following stages of activity:

1. Development of functional specifications for the system
2. Structural decomposition of functions into modules or system components
3. Project management of the coding of individual modules
4. Integration of individual modules to form the completed system

Generally, there is an emphasis on the first stage of this process, the development of functional specifications. Most often, this is the area in which the end-user, or client, for the system interacts most heavily with systems professionals. In most cases, once there is detailed agreement between the end-user and the systems professionals as to the system's ultimate functional requirements, the task is one of efficiently producing algorithms in a top-down, structured approach to project management. Such an approach is intended to maximize the efficiency of the development project and to ensure efficient, well-documented, and maintainable computer code.

This is inherently a "reductionistic" approach to systems engineering. It necessarily focuses on the decomposition of systems specifications into individual modules, or islands of function that are interrelated by the larger view of the system's ultimate role. Later in this chapter, this will be contrasted to a "holistic" approach, which is intended to maximize other criteria and results in other approaches to systems engineering that may be more appropriate for knowledge systems development.

It is important to understand that the end-user/client in Era I applications is largely uninvolved in all but the first stage, functional specifications. Once the system's ultimate function is described in detail, its creation is the task of systems professionals. This is possible because all the knowledge required for the decomposition of the larger task to modules, and the development of algorithms to meet the requirements of each module, is in the possession of the systems professional. During this stage of project development, the end-user/client has a relatively insignificant role, if any. "What the system will do" is the domain of the end-user/client. "How it will be done" is the domain of the systems professionals. This is in sharp contrast to the process of developing knowledge systems. As stated above, some of this contrast is a function of the level of maturity among knowledge systems development tools, and some is directly attributable to fundamental differences in just what is meant by "how it will be done," who possesses that knowledge, and how accessible that information is to either the end-user/client and/or the systems developer. Understanding these differences is important, as they have consequences for the process of systems design and development.

KNOWLEDGE ENGINEERING: DESIGNING AND DEVELOPING EXPERT SYSTEMS

In the traditional approach to systems design described above, a systems analyst, together with the ultimate end-users, or clients, for the project, will complete a functional specification of the system. At that point, the project is essentially in the hands of professional project management and programming staff, because that group possesses the knowledge and skill required to deliver the agreed upon features and functions. In the development of knowledge systems, this is simply not the case. Following the specification of function, a new problem arises. This is because it is not an algorithm that is being developed but knowledge that is being encoded for machine use.

The immediate problem is that traditional applications developers do not have sufficient knowledge of the applications area to complete the project from the starting point of a functional specification. This information generally exists in a variety of forms, depending on the applications area. In some cases an individual or group of individuals may uniquely possess the relevant knowledge. In other cases, the knowledge may exist in the form of published materials like manuals or textbooks. In still other cases, the knowledge does not presently exist at all, and must be created and developed along with the system itself. This is an extremely difficult circumstance. Further compounding this problem is a critical factor: Regardless of the form in which the knowledge currently exists, it is *not* in a form that is ready for use by a knowledge system. Someone must decide what knowledge is relevant and desirable for inclusion, acquire the knowledge, and represent it in a form suitable for a knowledge system to apply. In all but trivial applications the task of representing the knowledge requires not only coding individual "chunks" of knowledge, but also organizing and structuring these individual components.

Historically, owing to the remoteness and enigmatic quality of artificial intelligence technologies, the person doing the actual systems development and the "expert," or source of knowledge, were not the same. As is discussed below, the availability of tools, in place of enigmatic technologies, has had an impact on reducing this problem. Even if one can imagine the case in which the "expert" whose knowledge is to be modeled is also an "expert" with the use of artificial intelligence development tools, there still remains a sizable problem.

In the case where the knowledge resides with some practitioner or expert, it does not exist explicitly as a series of IF . . . THEN rules, ready to be encoded. Most practitioners and experts find it difficult to explain explicitly what they are doing while solving problems. They are not cognizant of the underlying rules they are applying. Their expertise has been developed from numerous experiences and involves highly developed pattern recognition skills and heuristics.

In the case where the knowledge to be included is contained in text material like manuals, regulations, procedures, and the like, the information is still not in a form ready for inclusion in an expert system. It must be remembered that one of the most often cited advantages of expert systems is that they make explicit the knowledge that is most often implicit and unavailable for review, evaluation, dissemination, and modification. The task of making knowledge both explicit and available for systems application is that of knowledge engineering. Most literature on the development and application of knowledge systems has identified the need for individuals skilled in knowledge engineering as a critical factor to widespread use of the technology.

As an example, earlier in this book a peak load management system for the Small Electric Utility Company (SEUC) was described. Briefly summarizing that application, the SEUC could better control its costs for electricity if it could accurately predict peak periods of its consumers' power requirements. During those peak periods, the SEUC could restrict power use, reduce the requirement for power production, and greatly lower its costs. A team of individuals was in charge of monitoring such data as current use levels, weather reports, historical use patterns, and the like. These managers were responsible for predicting the peak hour of power use in each month, and exercised control over power consumption at those times via a voluntary load control system. It was believed that the problem of combining these factors and predicting peak hours of electricity use was well suited to knowledge systems technologies.

This, in fact, was the case. Initial efforts to develop a prototype load control system were quite successful in representing the underlying rules that these individuals applied in predicting peak periods of power consumption. It was well recognized that one of the benefits of the process of expert systems development was the explication and refinement of these rules. What is of interest here, however, is that when first confronted with the task of explicating the basis of their decision making, these individuals had a most difficult time. Like most expert practitioners, they could do the job well, but they found the process of explaining their activity in a concise fashion quite taxing.

Two developments have helped to alleviate some of the difficulty in the knowledge engineering process. First is the advent of the type of readily available knowledge systems development tools described earlier. When knowledge systems development required esoteric technologies, using special artificial intelligence languages, it was not feasible for the "expert" to understand clearly what was being done with the information they provided. "Experts" were somewhat removed from the process; they had a hard time understanding what the systems developer was looking for and how their input would be useful. With the advent of knowledge systems development tools, it became possible for "experts" to be rather quickly instructed in the nature of the system being built. They could see with greater ease what type of knowledge was needed and why. This put "experts" in a more educated and proactive position relative to the entire systems development process.

Indeed, in the case of the SEUC, the individuals in control of the decision-making process learned to use simple PC-based tools to complete their own prototype system. In this case, the "expert" and the systems developer merged. Much of the emphasis on the difficulty of knowledge engineering has resulted from early attempts at systems development with older technologies. The availability of newer tools has reduced this problem by helping to educate the "experts" and involve them more actively in the process of providing useful information.

A second development is the introduction of "rule induction" software. This class of tool, often grouped with other "expert systems" or knowledge systems software, is intended to review examples of previous decisions and generate rules to explain them. These rules are then available for application to new problems. This type of system is a first step in the important challenge of creating programs that learn and modify their own behavior. Later in this chapter, the general characteristics, benefits, and limitations of this approach to "automated knowledge engineering" will be discussed. For the present, however, simply let it be said that the knowledge engineering process is getting somewhat easier, but still represents an important factor in differentiating knowledge systems development from that of traditional Era I systems.

Repeating a point made earlier, we note that currently available knowledge systems development tools make use of one of the two general schemes for representing knowledge—rules or frames. Within the rule-based category, which is clearly the more dominant in terms of applications in place and under development, inferencing systems can operate in forward- or backward-chaining modes. Again, the backward-chaining rule-based systems have been the more popular because the intuitive nature of the approach makes it relatively easy to learn, and the large set of applications areas makes it possible to leverage the time spent on the learning curve to numerous projects. However, regardless of the sophistication of the tool and its basic representation scheme, the fact remains that these tools greatly reduce the complexity of knowledge representation and systems coding partly by reducing choice and flexibility, but also by structuring and simplifying the task of knowledge representation. This is an inherent trade-off in the use of any tool.

Knowledge engineering involves acquiring, representing, and coding knowledge. The representation and coding aspects of systems development have been greatly impacted by these newly available tools. The speed with which prototyping can be accomplished has also helped reduce some of the difficulty in acquiring or refining knowledge. The knowledge engineer now finds it much less costly in time and effort to represent, code, and test early approaches to systems development, providing a more efficient feedback loop. This feedback loop is critical in the development of knowledge systems. The end-user/client for the project is, by nature, going to be much more involved in the systems design process than in traditional Era I-based systems, because that person is in possession of the evaluation criteria. The "programmer" often is incapable of deciding if the system is behaving properly, owing to a lack of fundamental knowledge about the applications area. This is simply not as strong a factor as in Era I development, where the programmer is capable of evaluating the accuracy and efficiency of algorithms. When the product is actionable knowledge rather than algorithms, the ability to evaluate project progress shifts to the end-user/client. This creates the increased emphasis on the feedback loop.

THE HOLISTIC APPROACH TO SYSTEMS DEVELOPMENT

The need for rapid prototyping, a short and efficient feedback loop, and the emphasis on "proof of concept" when evaluating the utility of a new technology creates a fundamental shift along the continuum from the well-understood "reductionistic" approach to a "holistic" one. By reductionism is meant the "top-down," structured approach to systems development. Repeating an earlier discussion, we note that in this approach, heavy emphasis is placed on the careful, detailed functional analysis of the system's performance criteria. Once these criteria, or specifications, have been developed, the individual components of the system are conceptualized through a top-down process of functional decomposition. This proceeds until individual units or modules of function have been identified. Planning then focuses on the interconnection of these units, the parameters they will receive as input, and the parameters they will provide as output. At this time, programmers are employed to develop and code the algorithms. The project can be managed like most engineering efforts. This results in an efficient approach to the development of fully documented, maintainable, efficient, and accurate systems. One downside of this approach is that it is often a very long time before the end-user/client actually "sees" or experiences the completed system. From the point of view of efficiency, this is not a problem, as the end-user/client generally has no substantive contribution to make to the process once functional specifications have been provided.

A holistic approach to systems development may be a much more suitable one for projects in which the end-user/client has valuable information that needs to be included in the system itself, and the prototype/feedback loop is critical. This approach is one of building the system in stages; each stage is a complete system with limited function. As the system moves through its stages, it becomes both more functional and more robust, or accurate, in its actions. In small, personal support systems characteristic of Era II applications, this is a dominant approach, for many of the same reasons that it matches well with knowledge systems development methodologies.

In order to clarify the nature of this approach and to better understand its contributions to the task of knowledge engineering, it will be useful to describe the technique in the context of the peak load management system for the Small Electric Utility Company (SEUC). It may be helpful for the reader to review the details of that project, described in Chapter 4, before proceeding.

In the SEUC case, the primary task was described as having two major components. First a decision had to be made as to whether any given day was one for which load control, or "hitting the switch," was appropriate. If, in fact, the conditions indicated that this was the day, then the right hour had to be chosen for load controls to be imposed. The developers decided to focus first on identifying the appropriate day, because this problem was highly similar to that of identifying the appropriate hour.

The preliminary description of the project included the types of data available to the decision makers, as follows:

1. Current, real-time data of the SEUC electrical load
2. Current, real-time data of the LEUC electrical load
3. Current, on-line weather conditions
4. Predicted, on-line weather conditions
5. Historical data on peak load patterns for the SEUC
6. Historical data on peak load patterns for the LEUC
7. Historical weather data
8. Present day of the week and month of the year
9. Knowledge of the patterns of electrical power use within the communities served by the SEUC

Those individuals responsible for load control had developed a variety of heuristics for predicting peak load periods. These heuristics were unknown to them in any explicit, articulated format. It was believed that they could be described and captured in an expert system. The objectives of the project were not only to relieve the decision makers of the "chore" of monitoring and assessing data. It was also believed that the availability of explicit knowledge, and the process of representing it, would result in the identification of areas where decision making could be improved. It would also relieve the SEUC of the problem of training new decision makers as they experienced turnover in these positions.

A key factor in this, as in all knowledge engineering tasks, was that there existed no algorithms for combining these data. Much of the reasoning was necessarily "fuzzy" and involved numerous uncertainties. As such, simply providing a functional description of the completed system would leave a programming staff in a very difficult position, because they would not know what to code. Another important component of this project was that a new technology was being investigated, and "proof of concept" was an important objective of the effort as well.

A holistic approach to systems development was undertaken. This view of systems design, when applied in the knowledge systems arena, can be characterized as progressively "backing the expert out" of the system by leaving his or her expertise behind. The approach begins with an easy, trivial exercise of creating a small set of rules that represent very little knowledge of the underlying task. This preliminary step results in a system that is usable only by the "expert," in that it contains little knowledge and is highly dependent on judgmental input from the user.

The first, trivial step in designing the peak load management system was to develop a two-rule representation of the decision-making process. These rules are stated in an English format, but could be easily translated into the syntax of any rule-based system:

"If this day of the month appears to be the one for which the LEUC demand will be the highest, hit the switch."

"If this day of the month appears not to be the one for which the LEUC demand will be the highest, do not hit the switch."

This trivial system would ask users to judge whether the current day is likely to be the peak for the month and would recommend whether to initiate load control. The system is essentially useless in this form, as the only feasible users are the experts themselves, and no substantive knowledge regarding the decision is represented. However, this becomes the basis for "backing the experts out" of the system, leaving some of their judgmental knowledge behind. It structures the knowledge acquisition process by focusing the process.

At this point the knowledge engineer would enter into a dialog with the experts and ask, "How might you determine whether or not the conditions are such that this will or will not be the day of the month on which peak use occurs?"

This dialog might result in the following expansion of the rule base for this system:

"If the predicted load for this day is higher than that for previous days in the current month, and it is unlikely that a higher load will occur later in the month, then this will be a peak day for the LEUC load."

This rule can then be expanded to the following:

"If the weather conditions for today exceed the historical pattern for the month, and predictions for the remainder of the month are substantially below the conditions for today, then it is unlikely that a higher load will occur later in the month."

This instantiation of the system can then be further expanded by asking questions like, "How do you determine whether or not the predictions for the remainder of the month are substantially below those for today?" This dialog results in another rule or set of rules that represent this reasoning process, and so on.

As the system matures, the "balance of knowledge" shifts from the knowledge source to the system. In early versions, the system must ask the user for substantial quantities of judgment. As this occurs, the question "How did you determine that?" is asked, and new rules are formed. The activity is that of examining the premises of very high-level rules and developing lower-level rules that can make the necessary judgments. In this way, the role of the knowledge source diminishes, as the expertise is progressively encoded into new rules.

This approach is fundamentally different from one of trying to determine the expert's "procedure." This is a critical distinction between developing knowledge systems and algorithmic systems. In an algorithmic approach, one might ask, "What do you do first?" and "What do you do after that?" Such an approach is cumbersome in terms of its ability to reveal the underlying rules of judgment being applied as it focuses on procedures. In small, simple applications, the distinction may be insignificant. However, in situations requiring complex judgment, the idea of developing an algorithm representing the expert's activity is simply infeasible and inconsistent with the goal of knowledge systems development. The objective here is to reveal "what the expert knows" and to make that explicit. The inferencing or reasoning component of the knowledge systems development tools creates procedures dynamically, given the knowledge available, the system's goal, and the specifics of the current situation.

Many individuals trained in traditional, procedural programming languages and algorithmic applications development find this aspect of knowledge systems development somewhat difficult to grasp. They are experienced at developing efficient and robust procedures. The emphasis in knowledge engineering is to develop an efficient and robust representation of knowledge. This requires a different approach to systems development.

Another advantage of the holistic process of systems development in the knowledge systems arena is that it provides the end-user/client with regular, tangible evidence of progress. This is not a "system" argument, but a political one. As the technology is new, and proof-of-concept is important, management may not be willing to invest in large-scale projects with prolonged development times. One outcome of "backing the expert out" of the system over time is that the system becomes useful, in stages, to individuals with less and less expertise. Over time, there is tangible, demonstrable progress in place of statements describing what the system will be like in 18 months or two years. This allows management to gain rapid insight into the cost/benefit ratio, and allows for a stage-oriented series of commitments to project development. At each stage, the functional qualities of the system expand, and decisions can be made as to the worth of further developing its power. In many organizations, commitments to small, specific projects with demonstrable short-range return and long-range, incremental potential are easier to approve than those requiring substantial allocations of resources before progress can be evaluated and value derived.

The dichotomy constructed here between reductionistic and holistic project management philosophies is, of course, an artificial one. Every project, regardless of its algorithmic or knowledge-based nature, incorporates elements of both. The image of knowledge engineering as the acquisition and coding of individual chunks of knowledge is too simplistic. Any nontrivial system has a need for structure. Revealing the underlying structure of knowledge required to perform in some domain and representing this structure with the appropriate tools is an important component of the systems development process. However, this structure is most often not analogous to decomposing a process into subroutines as in traditional programming. The structure of the knowledge is no more known at the beginning of systems development than are the individual knowledge chunks. However, as the structure is revealed during the systems development process, the organizational units of knowledge can be addressed and developed individually. This does allow for some amount of decomposition of the knowledge base itself, and leads to programming efficiencies. In this way, the act of decomposing the larger knowledge base into subparts is similar to reductionistic approaches. The difference is that this process is not completed as an initial step in systems design, but is most often an ongoing component of knowledge acquisition. The ability of tools to represent the structure of knowledge as well as the individual components, or chunks, of knowledge is a function that takes on increasing importance as the scope of a project expands. The need to deal with, and reduce, complexity through schemes for representing the structure of knowledge will become more and more important as organizations gain experience with the development and maintenance of knowledge systems.

REPRESENTING THE STRUCTURE OF KNOWLEDGE

While developing knowledge systems, it is common for the number of rules or chunks of knowledge in a system to follow a cyclical pattern. Early stages may result in several hundreds of rules. The understanding gained of the nature of the problem and the knowledge required to solve it often results in valuable insight and collapsing of multiple rules into smaller sets of more general rules. The initial rule representations may give way to very different structures. This may result in substantial system redesign. The intermediate step of the holistic approach may play an important role in revealing the structure of the problem itself and making possible new approaches to its solution. With the underlying structure revealed, the process of "reprogramming" the system from this new perspective takes place with a clearer vision of the final product and takes on some of the characteristics of traditional, reductionist techniques.

To clarify the function of inferencing systems like backward chaining, this book has presented a series of small, functionally trivial sample knowledge bases. This emphasis on simple knowledge bases is motivated by pedagogical objectives. However, there is an important drawback to this approach. The reader may conclude that by simply adding more and more rules and chunks of knowledge, systems can be developed to handle more and more complex problems. Unfortunately, this is not the case. As the number of rules increases, so do two other factors:

1. The difficulty of conceptualizing the system, which impedes development
2. The mass of rules considered during the inferencing process, which greatly reduces processing efficiency

Like all other systems, different methods of representing their functions are required at different levels of complexity. Each "layer" or "level" of description represents another increment in the system's abstraction. For example, some mathematical systems can be represented at the level of integer numbers, and the symbols, relations, and rules governing this level of complexity are appropriate to the task. However, as one moves up a level of complexity, other systems like matrix algebra are required to order the higher level of abstraction. One important distinction among knowledge systems development tools is their relative strengths at varying levels of knowledge representation.

In the development of small systems, the need to represent, order, and manipulate units of knowledge larger than individual rules is infrequent. A familiar analogy is spreadsheet modeling. Spreadsheets provide many functions and features for quantitative modeling; however, they provide no means for defining, relating, documenting, or manipulating components within large, complex models. For example, if one were to model a large, complex financial system composed of several business units, the tool provides no representation scheme for those subsystems in the larger model.

As humans develop more and more complex conceptual models, they must develop ever higher-order schemes for representing more and more general or abstract concepts. This distinction, the ability of a tool to support the development and management of more complex systems through increasingly abstract concepts and schemes, is a very important one in evaluating the utility of various knowledge systems development tools for projects of varying scope and complexity.

An often used example of this need to structure chunks of knowledge into higher-order units is the development of an expert system for engine fault diagnosis. Automobile engines are composed of numerous subsystems like the cooling system and carburetion. Very little if any of the knowledge relating to diagnosing problems in the cooling system is related to knowledge of the carburetion system. Indeed there are clearly cooling systems and carburetion systems specialists. These specialists may have difficulty if they were to attempt to ''cross over'' and solve problems in each other's areas. In developing a system for engine fault diagnosis, it may be helpful to organize knowledge in a fashion similar to the structure shown in Fig. 5-1.

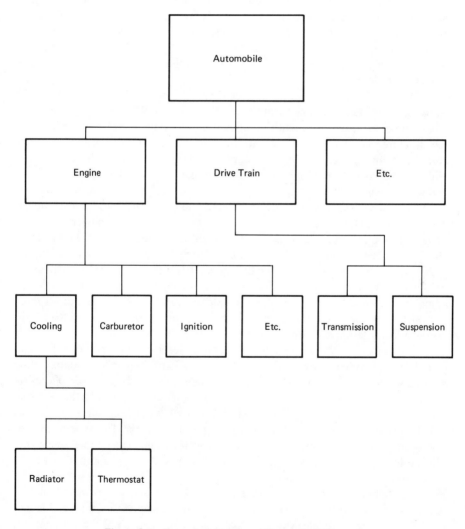

Figure 5-1 Conceptual Diagram of Engine Fault Diagnosis

In rule-based development systems, more sophisticated tools provide the support for representing, organizing, and managing structures like this. Each of the concepts in the diagram of Figure 5–1 can be thought of as a unit. In such systems, rules may "belong to" one or more units. At any one time, only one unit is allowed to be "active." Generally, individual rules are capable of activating other units and, consequently, their associated rules. Finally, procedures are available to restrict and/or allow one unit access to conclusions derived by another. In effect, the developer can write rules about the behavior of the units themselves. These rules define the structure of the knowledge and the flow of information within that structure.

This increased level of knowledge abstraction necessarily comes at a higher level of system complexity. It should not be surprising that this increase in systems power comes at a higher cost in terms of computation resources and a much steeper learning curve. The scope of problems that can be addressed by tools of this power is considerably greater. However, for many applications, this level of systems power is unnecessary.

In terms of maximum power and flexibility of knowledge representation, the frame-based or object-oriented systems are unsurpassed. When using systems with this orientation, users begin with the definition of "objects" or "concepts" and the structure that relates them. Again, this power and flexibility of these systems comes at a high price. The learning curve is relatively steep and long compared with rule-based systems, high levels of computation power are often necessary, and mainstream hardware support and systems integration are frequently missing.

As always, matching the power of the tool to the problem is a critical consideration. One might conceive of a graph of curves that relate the power of various knowledge representation schemes—unstructured rule-based, structured rule-based, and frame-based—with the difficulty of using tools based on each scheme. Figure 5–2 presents such a model. Although this model is entirely conceptual, it is intended to illustrate that each approach to tool design spans a different range of applications complexity. Some levels of problem complexity can be addressed with all three approaches, but for most problems, the choice of one representation scheme will result in lower levels of coding difficulty.

If this were all there was to tool selection, prescriptions would be easily and confidently provided. However, such factors as hardware and computing time constraints, the availability of trained support personnel, and varying emphases on development costs as opposed to costs over a system's life cycle make the selection process much more complex. The point of this discussion is that many individuals will argue that one scheme is "inherently" superior to others. This type of conviction is suspicious. If all other considerations were eliminated, no one underlying scheme for knowledge representation would be found the most appropriate across applications.

The field of knowledge engineering is far too immature at this stage of development to allow for the relatively systematic and prescriptive techniques for tool selection that are available for traditional systems design. Until the combination of increasing experience with knowledge systems tool development and use

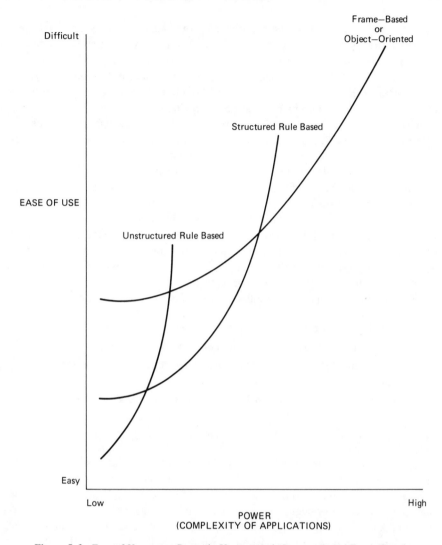

Figure 5–2 Ease of Use versus Power in Unstructured, Structured, and Frame-Based or Object-Oriented Knowledge Systems Development Tools

accumulates, only general criteria and relatively imprecise prescriptions are possible.

AUTOMATED KNOWLEDGE ACQUISITION: RULE-INDUCTION SYSTEMS

As described above, one approach to reducing the complexity of the knowledge acquisition process is to automate it in some way. One vision of such a technology would be a machine that monitors and questions experts as they work and derives an initial representation of their knowledge. As the machine begins to assume responsibility for decision making, it could be equipped with the ability to monitor its own success and both correct and update its knowledge base.

This vision of learning machines is a powerful one, but unfortunately, it is not yet attainable in any realistic sense. Although basic research is very active in this area of artificial intelligence, no generalizable technologies have emerged to date, and tools with these capabilities are not likely to be available in the foreseeable future. However, some early attempts to automate the rule-induction process have resulted in tools that can perform some knowledge acquisition functions. They are limited in the range of problems for which they are suitable; however, for problem areas that fit the constraints, they may provide a useful technology, and are described below.

First Class is perhaps the best known and most widely available PC-based rule-induction system. It features a user interface that adheres to the general criteria of ease-of-use associated with most quality business applications development software. This description will address the specific steps one would use in applying packages like this to a class of problem areas.

Using this rule-induction tool is a five-stage process:

1. Describe the criteria used in making a class of decisions
2. Enter a historical base of previous decisions to be modeled
3. Resolve any conflicting examples or inconsistencies in the historical base of examples
4. Induce the underlying rule structure that explains the examples in the historical base
5. Apply the newly derived rules to new cases

The general structure for defining the criteria for making decisions and for entering and reviewing the historical base of examples is an array. The screen interface for this step is similar to that for spreadsheet modeling and data base management. The user begins by listing column headings that represent the criteria used in decision making. For example, if one were interested in deriving the rules explaining the behavior of a consumer loan officer, the headings might be taken from the consumer loan application itself, for example:

1. Amount of the loan
2. Length of employment
3. Salary
4. Home ownership
5. Current debt obligation

Of course, other information like the applicant's credit rating may also be included. The final column in the model is reserved for the decision to be made—in this case, either to approve or deny the loan.

According to the description of this structure, a series of historical examples are entered as rows in the matrix. Values for all the criteria are entered under each column heading, with missing values being allowed. Finally, the decision that was reached regarding the application is entered in the final column. This process is repeated until all the examples are entered. Figure 5–3 displays sample screen from *First Class* with the headings defined and several sample historical entries.

At the time that examples are entered, the system detects inconsistencies, or "clashes." That is, if two examples have the same values on all criteria and have differing decisions associated with them, the system indicates a "clash." The user must resolve any clashes by correcting the decision entered for one of the examples. When all clashes are resolved, a command invokes the rule-induction process, and the system produces a multileveled decision rule that explains every example. The rules are constructed in such a way that they will fit every example provided. The rules are parsimonious in that they will use the smallest set of available criteria to explain the examples provided. Once the system has developed the rule set, the program can enter a "query" mode in which the system asks the user for values of the criteria used in the rules. Given these data, a decision is generated by applying the newly derived rules. Figure 5–4 provides an example of the hierar-

```
new_Example,  Replicate,  Change,  Activate,  Move,  Delete
        Files    Definitions   Examples   Methods   Rule     Advisor
[F1=Help]        10 Examples in LOAN             [F9=Definitions]  [F10=Methods]

          Loan        Employ       Salary      Home     Debt       RESULT
    1:    10000.      5.           23000.      yes      1450.      approve
    2:    23000.      10.          46000.      yes      1985.      approve
    3:    5000.       1.           12000.      no       1289.      deny
    4:    12000.      2.           15000.      yes      5000.      deny
    5:    7500.       3.           12500.      no       2000.      deny
    6:    1500.       4.           23000.      no       2500.      approve
    7:    2300.       8.           20000.      yes      1490.      approve
    8:    1000        3.           16000.      no       550.       approve
    9:    15400.      6.           37500.      yes      7500.      approve
   10:    15700       2.           23000.      yes      5000.      deny
```

Figure 5–3   Sample Screen from First Class: Input of Examples

```
Edit_rule,  Mark!examples,   Print_rule,    Statistics_on/off        line:
        Files    Definitions   Examples    Methods   Rule    Advisor
[F1=Help]        File = Loan                      [F9=Methods] [F10=Advisor]
---- start of rule ----
Employ??
[    <3.50:Loan??
|          |- <3000.00:--------------------------------approve
|          |- >3000.00:--------------------------------deny
| >3.50:----------------------------------------------approve
---- end of rule ----
```

```
Active examples:      10    Result's Examples:      1    Examples:   8
Result Frequency:  0.60    Result Probability:  0.10    Relative Probability:  1.00
Total weight:      10.00    Result weight:        1.00    Average weight:        1.00
```

Figure 5–4   Sample Screen from First Class: Display of Rule

chical rule structure derived from a small set of examples. This example uses the fictitious data displayed in Figure 5-3; it does not constitute an actual application.

Users familiar with the statistical procedures of multiple regression may erroneously jump to the conclusion that the system is in some way statistically based. However, whereas regression approaches estimate a statistical model to minimize some measure of error, and provide a "fit" to the data, it is extremely unlikely that the fit will be a perfect one. These tools do not result in an equation, but a set of hierarchical rules that will fit the examples perfectly, as they have no restrictions from underlying statistical assumptions, and no mathematical function to optimize.

Although this procedure does produce some potentially very useful results, it has a number of important weaknesses. First and foremost, whereas it does result in rules that resemble in many ways the IF . . . THEN structure used in rule-based knowledge systems, what is really derived is not a knowledge base as discussed here. In actuality, the rules are analogous to the traditional IF . . . THEN structures in procedural languages. The result is not a set of independent, modular rules processed by an inference system like backward or forward chaining. Instead, the result is an algorithm. It would be possible to take an example problem area like the loan officer and develop the modular, independent rules representing these decisions in the form appropriate for use in a knowledge system, and then run the same examples through the rule-induction process. The examples could be structured so that the resulting systems would function equivalently given the same set of new cases to examine. However, the other benefits of knowledge systems would not be available in the procedural rule model.

Another deficiency of this approach comes from the need for a historical base of examples that has the following characteristics:

1. The historical base must contain every factor used in coming to a decision. If other criteria were employed and are not available to the rule-induction process, they cannot appear in the resulting rule structure.

2. The decisions being modeled must be "right" decisions. That is, the resulting rules cannot produce any better decisions than the ones in the historical base. There is no opportunity to "gain insight" or improve the process during systems development.

3. The decisions must be consistent. Although this may not seem like a limitation at first, there are many examples in which inconsistencies are tolerated in the "real world." These include situations dependent on a high degree of judgment and inexact reasoning. It is precisely these environments that provide appropriate problem areas for many knowledge systems applications.

4. During the period of time in which the historical decisions were generated, there must be no change in criteria. That is, if some factor like a change in corporate policy or law resulted in different criteria being applied at different times, this would result in an inaccurate rule structure, as the system must account for all examples.

5. Fairly large numbers of examples are required relative to the number of criteria. That is, there should be a substantially larger number of rows than columns. If one listed ten criteria and three examples, the resulting rules would be highly questionable. This is a similar criterion to that for the ratio of observations to predictors used in multiple regression. Although rule induction is not statistically based, much of the same logic applies. It is possible to capitalize on relationships that are "meaningless" but do represent a viable pattern in the data.

6. There is an indeterminate number of possible rule sets that could be generated to fit the data, not just one. By rearranging the order of the columns, different rule sets can result.

The point of this discussion is simply that the knowledge engineering process is fundamentally different from traditional approaches to program development. It has been recognized that this process is critical and time-consuming. Several factors are reducing the impact of this constraint. These include the development of a variety of techniques for acquiring knowledge from human and printed sources, and the important role of relatively easy-to-learn prototyping tools to speed the feedback loop and help educate human experts so they can be more helpful in the type and quality of information they can provide. These factors are important in the emerging area of "knowledge management," which refers to the recognition of explicit, machine-usable knowledge as a capital good, a resource to be actively maintained and managed.

The prospects of automated knowledge acquisition and machine learning continue to be highly viable and interesting areas of basic research in the fields of artificial intelligence and cognitive science. However, the role of currently available tools and techniques is quite limited. Although in certain circumstances, these rule-induction technologies can be valuable productivity aids, they are not generally useful in the role of knowledge systems applications.

6

A Review of Development Tools: M.1 from Teknowledge, Inc.

There are very real differences in available knowledge systems development tools. These differences require the user to choose carefully in matching tool to application. In this and the next two chapters, three specific, rule-based development environments are described in detail—M.1 from Teknowledge, Inc., GURU from Micro Data Base, Inc., and the Expert System Environment from the IBM Corporation. Each of these has very different design objectives, is intended for different kinds of systems developers, and is best suited for different classes of applications. Although several other systems are available at this time and others are becoming available regularly, these have been selected because of the spectrum of features and functions they represent.

The discussion of each system begins with an overview of the package, noting something about its origins, general purpose, required hardware, and its intended audience. Following this, a description of each system's development environment is presented including such factors as the system's documentation, facilities for creating and editing knowledge bases, the ability to trace and monitor the system's activity while testing knowledge bases, the available methods for documenting the system, and the support for creating and manipulating the structure of larger knowledge bases. The discussions also include a description of each system's general processing capabilities. This includes the inferencing methods, facilities for dealing with uncertainty, provisions for noninferential processing, integration with the operating system and file structure of the host computer, and facilities to represent other data structures like arrays, tables, spreadsheets, text, and the like.

THE PROMOTION ADVISOR KNOWLEDGE BASES

In addition to the description of these three knowledge systems development environments, the Appendix contains sample knowledge bases written in all three systems that address the same problem. Each of the knowledge bases provides essentially equivalent functionality. This chapter and the two that follow end with a discussion/comparison of these knowledge bases as a means to highlight and clarify important distinctions among the development systems.

The objective of these knowledge bases is to provide advice to a new marketing manager regarding the promotion of a particular brand of a particular product that one might find in a supermarket. The structure that underlies each knowledge base is displayed in Figure 6-1. As shown, the ultimate outcome of a consultation with the promotion advisor is advice regarding which specific *promotion devices* the manager should employ. Promotion devices refer to methods like coupons, premiums in the package, mail in rebates, contests, and so on.

But before specific promotion devices can be recommended, the system must identify appropriate *promotion strategies*. Product promotion strategies used in the knowledge bases are taken from the following set:

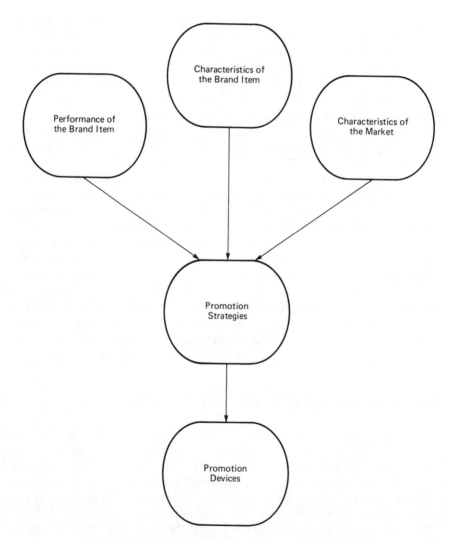

Figure 6-1   Conceptual Structure of Promotional Advisor System

1. **Trial**—This strategy is used to provide incentives and mechanisms for consumers to be introduced to the product and its benefits.
2. **Retrial**—Under certain conditions, when it is best for the consumer to experience use of the product more than one time, a retrial strategy is called for.
3. **Continuity**—Under other conditions, it is desirable to induce consumers to develop a pattern of purchasing the product repetitively. Continuity refers to continuity of purchase.
4. **Convenience**—Still other conditions will dictate a "convenience purchase" strategy. This approach induces the consumer to purchase substantial quantities of the product at one time.

Each of these promotion strategies is applicable under different conditions; however, conditions may overlap in such a way that more than one strategy may be appropriate at one time. To choose among available strategies, the promotion advisor requests information about the following circumstances:

1. Characteristics of the brand item
2. Performance of the brand within the market
3. Characteristics of the market

So, for example, a brand item like toothpaste has different characteristics in terms of product promotion, from potato chips. Also, a brand that is getting its share of the market and is widely known to consumers will be promoted differently from one that is a struggling new entry. Finally, the brand's market has relevant characteristics. If the market is growing, such as the market for soft drinks, one might promote a product differently than if the market is stable or declining.

Each of these chapters describing different knowledge systems development tools provides sample output from a consultation with the promotion advisor, as it is written in that tool. The sample knowledge bases themselves are provided in the Appendix and are referred to in the text of each chapter. The relevant distinctions among the knowledge bases, the experience of constructing each, and the prospects of expanding each are also discussed. These knowledge bases are prototypes intended for instructional purposes; however, they reflect many typical characteristics of prototype systems and provide a good point of departure for these discussions.

The prototype Promotion Advisor is intended to demonstrate ways in which a problem like this might be structured and represented for a knowledge systems application. Because of its prototype level of development, two aspects of systems implementation are discussed in the context of each of the three development environments. First, the experience of developing the prototype is described. Then, the prospects of expanding the system to a more complete, final form are explored.

As the prototype Promotion Advisor currently exists, it is a stand-alone system with very few requirements for representing anything but rule-based knowledge. Also, there is little call for processing anything other than rules. If the system were to be expanded, however, these simple requirements would be placed under considerable stress. As the reader will discover, the prototype Promotion Advisor requests the end-user to supply judgments regarding data. For example, the end-user may be asked

"Is the brand performing as expected with respect to market share?"

or,

"When compared with your competitors, is the percentage of your customers who are brand-loyal high, medium, or low?"

To answer such questions, the end-user must not only have access to relevant data, but must analyze them in an appropriate fashion, and then interpret them correctly. If the Promotion Advisor prototype's power were significantly expanded, it would be necessary for the system to access, analyze, and interpret these data. This is consistent with the approach discussed in an earlier chapter of "backing the expert out" of the system, and making the knowledge base more "self-reliant" and useful in the process. Therefore, comparing these development tools only in terms of their ability to implement the smaller prototype version of the Promotion Advisor might be misleading. With this in mind, the prospects of expanding the prototype within each development environment will also be described.

M.1 FROM TEKNOWLEDGE, INC.: AN OVERVIEW

The M.1 package from Teknowledge was the first commercially available knowledge systems application development tool for use with the IBM PC. As such, it has been highly visible, and has become a familiar package to many. Teknowledge is a corporation with ties to faculty at Stanford University, where a great deal of early knowledge systems research was conducted. As such, the M.1 system shows its heritage as a backward-chaining inference system similar at its foundations to the EMYCIN system developed at Stanford.

In large part, one could argue that M.1 was intended to test the proposition that knowledge systems development tools could be provided for an end-user without formal training in AI and be delivered on mainstream hardware. To that end, M.1 has been very successful, and has evolved quickly in response to comments and suggestions from its initial set of users. Teknowledge also offers a larger, mainframe system, S.1, which is similar to M.1. However, the two are not compatible. The company also offers extensive training and custom systems development consultation services. The M.1 system is, therefore, an important part of Teknowledge's line of systems and services. It is backed by a company that deals exclusively in the knowledge systems industry.

Orignally M.1 was written in the PROLOG language. However, since its original release, the package has been entirely rewritten in C. This has increased the system's speed and allows external processing routines written in C to be "linked" to M.1.

M.1 is regarded as a system for the novice developer, or end-user/client. Although it is certainly possible for professional developers to create sophisticated systems for nonprogramming end-users, the package's strengths lie in ease-of-use and the speed with which prototyping can be accomplished. Using M.1, programmers new to knowledge systems concepts can quickly gain insight into the fundamentals of backward-chaining inferencing and begin developing small- to medium-sized systems. This is because the tool is very focused in its ability, offering less choice in its use, and consequently less "overhead" in learning to use the system.

Although it is limited in the scope of appropriate applications, its range fits a large number of applications areas very well. If a developer has an application in this set, M.1 offers real advantages over systems designed for larger and more complex development projects. In many ways, it is similar to Lotus 1-2-3 in that it is aimed at a specific size and type of applications area. Within that domain it is powerful and easy to use. When the limits of that range are reached, it requires considerably more time and expertise to accomplish the task, and it is here that one must consider acquiring additional, more suitable tools.

THE DEVELOPMENT ENVIRONMENT

Documentation of the M.1 system consists of a single manual, although other materials and training are optionally available. The documentation is in the form of a "reference" manual, although some general overview and instructional materials are woven into the reference format. This is helpful because the world of knowledge systems is sufficiently unique that learning only from reference materials would be difficult; however, the materials provided may not be sufficient for the novice to come quickly up to speed. In most organizations, it would be beneficial for at least one person, designated for support, to attend the instructional program offered by Teknowledge. In most cases this experience should be sufficient to allow that person to conduct in-house instruction and train additional support personnel.

One characteristic of the tool is that it has been designed with many "default" decisions having been made for the developer. If the application fits these default conditions, only a minimum of coding is requried to get a knowledge base up and running. By specifying a goal for the system, entering some relevant IF . . . THEN rules, and typing the command "go," the inference engine will begin its task and even format the inquiry to the user for information that cannot be found as the consequence of rules. If the user wishes to modify the "default" settings, this requires additional effort; however, the default settings fit many applications well and allow for very rapid development, as ideas can be coded and tested quickly.

The support environment for creating and editing the knowledge base is somewhat limited, however, and this can cause problems as applications begin to grow. For larger applications, this has the effect of slowing the process in later stages of development. Although M.1 does have an internal rule-editing capability, the process of creating and maintaining nontrivial knowledge bases in M.1 requires the user to employ a word processor or text processor separately from the M.1 tool. Knowledge base files are maintained in an ASCII text format, and only minor editing and creating functions are available through the tool itself. The mechanics of development generally follow the following pattern:

1. The developer creates a knowledge base in a word or text processor, saving the result as an ASCII-formatted file.

2. The developer leaves the word or text processor and enters the M.1 environment.

3. Once in the M.1 environment, the developer loads the ASCII file. M.1 will "compile" the knowledge base and examine the contents for syntax errors. If any syntax errors are found, error messages are displayed.

4. If there are no errors in syntax, the inference engine can be invoked and the knowledge base "run" and tested.

5. To modify significantly the knowledge base to correct syntax errors or expand it, the M.1 environment is exited, and the word or text processor is reentered; then the cycle is repeated. Within M.1 the developer can add new elements and modify existing ones. These changes can then be saved. This editing capability is limited to one element at a time, however.

There are strengths and weaknesses to this approach. On the positive side, it requires no significant effort in learning new development and editing tools, as the user's familiar word or text processor serves that role. However, this means that the creation and editing environment is not specifically designed to respond to the structure of knowledge bases. Word or text processors do not know about "rules," "premises," "conclusions," "goals," and the like. To these processors, files are arranged in the units of characters, words, paragraphs, and format divisions. As such, the task of manipulating knowledge bases is not as efficient as in an environment specifically designed for the task. M.1's internal editor is helpful in solving some of these problems.

Aside from the problem of working in a generalized text environment for creating and editing knowledge bases, additional drawbacks arise because the developer spends time moving back and forth between the editing and knowledge systems environments. For more adept PC users, tools like IBM's Topview, Borland's Sidekick, or Microsoft's Windows allow for more fluid movement between tools. Also in keeping with M.1's emphasis on rapid, easy development for small- to medium-sized systems, the burden of "structuring" and documenting the knowledge base is entirely on the developer. If one does not want to bother with this task, the M.1 system does not require it. In this way developing systems with M.1 is similar to developing models with a spreadsheet package like Lotus

1-2-3. The developer is free to structure and document the system carefully or not. If it is worth the effort in a particular project to spend the time decomposing a model into subparts and relating them through documented references, this can be done. If the application calls instead for a quick test of some ideas, the ''structure'' of the model and its documentation may not be required; they can be avoided by omission. Also, as in Lotus 1-2-3, when the task requires structure and documentation, the tool provides little in the way of support for this approach. In M.1 the user can add comments to the ASCII file that are visibile only in the word or text processor. In M.1, when the knowledge base is viewed, these comments are not available, as they are simply ignored when the file is read.

It was noted in the previous chapter that in some instances it is highly desirable to structure a knowledge base by decomposing it to subparts. Each subpart contains knowledge about a particular activity. The example used was automobile engine fault diagnosis. In this case, it may be useful for the developer to isolate knowledge about carburetor diagnosis and repair from knowledge of the automobile's cooling system. This structuring leads to efficiencies in the processing of such knowledge bases and the maintenance of the knowledge itself. M.1 allows this type of problem decomposition to take place. The developer simply builds separate knowledge bases for each type of knowledge. A ''top level'' knowledge base can determine which of the ''lower-level'' knowledge bases are needed, remove itself from M.1's memory, and load the lower-level rules. However, there is no provision in the M.1 system for maintaining records of such components, their interrelations, or what information is to be shared and what is to be exclusively owned by a particular knowledge base. Later this approach will be contrasted with the ''focus control block'' structure of the Expert System Environment.

Once a knowledge base is loaded into M.1 and the testing and validation process begins, several useful features are available. M.1 provides a set of windows, called ''panels,'' to be displayed on the screen during a consultation. This panel provides a view into the internal operations of the inference engine while it is running. One can see what the system is trying to accomplish (goals and subgoals), what it concludes to be true as it concludes, what rules are being considered, why, and so forth. The ''speed'' of the panel can be controlled to allow careful monitoring of several components of the inference engine as it processes a knowledge base.

It is also possible to turn on a verbose ''tracing'' function during consultation and have a narrative description of all system activity during processing. This trace and any other output from the system can be routed to a file for later review or to the printer for a written reference to the system's behavior. In addition, at any time during the consultation, in response to any question, the user can ask the system to display either all the facts it has concluded and how it concluded them or just specific facts. It is also possible to inquire as to ''why'' the system is asking a particular question and view the rules currently under consideration.

If, during the consultation, the developer wishes to make an alteration in the current knowledge base by adding a rule, removing a rule, or altering the facts the system believes are true, this can be accomplished within a consultation. However, when the knowledge base is changed in this way within the M.1 environment, those changes are only temporary. For the changes to be permanent, they must also be made in the "source" file itself, via the word or text processor.

Lotus 1-2-3 freed the end-user/developer from considering many cumbersome details in getting something "up and running." In a similar way, M.1 eliminates the need to spend time with factors that may not be relevant for a particular application development project. The trade-offs between speed of development, ease-of-use, flexibility, and power are well known. Just as Lotus 1-2-3 is not suitable for all quantitative modeling applications, neither is M.1 suitable for all rule-based knowledge systems development projects. However, for those that it fits well, it is amazingly easy to learn and use.

INFERENCING AND DEALING WITH UNCERTAINTY

M.1 is a backward-chaining inference system. Some provisions for modifying this approach are made available through its "WHENFOUND" and "PRESUPPOSITION" functions. These allow for a temporary suspension of backward chaining under certain specific conditions. They do not allow, however, for an implementation of the forward-chaining inference process.

In its "default" mode the M.1 inference engine will backward chain first when searching for the values of needed variables; if the information cannot be found as the consequence of a rule, the user is asked to supply it. This sequence of searching for information can be modified with the "INITIALDATA" function, which tells M.1 always to ask the user for certain information before the consultation begins. This eliminates unnecessary searches for information that the system always needs and cannot find as the consequent of any rules. Examples of this type of information in the automobile fault diagnosis area might include the car's manufacturer, model, and year. In addition, the system provides a "DONTASK" function that tells the inference engine never to ask the user for certain information, even if it cannot be found by backward chaining through the knowledge base. This prevents users from being faced with requests for information that the system developer believes they will not possess.

These types of controls constitute important facilities to modify the backward-chaining process. They are useful in developing anything but the most trivial applications. Backward chaining as a basic approach to problem solving is very powerful, but its *exclusive* use would be very restrictive in the construction of meaningful systems. The developers of M.1 have emphasized keeping it simple and quick, but they still provide considerable control and flexibility within the bounds they have chosen.

M.1 provides mechanisms for reasoning with uncertainty through the concepts of "certainty factors" and "unknown" information. Certainty factors are one of the fundamental features of knowledge systems; they allow for reasoning to take place under "fuzzy," or unclear, conditions. In the process of decision making it is often the case that some facts lead one to believe, with varying levels of certainty, that some other fact may be true. Likewise, decision makers may have only some evidence that certain key components in a situation are present, but by the nature of the circumstances, they cannot be absolutely sure. Because reasoning involves chains of implications, and there may be uncertainties in both the premises and conclusions of rules, there must be some method for representing and combining certainties during the reasoning process. For example, refer to the following rules:

Rule 1:
IF A IS TRUE THEN C IS TRUE.

Rule 2:
IF B IS TRUE THEN C IS TRUE.

Rule 3:
IF A IS TRUE THEN C IS TRUE CF 80.

Rule 4:
IF A IS TRUE AND B IS TRUE THEN C IS TRUE.

Rule 5:
IF A IS TRUE OR B IS TRUE THEN C IS TRUE.

Rule 6:
IF A IS TRUE AND B IS TRUE THEN C IS TRUE CF 80.

In the examples above, Rule 1 states that A implies C, and Rule 2 states that B implies C. In the M.1 system, confidence in an assertion is represented by a certainty factor (CF) on a scale from −100 to 100. On this scale, −100 indicates that there is absolute certainty that the assertion is *not* true. A certainty factor of +100 indicates that there is absolute certainty that the assertion *is* true. A certainty factor of 0 indicates that there is no certainty one way or the other. Of course, values all along the scale are usable, but only in integer form. If a certainty factor is not provided in the conclusion to a rule or in a user's input, it is assumed that the assertion is made with CF 100.

If it were believed that A is true with a certainty factor of 70, and that B is true with a certainty factor of 90, and M.1 were to apply Rules 1 and 2 only, there are two independent sources of information regarding the truth of C. Because there are two independent indicators that C is true, belief in this assertion is strengthened. M.1 combines the certainties from the two rules in the following manner. Rule 1 will result in a belief that C is true with a certainty factor of 70, because that is the level of confidence in A.

Rule 2 increases the system's confidence in C. When Rule 2 is applied, confidence in C will increase to a certainty factor of 97. Because there is a certainty factor of 90 that B is true, the system's confidence can move 90 percent of the way from its previous level of confidence in C toward absolute certainty. Because there had been a confidence in C of 70, there is a distance of 30 between this position and absolute certainty. The new fact that B is true with CF 90 allows 90 percent of the distance to be traversed. This increases confidence that C is true by 27 points (.90 × 30) along the scale to a total of 97 (27 + 70). As described in an earlier discussion, this is very different from the concept of joint probabilities, and should not be confused with the mathematics of that concept.

In Rule 3, the conclusion is that C is true with a certainty factor of 80. If only this rule were encountered, and the system had knowledge that A were true with a certainty factor of 30, then it would conclude that C was true with a certainty factor of only 24. In the simple condition of passing the confidence in the premise on to the confidence of the conclusion, the rules of combining probabilities are followed, and the two certainty factors are multiplied (.30 × .80).

Rule 4 has a compound premise, requiring BOTH A AND B to be true in order to conclude for C. If the system believed that A were true with a certainty factor of 70, and that B were true with a certainty factor of 80, then if it consulted this rule only, it would conclude that C is true with a certainty factor of 70. Because BOTH A AND B are required, the lower of the two confidence factors is used in calculating the confidence in the conclusion. This is equivalent to passing on the weakest link in the chain because BOTH are required.

In Rule 5, however, the truth of EITHER A OR B will allow one to conclude for C. If only Rule 5 were considered, and the system believed that A were true with a certainty factor of 70 and that B were true with a certainty factor of 80, then it would conclude that C is true with a certainty factor of 80. Because the premise states that EITHER A OR B will provide evidence for C, then the strongest evidence is carried forward.

Finally, if only Rule 6 were encountered, and the system believed that A were true with a certainty factor of 70, and that B were true with a certainty factor of 80, then it would conclude that C is true with a certainty factor of 56. Because BOTH A AND B are required, the system's confidence in the premise of Rule 6 is only 70. This is "passed on" to the conclusion through the multiplication of .70 and the conclusion's confidence factor of 80, to produce a final certainty factor of 56 for the truth of C.

The methods described above for combining certainty factors have their roots in early knowledge systems research and development. They are examples of "certainty factor algebra." There are many other possible variations. However, the methods described above are the only methods available for use in the M.1 system. Although they have proven in many cases to be robust and generally useful, there are circumstances in which the developer may wish to employ different certainty factor algebras. In the M.1 system, no options regarding certainty factor calculations are available. Again, this simplifies development by reducing choice. And again, the choices made by the developers of M.1 fit most application areas well.

As in all other rule-based knowledge systems, M.1 allows the developer to represent and reason with unknown information. It is possible to indicate that the value for any expression is unknown, and to test in the premise of a rule whether or not something is known or unknown, and indicate what action to take under such conditions. One such action might be to assign some default value when no value can be attained from the user or from the examination of rules.

INTEGRATION AND NONINFERENTIAL PROCESSING

M.1 is essentially a stand-alone knowledge systems development tool designed for backward chaining. Although M.1 provides access to external files and some noninferential processing, these aspects of the system are minimal and, in some cases, require writing external routines in the C or asssembler language. These, again, seem to be design decisions that reflect its intent to be used as a straight-forward prototyping environment.

There are two forms for representing information in M.1. There are statements of fact, such as

```
preferred__wine = 'burgundy' cf 80.
```

as well as the familiar rule structure. M.1 provides the ability to collapse more complex statements of fact into a table form like the following:

```
wine(white,light,dry) = 'soave'.
wine(white,light,sweet) = 'chenin blanc'.
wine(red,medium,sweet) = 'gamay'.
```

This allows the system to do some table lookups using "variables." Variables in M.1 are powerful tools for collapsing many rules into one. Any character string beginning with a capital letter that is not contained in quotes is regarded as a variable, or wild card, that can take on any value. For example, if the system had asked the user for such factors as preferred wine color, preferred wine body, and preferred level of sweetness, then the following rule would do a table lookup to find a recommended wine:

```
If preferred__color = X and
   preferred__body = Y and
   preferred__sweetness = Z and
   wine (X,Y,Z) = W
then recommended__wine = W.
```

The rule construction above is a bit unconventional in appearance. This has much to do with the fact that M.1 is not designed for table lookups in the conventional sense. However, with such "bending" of the system, it is possible to provide some of the capabilities of other schemes for representing information. The availability of tabular structures of this type is a step in the right direction; however, there are many limitations on its use. It would be a serious mistake to conclude that this approach duplicates anything but the most trivial functions of a data management system. What it offers, mainly, is efficiencies in the space required to construct knowledge bases. Without the use of variables, this rule would have to be repeated with specific values, in a form such as

```
If preferred__color = white and
   preferred__body = light and
   preferred__sweetness = dry
then recommended__wine = soave.
```

Variables in M.1 can be used for much more than efficiency in numbers of rules. They represent an important feature in adding flexibility to more creative knowledge engineers. Consider, for example, the following rule:

```
If temp = X and
   X > = 50 and
   X < = 100 and
   X − 50 = Y and
   Y × .2 = Z
then weather = hot cf Z.
```

This rule determines whether the temperature is in the range of 50 to 100 degrees. If it is within that range, the rule maps the temperature into a certainty factor for the conclusion that weather = hot. If the temperature is 50 degrees, the conclusion is that weather = hot is drawn with a certainty factor of 0. This corresponds to no belief. If the temperature were 60 degrees, the conclusion would be that weather = hot with a certainty factor of 20 (the bare minimum to conclude something is true). At 90 degrees, the conclusion would be that weather = hot with a certainty factor of 80. And at 100 degrees the fact that weather = hot would be concluded with absolute certainty. As can be seen in this example, the use of variables allows for procedural, numeric processing to take place within the constraints of rule syntax, although the structure appears awkward.

M.1 provides some mathematical capability. However, a simple procedure for computing the fare for a taxi ride would take the form of the following rule:

```
If fare__per__mile = X and
   total__distance = Y and
   X × Y = Z
then cost = Z.
```

This structure shows how procedural programming results can be accomplished in M.1 within the constraints of rule-based inferencing processors. It looks awkward, and certainly takes some getting used to; but it is possible to "bend" the system to accomplish some basic mathematical processing.

In the case of the above rule, if the system had a goal or subgoal of "cost," this rule would be "relevant" in that it concludes a value for cost. When examining the rule's premise, M.1 would need to have a value for "fare-per-mile." If it did not have one, it would back chain to find one from another rule, or if that failed, ask the user. In any case, assuming that the system could derive values for "fare-per-mile" and "total-distance," it would "bind" these values to the variables X and Y, respectively. It would then multiply X and Y and "bind" the result to Z. In the conclusion, the value of Z would be linked to cost by the statement "cost = Z." This strange format is a function of both M.1's underlying representational scheme and its lack of any procedural processing capabilities. Within these restrictions, M.1 offers the following numerical processing:

- Arithmetic operators for addition, subtraction, multiplication, division, integer division returning the quotient, and integer division returning the remainder.
- Arithmetic functions for converting numbers between integer and floating point formats, rounding real numbers, truncating, and finding square roots.

However, the construct of an "array" does not exist, and accomplishing a relatively simple procedural task like sorting a list of values becomes difficult. To achieve any significant level of noninferential processing, it is necessary to "link" M.1 to external functions written in C or assembler. This is certainly an important extension of the M.1 system, and is not to be taken for granted. Some other stand-alone inferencing systems do not have this capability. In addition, M.1 allows one to write to and read from external files. These files can be read and/or written by programs running independently of M.1.

The M.1 reference manual cautions, however, that preparing external functions is likely to require two individuals to play distinct roles in the process:

- Someone familiar with M.1, responsible for knowledge engineering, and,
- A programmer with knowledge of the IBM PC/XT/AT computer DOS operating system, C, or assembly language, LINK, and related utilities.

THE PROMOTION ADVISOR IN M.1

Figure 6–2 documents a consultation with the Promotion Advisor knowledge system. A complete listing of the knowledge base is provided in the Appendix. In the consultation in Figure 6–2, the manager seeking advice was thinking of introducing a new soft drink product when answering the system's questions. To follow the consultation, it will be helpful to describe the general structure of the knowledge base as listed in the Appendix.

Remember that the M.1 knowledge base is created in a text or word processor. In that document, the developer is free to insert comments to provide structure and clarification. As is discussed in more detail below, this is in no way

```
M.1> go

---------------------------------------------------
| Would you say that preference for this brand |
| is overwhelming among those consumers who    |
| have tried it?                               |
---------------------------------------------------

     1.   yes
     2.   no
>> 1 cf 80


---------------------------------------------------
| Would you say that market share is developing |
| normally for this brand?                      |
---------------------------------------------------

     1.   yes
     2.   no
>> 2


---------------------------------------------------
| Would you say that the past 12 month trial rate |
| for this brand is high, medium or low?          |
---------------------------------------------------

     1.   high
     2.   medium
     3.   low
>> why

Your answer will help determine what
promotion strategy to use.

What is the rate of trial for this brand over
the past 12 months?  In other words, of all
purchases of this brand, what proportion are
trial (rather than retrial or continuity)
purchases?


---------------------------------------------------
| Would you say that the past 12 month trial rate |
| for this brand is high, medium or low?          |
---------------------------------------------------

     1.   high
     2.   medium
     3.   low
>> 3 cf 70


---------------------------------------------------
| Is this a brand with high consumer loyalty? |
---------------------------------------------------

     1.   yes
     2.   no
>> 1


---------------------------------------------------
| Would you describe the market for this brand |
|as growing, stable or declining?              |
---------------------------------------------------

     1.   growing
     2.   stable
     3.   declining
>> 1
```

Figure 6–2   Consultation with the Promotion Advisor in M.1

```
----------------------------------------------------
| Would you describe the numbers of consumers who  |
| have used this brand in the past month as lower  |
| than the number who used it over the past six    |
| months?                                          |
----------------------------------------------------
```

```
       1.  yes
       2.  no
>> 1 cf 80
```

```
--------------------------------------------------
| How would you compare the percent of your      |
| customers who are totally brand loyal versus    |
| the percent for your competitors?               |
--------------------------------------------------
```

```
       1.  low
       2.  medium
       3.  high
>> 3
```

```
----------------------------------------------
| Is this product one for which multiple     |
| purchasing keeps consumers out of the      |
| market?                                    |
----------------------------------------------
```

```
       1.  yes
       2.  no
>> 1 cf 70
```

```
-------------------------------------------------
| Is this a brand for which consumer inventory  |
| is correlated with user consumption?          |
-------------------------------------------------
```

```
       1.  yes
       2.  no
>> 1
```

```
-------------------------------------------------
| Is it true that a consumer must use this      |
| brand several times in order to appreciate    |
| this brand's benefits?                        |
-------------------------------------------------
```

```
       1.  yes
       2.  no
>> 2
```

The strategies the system recommends are:

```
       sys_strat = trial (86%) because rule6 and rule4 and rule1.
       sys_strat = convenience (67%) because rule10 and rule9.
       sys_strat = retrial (64%) because rule7.
```

```
--------------------------------------
| Do you agree with this strategy? |
--------------------------------------
```

```
       1.  yes
       2.  no
>> 2
```

Figure 6–2   (*cont.*)

```
-------------------------------------------
| Select the strategy(ies) you prefer      |
| from the list below.  You may include    |
| certainty factors.                        |
-------------------------------------------

    1.  trial
    2.  retrial
    3.  continuity
    4.  convenience
>> 1 cf 90,4 cf 60
```

```
        **  The system is now seeking marketing device.  **


    device = own_brand_coupon (93%) because rule17 and rule14.
    device = sampling (90%) because rule17 and rule14.
    device = trial_size (90%) because rule17 and rule14.
    device = pack_premiums (82%) because rule17 and rule14.
    device = container_pack_premiums (81%) because rule17 and rule14.
    device = bonus_pack (81%) because rule17 and rule14.
    device = refund_coupons (76%) because rule17 and rule14.
    device = free_mail_in_low_proof_premiums (72%) because rule17 and rule14.
    device = high_value_single_unit_refunds (72%) because rule17 and rule14.
    device = group_refunds (72%) because rule17 and rule14.
    device = high_value_smaller_sizes_price_pack (72%) because rule17 and rule14
    device = generic_refunds (70%) because rule17 and rule14.
    device = feature_display_allowances (70%) because rule17 and rule14.
    device = promotion_advertising (70%) because rule17 and rule14.
    device = progressive_refunds (66%) because rule17 and rule14.
    device = free_mail_in_premium_high_proof_required (60%) because rule17 and
rule14.
    device = contests (54%) because rule17 and rule14.
    device = in_pack_games (54%) because rule17 and rule14.
    device = high_value_multiple_unit_refunds (48%) because rule17 and rule14.
    device = off_invoice_allowances (43%) because rule17 and rule14.
    device = continuity_catalog_premiums (36%) because rule17 and rule14.
    device = cross_ruff_coupons (0%) because rule17 and rule14.
    device = self_liquidating_premium (0%) because rule17 and rule14.
    device = low_value_refunds (0%) because rule17 and rule14.
    device = normal_low_value_price_pack (0%) because rule17 and rule14.
    device = high_value_multiple_unit_price_pack (0%) because rule17 and rule14.
    device = sweepstakes (0%) because rule17 and rule14.
```

Figure 6–2   (*cont.*)

required. The M.1 knowledge base in the Appendix has been written taking advantage of these features. Comments appear between "/*" and "*/" indicators. For example, at the top of the knowledge base is a "box" of comments. In other places, main sections of the knowledge base are enclosed in boxes of stars, like the following:

```
/****************************************************************/

/*                           GOALS                          */

/****************************************************************/
```

Each of these is a comment to the system developer/maintainer, and is simply ignored by M.1 when the knowledge base is being loaded. The comments are not available within the M.1 environment when the knowledge base is listed by M.1, because they are simply skipped when the file is read.

For illustrative purposes, the Promotion Advisor knowledge base in the Appendix is arranged into the following sections:

1. GOALS
2. DATA FROM MARKETER
3. REVIEW SYSTEM STRATEGY WITH USER
4. SYSTEM FINDS MARKETING DEVICE
5. CONFIGURATION

In the GOALS section, the system is told that its objective is to find a value for *device*. It is also told that before seeking its goal, it should first determine values for *sys-strat* (this is the promotion strategy, or strategies that the system will recommend), and *strategy* (this is the final promotion strategy, or strategies the system will use to find a value for promotion device). It will either be the same strategy or strategies the system recommends in *sys-strat*, or strategies that the user supplies after a review of the system's recommendations. "Goal" and "initialdata" are called *Meta-Facts* in M.1.

Other important Meta-Facts in this initial section labeled "goals" are "legalvals" and "multivalued." Legalvals tells M.1 what the possible set of values is for some expression it is seeking. For example, in this section, legal values are provided for *strategy*. These are trial, retrial, convenience, and continuity. By declaring legal values, the M.1 system can identify errors in user input (for example, if a user typed "trail" instead of "trial"), inform the user of the error, and ask for the information to be retyped. This also allows for the generation of the menus of choices displayed during consultation. Legalvals statements are very helpful but are in no way required in M.1.

The "multivalued" statement is a very important Meta-Fact in M.1. It allows an expression being sought (e.g., strategy) to have more than one value with absolute certainty at one time. If an expression is not declared as being multi-valued, the system assumes it is "singlevalued." Under these conditions, if the system were seeking "strategy," it would stop doing so as soon as a single value were found with absolute certainty. Since the expression "strategy" is multi-valued, the system will continue to seek values until all its resources have been employed, even if a value is found with absolute certainty. This ability is necessary in any application other than the most trivial.

Moving to the section labeled "DATA FROM THE MARKETER," we see that there is a repetitive format within the knowledge base. Within this format, each concept used in developing a set of system-recommended strategies is treated separately. The first is the concept of "overwhelming product preference." This section is set off with the comment

```
/* OW (OVERWHELMING) -------------------------------------*/
```

Within this section, the rule that uses the concept of "overwhelming product preference'' is listed first, and is labeled rule1. This simple rule states that

If ow = yes then sys__strat = trial cf 50.

This means that if it is known that consumers have an overwhelming preference for this product, there is a certainty factor of 50 that an appropriate strategy for promoting it is to induce consumer trial.

Following the rule is another Meta-Fact, ''question.'' This tells M.1 that if it needs to ask the user for a value of ''ow'' it should use the following question. The ''nl''s included in the question Meta-Fact indicate ''new lines'' to be printed on the screen. The question Meta-Fact is also optional. Without it, when M.1 needs to ask the value for an expression, it will generate its own, standard question. If it were seeking ''ow'' and had no question Meta-Fact for ow, it would ask the user the following:

What is the value of: ow?

The question Meta-Fact, therefore, is one way to control the user interface.

Also in this section dealing with the concept of ''overwhelming product preference'' is a declaration of the legal values for ''ow'' and two other Meta-Facts, ''automaticmenu'' and ''enumeratedanswers.'' These two Meta-Facts direct the system to use the legal values previously declared for ''ow'' to generate a menu of possible answers, and to allow the user to select the desired answer by its number in the menu.

Finally, another Meta-Fact is used, ''explanation.'' This controls the information sent to the screen when the user asks the question ''why'' in response to a question. As described in earlier chapters, the ability of knowledge systems to explain what they are doing during the reasoning process, as well as at its completion, is an important characteristic of the technology. As with each of the other systems described here, the user is free to ask ''why'' at any time. If there is no ''explanation'' Meta-Fact, the system will generate its own text to explain its reasoning, in much the same manner as it generates its own questions in the absence of a ''question'' Meta-Fact. However, as in the system-generated questions, the explanation M.1 generates is tied to the language of the knowledge base. In this case, the text of the active rule would be output to the screen for the user to review. As the text of this rule would be almost unreadable by the user, the ''explanation'' Meta-Fact allows the developer to provide text to be substituted for the more cryptic rule during explanations.

This structure of listing rules, ''questions,'' ''legalvals,'' ''automatic-menus,'' ''enumeratedanswers,'' and ''explanations'' is repeated for each of the concepts throughout the ''DATA FROM THE MARKETER'' section of the knowledge base. The impact of the Meta-Fact statements can be seen when the consultation is reviewed in Figure 6–2.

The consultation in Figure 6–2 begins by asking the user for information by presenting the structured question and menus specified by the developer in the knowledge base. The reader should be able to connect, in a general way, the format of the interaction with the content of the knowledge base in the Appendix. Note the use of the "why" response to the question regarding the "past 12 month trial rate" for the product, and the ability to use the menus and certainty factors in answering questions. After asking a series of questions about the characteristics of the brand, the performance of the brand in its market, and the nature of the market, the system recommends its strategies for promoting the product. These are trial (with 86 percent certainty), convenience (67 percent certainty), and retrial (64 percent certainty). At this point, the user is allowed to review and change these strategies before the system moves on to recommend particular promotion devices. In the consultation in Figure 6–2 the user chooses to override the system's recommendations, and directs the system to use a trial strategy (with 90 percent certainty), and a convenience strategy (60 percent certainty).

These values are used to generate the final set of recommendations for promotion devices. They are listed by the system in descending order of confidence, including those with confidence factors of zero, indicating no confidence in these devices.

One of the important features that has been described in M.1 is the way in which the system uses "default" methods of processing in the absence of user-supplied controls and the resulting rapid nature of prototyping. To illustrate these characteristics, the M.1 Promotion Advisor knowledge base in the Appendix is followed by a "simplified" version. In this version, all the optional Meta-Facts and comments have been stripped from the first version. What remains is the essential information M.1 needs to conduct a consultation. The resulting consultation is much less rich, and has the danger of allowing mistyped user input, as no "legalval" Meta-Facts are used. A consultation with the simplified version of the M.1 knowledge base is included in Figure 6–3. The responses to all the questions are the same as in the consultation in Figure 6–2. It should be noted that without the "question" and "legalval" Meta-Facts, the user must know exactly what is anticipated in terms of responses, as the system cannot provide any indication, and will not correct any user errors.

The point of providing the simplified version of the knowledge base and the sample consultation with it is to demonstrate that very quick prototyping can be accomplished with M.1, and a general approach to the development task can be derived without investing the time in specifying all the "bells and whistles" one would want in a completed application. There may be several attempts to develop an approach to a problem like the Promotion Advisor, each one implemented at the level of the "simplified" version of the knowledge base. Each of these may lead to another approach, with earlier versions generally discarded. When an appropriate structure emerges, then more complete systems development efforts may proceed. This is important for new developers especially, in that the speed with which attempts can be constructed and evaluated leads to a much more rapid path along the learning curve.

As might be expected, getting a model of the Promotion Advisor running with the M.1 system proved to be easier than with either GURU or the Expert

```
M.1> go
What is the value of:   ow?
>> yes cf 80
What is the value of:   share?
>> no
What is the value of:   past_12?
>> why
      M.1 is trying to determine whether the following rule is
      applicable in this consultation:

      kb-8:
              if past_12 = medium
              then sys_strat = continuity cf 80.

      The following entries are also under consideration:

          kb-2    (an initialdata)

What is the value of:   past_12?
>> low cf 70
What is the value of:   loyalty?
>> yes
What is the value of:   growth?
>> growing
What is the value of:   six_to_one?
>> yes cf 80
What is the value of:   share_of_con_p?
>> high
What is the value of:   lock_up?
>> yes cf 70
What is the value of:   use_corr?
>> yes
What is the value of:   con_purch?
>> no


The strategies the system recommends are:

      sys_strat = trial (86%) because kb-11 and kb-9 and kb-6.
      sys_strat = convenience (67%) because kb-15 and kb-14.
      sys_strat = retrial (64%) because kb-12.
What is the value of:   user_agrees?
>> no
What is the value of:   user_strat?
>> trial cf 90, convenience cf 60


              **   The system is now seeking marketing device.   **

   device = own_brand_coupon (93%) because kb-23 and kb-20.
   device = sampling (90%) because kb-23 and kb-20.
   device = trial_size (90%) because kb-23 and kb-20.
   device = pack_premiums (82%) because kb-23 and kb-20.
   device = container_pack_premiums (81%) because kb-23 and kb-20.
   device = bonus_pack (81%) because kb-23 and kb-20.
   device = refund_coupons (76%) because kb-23 and kb-20.
   device = free_mail_in_low_proof_premiums (72%) because kb-23 and kb-20.
   device = high_value_single_unit_refunds (72%) because kb-23 and kb-20.
   device = group_refunds (72%) because kb-23 and kb-20.
   device = high_value_smaller_sizes_price_pack (72%) because kb-23 and kb-20.
   device = generic_refunds (70%) because kb-23 and kb-20.
   device = feature_display_allowances (70%) because kb-23 and kb-20.
   device = promotion_advertising (70%) because kb-23 and kb-20.
   device = progressive_refunds (66%) because kb-23 and kb-20.
   device = free_mail_in_premium_high_proof_required (60%) because kb-23 and kb
   device = contests (54%) because kb-23 and kb-20.
   device = in_pack_games (54%) because kb-23 and kb-20.
   device = high_value_multiple_unit_refunds (48%) because kb-23 and kb-20.
   device = off_invoice_allowances (43%) because kb-23 and kb-20.
   device = continuity_catalog_premiums (36%) because kb-23 and kb-20.
   device = cross_ruff_coupons (0%) because kb-23 and kb-20.
   device = self_liquidating_premium (0%) because kb-23 and kb-20.
   device = low_value_refunds (0%) because kb-23 and kb-20.
   device = normal_low_value_price_pack (0%) because kb-23 and kb-20.
   device = high_value_multiple_unit_price_pack (0%) because kb-23 and kb-20.
   device = sweepstakes (0%) because kb-23 and kb-20.
```

Figure 6-3 Consultation with the Simplified Promotion Advisor in M.1

System Environment. The "simplified" version of the knowledge base provided in the Appendix shows the compact nature of the minimal code required to create a functioning system. During initial stages of development the process of moving between the systems tool and word processing seemed cumbersome in the context of other aspects of systems development being quite easy.

Another problem was created by the need to perform simple procedures in the context of the rule structure, for example, the following rule from the Promotion Advisor:

Rule 12:

```
If display ([nl, nl, nl, nl, nl,
    'the strategies the system recommends are:',
    nl, nl])
and do (show sys__strat)
and user__agrees = yes
and sys__strat = A
then strategy = A.
```

This "rule" is neither clear nor straightforward. No end-user could look at this and quickly determine its function, because procedural activities and control of the user interface are intertwined in the backward-chaining rule structure. Learning to "bend" the system to fit these needs took some getting used to. The speed with which some aspects of the system could be quickly implemented was offset to an extent by having to learn "tricks" like this one.

The prospects of expanding this prototype to a full-scale system in M.1 are not too promising. The requirements of accessing and processing any substantial amount of external data place this problem outside the tool's range. If these data were stored in another computer, such as a mainframe, the additional burden of downloading the information would be added. Any such capabilities would have to be performed by external programs. The links between M.1 and these other tools would need to be "hand-crafted" using C.

Also, as the rule base expands, the dozen or so rules now employed may expand to hundreds. There would then be a group of rules that relate "performance of the brand in the market" to promotion strategies, instead of the handful in the prototype version. As the knowledge base expands, the need to organize rules into a larger conceptual framework emerges. M.1 provides no representational scheme for such units. As such, the burden falls on the developer to manually organize, relate, and maintain this structure.

The M.1 system, however, is an excellent environment for "getting a handle" on the problem and gaining insight into an approach to developing a knowledge system in a specific application area. In the development of the prototype system for the Promotion Advisor, these strengths were obvious and appreciated.

SUMMARY

The M.1 system is intended to support relatively novice users interested in gaining insight into the world of rule-based backward-chaining knowledge systems. It is also aimed at more experienced users developing prototype systems that may be expanded later into other development environments, or that may not require processing significantly beyond M.1's capabilities. It makes an excellent learning tool, and is well received for its support of rapid prototyping with a minimum of systems interference.

It is backed by a company with significant academic credentials in the knowledge systems field. Teknowledge offers a series of educational programs for its products, and backs them with strong technical support. It has been involved in consulting and customized systems development for some time, and has the breadth and depth of knowledge to support its products and guide their evolution.

M.1 is, however, less than an "industrial strength" applications development tool. It provides little support for building and maintaining large systems with a range of processing needs. Some noninferential processing and data representation can be accomplished by "bending" the system to fit these needs. However, the novice users who are one of the target groups for this system find limiting the need to "bend" a straightforward process to fit the needs of a backward-chaining inference engine, or the need to construct external processing routines in another language.

7

A Review of Development Tools: GURU from Micro Data Base Systems

The preceding chapter described M.1 from Teknowledge. Here a parallel discussion of the GURU application development system is provided, along with a description of the prototype Promotion Advisor knowledge base, written in GURU, that appears in the Appendix. The use of GURU in developing that prototype, and the anticipated strengths and weaknesses of GURU for expanding the prototype to a fully developed system, will be presented.

OVERVIEW

Where M.1 reflects its roots in the rule-based expert systems research and development laboratories, GURU is a system resulting from the integration of knowledge systems concepts and a preexisting information systems development tool, KNOWLEDGE MANAGER (K MAN). K MAN is an integrated applications development package incorporating spreadsheets, relational data bases, graphics, report writing, text processing, procedural programming, and remote communications. This system has been augmented further by the addition of a powerful rule-based knowledge systems development environment. When one takes all the components of K MAN and adds the knowledge systems development features, the result is GURU.

The most striking characteristic of the GURU package is the relatively seamless integration of these systems components. That characteristic also creates some difficulties in fully describing the system. The knowledge systems components of GURU allow the developer access to all the functions of the K MAN environment from the rule system. Among other things, a rule's premise can reference spreadsheet cells, fields in relational data tables, and data values downloaded from a remote computer service. The conclusions of rules can initiate consultations with other knowledge systems, update data tables, create or modify spreadsheets, call a preprogrammed procedure, dial a remote computer, write a report, or present a graph to the user for review, for example. It is possible for a spreadsheet to have a cell defined in such a way that when the spreadsheet is recalculated, a knowledge system is consulted to provide the value for that, and other, cells.

Because of this, a particular application may have a rule-based knowledge system as a component of a larger information system, support the knowledge system with some data management via the other processing functions, ignore the knowledge systems development environment altogether and employ only the more traditional business information processing features, or use the knowledge systems development environment exclusively. In the interest of simplicity and because of the topic of this book, this discussion will focus primarily on the knowledge systems features and functions of the GURU package.

GURU is written in the C language and will run under both the DOS and UNIX operating systems. It is available in a stand-alone form for the IBM PC and compatibles, having 640 k of RAM memory and a hard disk. There is also a version of GURU that runs under the NOVELL NETWARE 286 operating system, supporting a variety of IBM PC networking protocols. The GURU networking version is a true local area network implementation that allows for multiple levels of password protection for access to shared files and the like. Under the UNIX operating systems, GURU is available to run on the IBM RT and DEC VAX computer systems.

GURU is at its best when in the hands of an applications development specialist. It is possible to use only small subsets of the system's features, and therefore greatly simplify the learning process: In this mode many relative novices can develop applications in GURU; however, it is the ability to represent and act on information in many different formats that provides the uniqueness of this tool. Fully utilizing this capability requires learning how to use each of the system's data management systems, move information among them, and integrate them with the knowledge systems components.

In terms of the ''size'' of applications appropriate for development with GURU, it is useful for medium- through large-scale applications, depending to a large degree on the power of the underlying hardware system. From the perspective of data management, there are no real limits on the sizes of data files, the number of files being accessed at one time, and so forth. Spreadsheets are, however, limited in size to 256 by 256 cells.

In terms of the rule bases, large systems can be ''decomposed'' into smaller ones, as one knowledge system can dynamically call another, much like a traditional program uses subroutines. There is, however, no system for structuring, relating, and managing these knowledge systems. This results in an additional burden on the systems developer when ''linking'' various smaller knowledge systems to form larger ones. For example, it is possible for one knowledge system to inadvertently redefine a variable used in another. Therefore, as systems become quite large, the developer must devote more effort to monitoring such factors explicitly.

THE DEVELOPMENT ENVIRONMENT

Documentation for GURU is provided in a four-volume set consisting of two volumes of reference material. There is also one user's guide each for the menu and command-oriented interfaces. GURU has been developed so that the user can either employ a hierarchical arrangement of menus to build and work with the knowledge and information systems facilities or enter commands directly through a prompt. The developer can move between these interfaces, usually employing the command mode when in a familiar area and relying on the menus when breaking new ground. The user's guides document the use of these two modes of systems interaction.

Like Teknowledge and IBM, MDBS offers instruction in the use of GURU, as it does in the use of the rest of its product line. These courses are offered in various sites on a rotating schedule. It is also possible to purchase special, high-priority help line assistance. This enables the user to request a prespecified amount of in-depth technical assistance, with a guaranteed response time to questions.

Describing the development environment of GURU is somewhat more difficult than for M.1. This is not because the system is more difficult to use; rather, it offers many different faces depending on the applications being developed and the preferences of the developer. It is perhaps best to think of GURU as providing a variety of methods for representing and managing information. For example, data can be represented in the form of single-variable values, arrays, relational tables, spreadsheets, and the like. Using various forms of the CONVERT command, the user can move this information from one form to another. The commands, functions, and features of the data tables might be best for solving new problems using data that have previously been stored in a spreadsheet, for example. It is also possible to "imbed" procedural language programs and/or knowledge systems in spreadsheets. A cell in a spreadsheet can be defined as "CONSULT ADVISOR," where ADVISOR is the name of a knowledge system. Each time the spreadsheet is calculated and this cell is encountered, the knowledge system, ADVISOR, will be processed by the inference engine. Alternatively, a knowledge system can request processing from procedural programs, data from spreadsheets, and so forth, as well as issue any command defined in the system. Again, all this flexibility makes it somewhat difficult to describe just what building a system with GURU is like, as it is so much a function of the application. Therefore, it is most appropriate to disregard the other components of GURU and focus primarily on the knowledge systems development environment, as if one were concerned only with building a rule-based, stand-alone system.

To begin, one might build a knowledge base (called a "rule set" in GURU) using either the text editor or the menu interface. The text editor is a general-purpose tool that can be used for text composition. It is only when a text file is defined as having ".rss" (rule set source) extension that the system recognizes it as anything other than a normal text file. If the developer is capable of remembering all the necessary syntax and sequencing of elements in a GURU rule set, then the system could be constructed entirely in the text editor, much like an M.1 knowledge base. However, this is one place where the menu-oriented support is most welcome, even for the experienced developer. The text editor is most useful when searching a preexisting rule set for particular information, or when making "global" changes to the rule set. For example, one might want to change the phrase "enough" to "sufficient" in every occurrence. The text editor is efficient and well suited to these types of tasks.

A rule set in GURU consists of five main parts, although some of these are optional, depending on the application; most development efforts will require that all five be defined. These include

1. *An initialization section.* Any procedures for opening any needed files or tables, resetting the values of variables, asking the user for any information needed to start the consultation, and so on are described here. The instructions in the initialization section can be any legal GURU command, and will be carried out before any consultation begins.

2. *Definitions of goals, windows, and the like.* The definition section of a rule set can contain something other than a goal statement, but this is the most frequent use. Whether or not the developer includes a goal, it is possible for the user to tell GURU's inference engine what goal to pursue when the consultation is requested. This will become the goal of the consultation and will override the goal statement, if one is provided. In actuality, most all knowledge systems have a specific goal that is predefined, and this is the place for it in GURU.

3. *A rule section.* This section contains all the rules that the inference engine is to process in finding the goal. For each rule several optional features can be defined. They are included in this rule section and are described in detail in the discussion of inferencing below.

4. *A variable section.* Here the developer has the opportunity to define how the values of variables will be found. There are weak analogies to this capability in the M.1 package. However, when the Expert System Environment is described in the following chapter, the reader will note the strong similarity between this control mechanism and the Expert System Environment's "sourcing sequence." It should also be noted that "variables" in GURU have the same meaning as "expressions" in M.1, and should not be confused with the way in which M.1 uses the variable concept.

5. *A completion section.* This section describes the actions the knowledge system is to take when a value for its goal has been found, or when it has failed to make a conclusion. For instance, the system may update a spreadsheet, write a report, join some tables, inform the user on the screen, or carry out any other GURU instructions. The completion section is optional, but in most practical applications, it will contain instructions.

The menus for building a knowledge system rule set provide the developer with choices about which of these sections are to be worked on. Specifically designed, window- and menu-oriented interfaces are provided for each of the five areas of rule set development. A reproduction of the menu-oriented interface for creating and editing rules is provided in Figure 7-1. This screen provides the developer with several "windows," which correspond to the various components

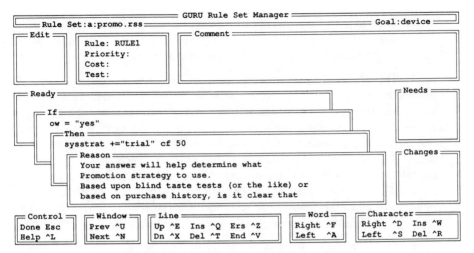

Figure 7-1 Sample Screen from GURU: Rule Editing

that the user might want to address in defining a rule. Although the form is different, the effect is very similar to the rule editing environment in the Expert System Environment described in the following chapter. Each rule has various "components," some of which are required and some of which are optional. Because they are organized on one screen, allowing the developer to move among them in one visual field, the task of coding becomes one of recognizing, rather than recalling, what needs to be acted on. In this way, the developer does not need to remember the syntax for various commands, as the screen is essentially a "form" for entering information about rules.

Some of the "windows" in Figure 7-1 include the following:

1. The "Rule" window, where the developer can choose to assign such things as relative costs and priorities to the rules. These factors can be used later by the inference engine to select among rules when searching for a goal. The effects of these controls on the inferencing process are discussed in the following section.

2. The "Comment" window, in which any notes or comments relevant to this rule can be maintained by the developer.

3. The "Ready" window allows the developer to specify any actions that need to be taken before a rule's premise can be considered. For example, it may be necessary to open a table, or check for the existence of some text file.

4. The "If" window contains the premise for the rule.

5. The "Then" window contains any actions that are to be taken if the rule fires. This can contain any valid GURU commands.

6. The "Reason" window allows the developer to describe the rule's underlying rationale. If the user were to ask the equivalent of "why" during a consultation, this is the text that is presented in explanation.

7. The "Needs" window is very optional. It orders the inference engine's activities in resolving the values of variables in the rule's premise. That is, if the premise contains several variables arranged with "and" clauses, the developer may want to list these variables in another order in the "Needs" window. When the inference engine attempts to resolve the truth of the rule's premise, it will examine the values of these variables in the order in which they appear in the "Needs" window, rather than the natural order in which they appear in the rule's premise. The developer may know that certain variables can have their values checked more efficiently than others, and under these conditions may want to direct the activity of the inference engine to these variables first to increase efficiency.

8. The "Changes" window is similar to the "Needs" window in that it restates the activity of the conclusion section of the rule. It is possible for the conclusion of a rule to call a programmed procedure, which will result in a new value for a variable like "internal rate of return." The procedure may be called "IRRCALC" by the developer. If the rule concludes:

THEN PERFORM IRRCALC

there would be no way for the inference engine to know that the procedure assigns a value to the variable "internal rate of return." If the inference engine were seeking a rule to help find a value of "internal rate of return," it would bypass this rule if it examined only the literal content of its conclusion, because "internal rate of return" is not explicitly referenced. Under these conditions, the developer may want to declare "internal rate of return" in the "Changes" window. The inference engine will examine the contents of the "Changes" window instead of the literal contents of the rule's conclusion, when backward chaining, if the developer provides it. Otherwise, the conclusion of the rule will be examined. As another example, the conclusion of a rule may be

THEN CONSULT ADVSYS

where ADVSYS is another rule set. In this case, too, just what variables the ADVSYS knowledge system changes is not available to the inference engine unless they are listed in the "Changes" window.

At any point in the process of using the menu-oriented interface, the developer can access on-line, context-sensitive help. This is similar to the help facility provided in Lotus 1-2-3, with which the reader may be familiar. When using the command-oriented interface, the developer may enter the command "Help" followed by a command name to receive similar on-line support. For example, the command "Help calc" will provide a description of the GURU spreadsheet facility.

Using the menu-oriented screens for rule set development results in a formatted text file that contains all the components of the rule set. The Appendix contains such a file for the Promotion Advisor rule set. When a file is created with the menu interface, it has a file extension of ''.rss'' appended to its name. By entering the GURU text editor, the developer can request this file and edit it directly as any other text file. On the other hand, the file can be completely or partially created in the text editor, and then modified or added to by using the menu interface. There are editing and creating tasks for which one environment or the other is preferable, and the developer can move between them.

Similarly, variables can be defined in some detail in the GURU system. One of the most important aspects of a variable's definition in GURU is the ''Find'' window. As one might expect, this window controls just how the value is to be determined. This window may contain the name of a program to run, a relational data base call, a query to the user, or whatever other method the developer might specify for resolving its value.

Once a rule set has been developed, and a ''.rss'' file created, the developer invokes the rule set compiler. The compiler checks for any errors in syntax in the rule set, and also warns the developer of a number of apparent logical inconsistencies, or missing components. For example, the compiler might inform the developer that a variable is referenced in the premise of a rule, but it is not defined, has no ''Find'' window, and its value is not determined by any other rule. This type of checking and warning is most useful and far exceeds simple syntax checking.

Even though the focus here is specifically on the development of rule sets, it is impossible to describe the GURU environment without the concepts of ''environment variables'' and ''utility variables.'' GURU has approximately 150 of these ''controls'' that can be set and reset as needed. They control a wide variety of systems functions. For example, the environment variable e.rigr controls the veracity with which the inference engine will search for a variable's value. The environment variable e.lstr sets the limit on the number of characters allowed in a character string variable. The background colors displayed in the text processor, graphs, spreadsheet, and so on are controlled by e.bacg. The ability to alter the values of these variables offers extensive flexibility to the systems developer. Of course, each of these variables has a systems-supplied default value. However, anyone who enters into more than a superficial systems development task needs to learn how each of these works. This is more reason why the real power of the GURU system is more accessible to experienced applications developers than casual end-users.

GURU gives the developer access to the operating system of the host computer on which it is running, as well as allowing the transfer of files in various formats into GURU arrays, tables, and spreadsheets. These functions are extended by the inclusion of a remote communications module that allows GURU to initiate dialing, connection, and communication with remote computers. They are more fully described in the section below on noninferential processing.

INFERENCING AND DEALING WITH UNCERTAINTY

GURU provides many options that control the inferencing process. GURU gives the developer the ability to describe variables in such a way that the methods for finding their values are a part of their definition. These are described to the system in the "Find clause" for each variable.

When backward chaining for the value of some variable, GURU identifies a set of "candidate rules" for consideration. The conclusions of these rules have the ability to assign a value to the variable in question. Once this set of candidate rules is identified, there are also many options as to how to choose among them. In M.1 the order is simple. The inference engine considers them in the order in which they appear in the knowledge base. In GURU the selections can be made on multiple criteria and are controlled through the value of an "environment variable"—e.sord. This variable has as its value a character string of one or more letters that describe the criteria GURU is to apply when selecting among rules in a set of candidates. The variable e.sord can be assigned the following values, or any combination of them:

> F—Select the rules to be fired considering the first rule that appears in the rule set, and then each additional candidate rule in the sequence in which they appear. M.1 uses this method.
>
> P—Order the candidate rules by their "priorities." When creating rules, the developer has the option of assigning a "priority" on a scale of 1 to 100 to each rule to explicitly control the order of their consideration.
>
> C—Order the candidate rules on the basis of their "cost factors." The developer also has the option of describing a cost on a scale of 1 to 100 for each rule. This cost may reflect the developer's relative judgment of the difficulty in attaining the information required to evaluate the premise, or the cost of executing the conclusion of the rule.
>
> U—Order the candidate rules according to the number of unknown values in their premises. This is a "minimal effort" constraint as well. It orders rules in terms of some measure of the amount of effort involved in resolving the values of the variables in the premise.
>
> H—Order the candidate rules by the strength of the certainty factors with which they conclude a value for the variable of interest. That is, first consider rules that will conclude with the highest certainties.
>
> R—Fire rules in a random order from the candidate set.

These character string values can be combined. For example, e.sord could be set to the string "UHR." If this were done, then the candidate rules would be ordered first by the number of unknown values in their premises. Then, if there were "ties" among the rules, these subsets would be sorted so that the rules with the highest certainty factors in their conclusions would be considered first. And, finally, if there were still groupings of rules "tied" for ranking in consideration, they would be selected in a random order. It is unlikely that many applications would call for multiple levels of specification in the e.sord character string, but it is possible to create highly specific controls for the inference engine through the e.sord environment variable.

Another important control, in either forward- or backward-chaining modes of inference, is that of "rigor." Imagine that the system is pursuing a goal or subgoal such as "promotion strategy." At what point does it stop pursuing this goal? GURU allows the user to specify three levels of "rigor." These are controlled globally by an environment variable, e.rigr. This variable can have the value "A" for absolute, "M" for minimal, or "C" for compromise. If the value of e.rigr is set to "A," then the inference engine will consider all possible rules when either backward or forward chaining to acquire the value of a variable, and if a value for the variable is found with absolute certainty. If e.rigr is set to "M," then the inference engine will stop searching for a value as soon as the variable in question has a value with a certainty factor over the "threshold of belief." In M.1, the threshold of belief is set to a certainty factor of 20. That is, if the certainty factor for a variable's value is over 20, then there is some evidence that that value is true. If the system believed that "strategy = trial cf 19," then any rule with "If strategy = trial" in the premise would not fire, as the certainty factor is below the "threshold of belief." If it were believed that "strategy = trial cf 25," however, the rule would fire. The level that the system uses for threshold of belief in GURU is user-selectable. Whatever that level might be, if e.rigr = "M," the inference engine will stop searching for the value of a variable as soon as it has a value with a certainty factor over this level. Therefore, if the inference engine were backward chaining and had identified 12 candidate rules for the variable "strategy," and the first rule tested concluded that "strategy = trial cf 30," the inference engine would abandon the remaining group of rules, never testing them.

Finally if e.rigr = "C," a compromise method would be used. If one rule in a set of candidate rules concluded for the variable in question with a certainty factor over the "threshold of belief," the system would consider all the other rules in the candidate set but would do no backward chaining to resolve values of any unknown variables in the premises of those rules. That is, if the system already knows enough to fire a rule with no further processing effort, it would fire those rules before abandoning the search.

By combining various settings for e.sord, and e.rigr, the inference engine will perform quite differently. It must also be noted that individual variables can be associated with "local" settings for rule selection order and rigor. The developer can say, in effect, "When you are looking for this variable, regardless of the value of e.rigr, use absolute rigor." This control will be in effect while that specific variable is being sought. When this search is complete, the global setting, stored in the value for e.rigr, will be reinstated as the control for the inference process. GURU provides opportunities for the developer to control the inferencing process locally and globally. In many applications, the developer will probably leave the settings in one standard position. However, the ability to control these actions is an important source of flexibility that eliminates the need to "bend" less adaptive inference engines.

Similarly, there are controls that affect the ways that certainty factors are computed. These, too, are managed globally through environment variables, and locally in the act of defining variables. The developer can control whether or not a variable can have certainty factors, if so, how many values the system will maintain, and whether or not the certainty factor of a variable will be output with its value when printing reports or writing to the screen.

GURU also provides a number of different methods for computing certainty factors. For example, these control the ways in which the certainty factor for a premise is computed under a variety of conditions involving multiple clauses connected with "and"'s and "or"'s. They also control the ways in which the certainty factors of premises are passed on to conclusions. Finally, they affect the way the system updates and maintains certainty factors for a particular variable, as evidence accumulates from various sources.

One of the surprising outcomes from the integrated way in which GURU maintains information in many different formats is that any variable in GURU can have a certainty factor associated with it. This includes spreadsheet cells, table values, character string variables, and so on. There are even methods for controlling the ways in which certainty factors might be computed for numerical expressions. For example, if it were believed that $X = 100$ with cf 80, and that $Y = 3$ with cf 63, the system could compute that $Z = X$ to the power of Y. If this were done, the value of Z would also have a certainty factor. Choices are available to the developer controlling how such computations are made.

Finally, GURU allows for multivalued and single-valued variables, as does M.1. Unlike other packages, however, this dimension is not controlled with a declaration when the variable is defined. It occurs when a variable is assigned a value. If a statement like "strategy = trial" is found, then the variable "strategy" is assumed to be single-valued. If, however, the statement "strategy = {trial cf 80, retrial cf 78, convenience cf 45}" were encountered, it would be assumed that it was to be multivalued. Alternatively, the developer could write a statement like "strategy + = trial." The plus sign sets up a multivalued strategy. This would indicate that "Whatever the current value(s) of 'strategy' may be, add 'trial' to the list." It is also possible to declare "strategy − = trial," where the minus sign translates into "Whatever value(s) strategy might have at the present time, take 'trial' off that list." The compiler will inform the developer of any inconsistent use of =, ={ }, + =, or − = in the rule set so these might be corrected.

INTEGRATION AND NONINFERENTIAL PROCESSING

GURU allows the user to write any sequence of valid GURU commands, programs, and so forth to ascertain the value of variables. The effect is very similar. Other systems like M.1 also provide an ability to access external information through the creation and linking of an externally written routine. However, there is an important distinction with GURU. Instead of having to run an external routine to get a value, in many cases this is unnecessary in GURU. For example, if data are stored in a GURU spreadsheet, data tables, and the like, the rules in GURU can simply reference these variables directly. For example, consider the following rule:

```
IF #a3 > #w89
then obtain record from mydata for age > 40 and convert name, age
from mydata to cell #k3 and perform classify.
```

This rule references two spreadsheet cells (#a3 and #w89) directly in the premise. In the conclusion, it directs the system to obtain a record from the already opened data base file, converts some records from another data base file to cells in the spreadsheet, and performs a developer-written procedure named "classify." Just what variables these actions would alter would be declared in the "Changes" window for this rule, so the backward-chaining inference process would see the rule as relevant when pursuing values for any of these variables.

Therefore, the point is that when creating rules and variables, there is no need to define an external procedure for acquiring their values if they are stored within one of GURU's other formats. They can be referenced directly in the rules because they are supported inside of the GURU package. Of course, the user could define the cell names #a3 and #w89 more meaningfully, either in the spreadsheet or in the knowledge system, and refer to these names in the rules. For example, #a3 could be defined as "first quarter sales" and #w89 as "average annual sales." This sort of renaming can make the rules more readable, but the point would be the same: these names directly reference cells in the spreadsheet, and no external routine is required to assign them values.

The conclusion of this rule directly calls other information management routines, which the developer might need if using the information management routines through the keyboard. This provides a very natural "feel" to the development of rules and variables. They appear as they would to the user of the information system if the knowledge systems components were not present.

Under either or both of the following conditions, this can be a very powerful feature:

1. When the information to be managed by the knowledge system is stored in GURU, or is appropriate for management in GURU
2. When the knowledge system itself is better supported through the ability to create and process its own information in a variety of formats, beyond rules and facts

Point number one is quite important. If the application is going to access data that are already stored and processed in some other information system, and it is not feasible or desirable to transport them to GURU for permanent management, then these features have little value. GURU provides the ability to convert information from various file formats into GURU tables, spreadsheets, arrays, and so on, but these steps in the process of importing data are similar to those in other systems.

The ability to represent and manage data in multiple formats is best applied when the data are either moved from some other source into GURU, and then left there for additional processing without the need to frequently "return" the processed data to their source format, or when the application is new or being rewritten, and the entire data management process can be handled by the GURU facilities. These considerations are similar to those any developer finds when using any integrated package.

Point number two, which is also important, is that it is often very helpful to represent knowledge of a variety of formats, even when the developer is thinking only in terms of the knowledge system itself. That is, in working with information, regardless of the form in which it is originally stored, it is often helpful to think of it and manage it in terms of these other business information processing formats. When inferencing, it may be useful to create a table to manage information that the knowledge system is creating for its own internal use. As a simple example, a more complete version of the Promotion Advisor takes advantage of storing information relating various promotion strategies, devices, and characteristics of brands and markets in a series of relational data tables. Having the information in this form might well replicate the way in which a decision maker would arrange the information on sheets of paper for later reference. This flexibility in representing and processing information creates a directness and clarity in creating management-oriented knowledge systems that are distinct from the ability to access data from external files and call external processes. The ability to directly create, reference, and process information in a variety of formats is of value for many management applications even if these formats are not used to manage the data for use outside the knowledge system itself.

GURU allows access to the host computer's operating system, files, and programs. The system running under PC DOS can execute a command like "run copy a:*.* c:" or any other DOS command. In addition to DOS commands, GURU can directly run an external program written to run under DOS. For example, consider the situation in which the developer had a program called "REGRESS" that computes a simple regression equation using data in an external file. This program may be written in some other language such as PASCAL and compiled on disk. GURU could call this program and have it executed with a command like "RUN REGRESS." Finally, if the developer would like to create new functions or routines in GURU, for example, a routine to compute the net present value for a series of cash flows, this routine could be written in the C language and "linked" to GURU. These types of modifications of the system and links to the operating system are not for the novice. However, the full power of this type of system is not designed for this audience.

GURU also provides a number of file transfer utilities, both for moving data from format to format within GURU and for transferring files in and out of GURU. These are "conversion" utilities that move information between arrays, spreadsheets, tables, and external files. These utilities allow the external files to be read and created in several formats. This integration at the file level is further supported by a "remote communications" facility that allows control of a modem and connections to external computing systems.

Other features of GURU not described in detail here are the graphics, report writing, and forms. These capabilities can be called on when the application requires their use. They are not described in this context, as they do not directly correspond to a method of information storage or knowledge representation, but are methods for the display and input of information. Like all other GURU components, they can be called on by the knowledge system to provide more flexible interactions with users in either gathering or preparing information for presentation.

THE PROMOTION ADVISOR IN GURU

The Appendix contains a sample knowledge base for the Promotion Advisor written in GURU. This is the "rule set" as it would appear when viewed in the text editor. It was created with the menu-oriented rule set building screens. The five sections of a GURU rule set, or knowledge base, are included.

The goal is obviously defined in the first line, labeled "GOAL:". Also defined in this "definition" section is a "window," which tells GURU where on the screen to write the "reason" section of a rule when the user requests an explanation of why the system is asking for information.

Following the "definition" section, the label "INITIAL:" introduces the initialization section, which can contain anything the developer may want the system to do before beginning the actual consultation. In the prototype Promotion Advisor rule set, this section assigns values to various variables. Some of these are variables used in the rules like "share" and "device." Here they are set to "unknown" in anticipation of the user's running more than one consultation. If the variables are not explicitly reset to "unknown," the system will retain their values from the first consultation. Other variables set to explicit values are the "environment variables" like "e.rigr." This section could also open any needed tables, ask the user some initial questions, plot a graph, connect with a remote computer system, and complete any other valid GURU commands.

The "DO:" label introduces the "completion" section, which describes the actions to take when the system has completed processing the rule set. Again, the developer may include any valid GURU commands here. In this simple prototype, the system is instructed only to clear the screen and then output the findings for the user to review.

Following this section, individual rules are defined with the label "RULE:". In this example, the rules consist of "IF," "THEN," and "REASON" definitions. If the developer took advantage of the other components of rules that are available for definition (e.g., "Priority" or "Cost"), these would appear in this section as well.

Finally, the section appears in which the variables are defined. The variable definitions in this prototype are simple, and include only the "Find" clause, which directs the system in finding the variable's value, and the "label," or long name for the variable. Other aspects of each variable could be described here such as the ways in which to choose among candidate rules when finding the variable's value. And so on. The "Find" instructions could include any valid GURU commands like a "lookup" in a spreadsheet, or an "obtain" from a data table.

Learning enough of the GURU system to implement the prototype knowledge advisor is not a difficult task, as it uses very little of the system's capability. The menu-oriented rule set building environment is very helpful in reminding the developer of needed information, as are the messages from the compiler that point out syntax errors. Also, the ability to enter GURU's text processor and modify the rule set is helpful. For example, after developing the system, one can decide to modify the name of one of the variables. It is then possible to enter the text processor and issue GURU's "modify" command to change every instance of one text string, "trialrate," to another, "past12." Without this ability, one would find it necessary to make the change individually in several locations in the rule set by calling them up in the menu-oriented interface.

The strengths of GURU would come into play if the prototype system were expanded to include the management and access of data. Under these conditions, the use of multiple formats to represent and process information and the integrated nature of the package's features would be highly beneficial. One can easily imagine data tables and/or spreadsheets that contain data regarding product performance in various markets, for example. The ability to provide graphic presentations of some of these data and request the user's opinion in some regard is also quite achievable. In general, the ability to directly represent information in the knowledge system in a variety of forms that a manager would employ when solving these problems is very inviting. This is in comparison with "translating" information stored in one format into another format so it can be referenced by rules and the inference process.

GURU goes a long way in melding the functions of management information systems, decision support systems, and knowledge systems. It achieves this by attempting to provide many of the functions a developer would want in a single package. As with all integrated software, there are some problems with this approach. First and foremost, it is an attempt to avoid the current technical bottleneck that has arisen in the area of direct program-to-program communications. It is quite difficult to get one program (e.g., a data base management system) to talk easily to another program (e.g., a spreadsheet). Since there is often a need to move data freely from one of these environments to another, and this is often difficult, a shortcut is to provide the functions of both in one package. Since a single developer creates that one package, the facilities for referring to and moving data across applications is under control. This works well when two things are true. One, the bulk of the data are not permanently stored in some other system and are amenable, for whatever reason, to being translated for use in the integrated package. Two, the functions offered in the various components of the integrated package must be robust and powerful enough to do the necessary processing. That is, if the spreadsheet in an integrated package lacks necessary functions and features found in a stand-alone spreadsheet, the integrated package fails as a solution.

These are important factors when considering the use of GURU. As a stand-alone knowledge system, GURU is powerful and flexible. It also allows the stand-alone knowledge system to represent and process data in important formats unique in knowledge systems software. However, to realize the loftier objective of creating an integrated information management, decision support, and knowledge-based system in one package, each of the subparts must be up to the requirements of its task, or the application cannot succeed.

When this type of system is the objective, one must consider the power of each of the relevant subparts of GURU—the spreadsheet, data base management system, report writer, text processor, graphics, remote communications, and so on. The requirements placed on each of these components will vary across applications areas. However, the system is based extensively on K MAN. This package has several years of development behind it, and has been well received for its flexibility and power. Consequently, GURU offers a solution to the problems of complex, multifunction systems for a variety of applications areas.

8

A Review of
Development Tools:
The Expert System
Environment from IBM

The two previous chapters reviewed the M.1 system from Teknowledge and GURU from Micro Data Base Systems. The discussions focused on the general characteristics of the packages and their strengths and weaknesses in the context of implementing and expanding on the prototype Promotion Advisor knowledge system listed in the Appendix. In this chapter, a parallel description is presented of the Expert System Environment from the IBM Corporation.

OVERVIEW

Like the M.1 system, the Expert System Environment (ESE) has a lineage that extends to the artificial intelligence research community of Stanford University. ESE was an internal IBM system developed at IBM's Palo Alto Scientific Center. At that time, the system was known as PRISM (PRototype Inferencing SysteM). The designers of ESE have maintained formal and informal contact with the artificial intelligence research and development community at neighboring Stanford University, among others. ESE's rule-oriented representation schemes reflect some of this heritage.

M.1 can be viewed as covering a range from small- through mid-sized systems, with its real strength diminishing as the size of development projects move through that range. It is used to greatest advantage by the developer new to knowledge systems development. GURU is best used by professional applications developers and is well suited to mid- to large-sized systems. Although ESE also covers a range from mid- through large-sized systems, it seems to provide considerable ease-of-use for relative novices if the application does not call for access to external data or procedures. However, ESE is at its best when used by developers with mainframe systems development experience. The support environment for developing and editing knowledge bases in ESE is very strong and well suited to users new to knowledge systems concepts. However, one of the real strengths of this package is its ability to interface with external programs and data. This is described in detail below; however, using this strength requires knowledge of the world outside of ESE. In many ways, ESE represents the opposite end of the scale on several dimensions when compared with a package like M.1. Like M.1, however, it represents a first. ESE is the first commercially available knowledge systems development environment offered by IBM, and it is the first to run under IBM's mainframe operating systems, CMS and MVS.

ESE is written in IBM PASCAL, but it requires that other IBM products also be available. Its interface with the screen is accomplished with IBM's Graphic Data Display Manager (GDDM) system, and all documentation of knowledge bases is formatted and printed by IBM's SCRIPT text processor. Finally, PASCAL itself is needed to construct "external" program and file interfaces.

ESE is well suited for large-scale development projects. It offers the ability to structure knowledge bases into blocks of rules called "focus control blocks," or FCBs. Within any FCB, it is possible to implement either forward- or backward-chaining inferencing. And within either forward or backward inferencing modes, ESE offers the developer considerable control over how rules are processed. As described below, ESE offers specially designed systems editors for developing and maintaining knowledge bases, the ability to generate systems documentation from the knowledge base itself, and access to the operating system and file structure of the host computer system.

In general, ESE has a learning curve similar to the Structured Query Language (SQL) and Data Base 2 (DB2) relational data base tools with which some readers may be familiar, or other fourth-generation application development packages. For readers familiar with mainframe development, running the ESE system under the Virtual Machine (VM) operating system requires the developer to define a three-megabyte virtual machine, so the development system is fairly large.

THE DEVELOPMENT ENVIRONMENT

The documentation for systems development with ESE is a reference manual. As have the developers of most all knowledge systems development tools, the writers of the reference manual have included some material regarding the general nature of the world of knowledge systems development. But this is minimal. The manual is not wordy and in many cases seems lacking in either content or structure. In fairness, much of this is due to the fact that there have not been manuals for such systems before, and there have not been communities of new users from outside the AI community. Therefore, just what needs to be in printed form and how to organize it for systems developers requires experience that few individuals have. An important additional feature of the ESE system is on-line help, however. When one forgets some details regarding the syntax for a command, it is possible to request help without having to consult the manual, as with GURU.

Like Teknowledge and MDBS, IBM offers instruction in the use of ESE. This takes place in the familiar context of IBM courses offered on a regular basis in various customer education centers around the country. These courses are divided between general concepts in the domain of knowledge systems development and the specifics of the ESE system. Also, IBM has recently offered the concept of the "solution pac." Solution pacs are bundles of products and services at reduced prices to meet the needs of particular groups of customers. There is now an ESE solution pac that bundles software, courses, and consultation services for a single price.

The ESE product is divided into two components: the Expert System Development Environment (ESDE), and the Expert System Consultation Environment (ESCE). As might be expected, the consultation environment allows the running of systems created with the development environment, without the additional cost and overhead of the development tools. This allows the dissemination of completed systems on machines licensed for the ESCE without the cost of individually licensing each delivery machine with the development tools.

As a systems development tool, the ESDE is about as different from M.1 as could be. It includes three special editors, one each for "parameters," rules, focus control blocks (FCBs), "groups," and interface screens. These editors have the same structure and operate in the same way, giving a consistency to the systems development process. A sample screen from the rule editor is provided in Figure 8-1.

Editing screens have four major sections. On the extreme bottom is the "command line," where systems commands can be entered. These include moving to other editors and running consultations with the currently defined knowledge system. The column on the left contains all the properties of a rule that can be displayed and/or edited. The remainder of the screen is divided into the areas where actual editing takes place. By moving the cursor under one of the properties in the list on the left and pressing the correct "function key," that property is moved into either the top or bottom editing area. Here the property can be viewed and, if it is a property that can be edited, changed.

```
Rule:      RULE0001                      Last Updated:   12/02/86 18:42:41

                                         For HELP press PF1

Property:           |      Edit:      Owning FCBs
Rule text           |  1 x    : FCB:F2_DATA_TO_STRAT
Owning FCBs         |  2      : FCB:F3_STRAT_TO_DEVICE
Rule type           |  3
Comment             |  4
Justification       |  5
Name                |  6
Print name          |  7
Author              |-------------------------------------------------------
I ref it list       |      Edit:      Rule text
It ref me list      |  1 FIF f2_ow_product_pref is true
Error Report        |  2    THEN there is .5 evidence that
                    |  3        f2_strategy= 'trial'
                    |  4
                    |  5
                    |  6
                    |  7

==>
```

Figure 8-1 Sample Screen from Expert System Environment Development System: Rule Editing

For example, one of the properties might be the rule text itself. Another would be the list of "parameters" that the rule references. In this case, it is not an editable property, because the system keeps track of this list for the developer. Still another property would be the FCB to which the rule belongs. (FCBs are discussed below.)

If, for example, the developer were to create a new rule in the rule editor, and that rule referenced a new "parameter" like "market share," the system would alert the developer that this parameter is new, and that the system has none of the necessary information about it. This notification takes place when the rule text is created. This is a most valuable feature of the development environment. The system is checking for logical consistency, not just syntactical consistency. And this checking is dynamic. The developer does not have to wait until a "compilation" has taken place to find errors; they are flagged as they occur.

At this point the developer can move directly to the parameter editing screen and create the currently undefined reference. While in the parameter editing screen, the developer may create a constraint for the parameter, describing the type of parameter it is and the list of legal values it can take. A prompt could also be created so that the system can ask the user for a value if called on to do so, and so forth.

Once the parameter is created, the developer can return to the rule editing screen and continue with this task. In this way, the system keeps track of the relations between elements of the knowledge system and eliminates the possibility of errors of omission and misspelling. In a large system, the possibility of errors of this type are very real, and the possibility of their being overlooked can have important implications. The ESE development environment eliminates this possibility. Even such errors as creating a parameter as a numerical variable and then referencing it as if it were a string within the text of rule can be detected and flagged for the developer.

There are obvious advantages to a system with this level of support for systems development and editing. But, of course, it comes with a price. In the M.1 environment, the user is free to enter rules without any need to describe to the system the nature of the parameters those rules reference, what focus control block they belong to, and so forth. For rapid testing of ideas and for very small systems, the "overhead" of ESDE's structure could be burdensome. But for any system of significance, the additional support from the editing environment is most welcome.

Focus control blocks (FCBs) are important conceptual units used by ESE to structure and control processing within a knowledge base. Each FCB consists of collections of rules and parameters that focus on a particular area of the application. FCBs are arranged hierarchically, with one FCB, the "ROOT," located at the top of the hierarchical tree.

Each FCB's activity, at a high level of abstraction, is determined by its "control text." For example, control text for one of the FCBs in the Promotion Advisor listed in the Appendix is

```
ASK f3__Usr__to__Set__Strategy
DETERMINE f3__Usr__Strategy
DETERMINE f3__Device
DISPLAY f3__Sys__Strategy
DISPLAY (f3__Strategy, f3__Device)
```

The key words ASK, DETERMINE, and DISPLAY tell the FCB first to ask the user for some information, then to use backward chaining to DETERMINE the values of some parameters, and finally to DISPLAY some results. Other keywords that can be used in the control language include

ACQUIRE—acquire external data

DISCOVER—forward chain for the values of some parameter(s)

ESTABLISH—give control to another FCB

PROCESS—put ESE data in an external file for processing by another program

In this way, the control text is part of a "control language" that directs the activity of an FCB in a procedural fashion. It is possible to add some limited conditional statements, so that certain activities will be carried out only under specified conditions. Every time an FCB is "established," its control text determines its sequence of activity.

In the context of the Promotion Advisor, an FCB could be constructed for knowledge relating the nature of the brand item to the appropriate promotion strategies. Similar FCBs could be constructed for knowledge relating information about the brands' performance in a market, and the nature of the market itself, to promotion strategies. In ESE, these FCBs can be regarded as separate, smaller knowledge bases, each with control over how processing proceeds within that FCB.

There must be a "ROOT" FCB that serves as the "controller" for the system. The remaining FCBs are arranged hierarchically, much as an organizational chart would be. The structure of these FCBs is modifiable through the FCB editing screens. Here the developer can address the structure of the larger system and control its components. There are controls available to govern which rules and which parameters are owned by which focus control blocks, and which ones can access information concluded in others. Under some conditions the developer may want information attained in one FCB to be "local" to that FCB, and under other conditions, the developer may want those findings to be available to other FCBs.

It is also possible to declare an FCB as able to be "instantiated" once or multiple times. A developer may create an FCB to reason about some concept like coupons. In the course of the consultation, it may be necessary to refer to several different coupons that have been used in the past. By declaring the "coupon FCB" to be capable of multiple instantiations, each coupon considered by the system will be created in its own FCB.

In short, FCBs are both powerful concepts and complex constructs. The learning curve for FCBs is not trivial, but neither is the power and flexibility they provide. A minimal level of understanding is absolutely required to use ESE, as FCBs are not "optional." It is possible for the developer to minimize the use of FCBs and essentially create systems in a single FCB. However, in the development of large systems, the use of FCBs is essential for efficient development and maintenance.

INFERENCING AND DEALING WITH UNCERTAINTY

"Parameters" in ESE are objects that can take on values. They might be equated with variables in traditional programming languages or be called "expressions" in M.1. An example of a parameter in the Promotion Advisor would be "strategy," "device," or "inventory__use__correlation." In ESE parameters can take on values in four ways:

1. As the consequence of a rule
2. From user input
3. From a default value
4. From the execution of some external function

When parameters are defined in the parameter editor, the ways in which the system is allowed to determine values for a parameter and the order in which these methods are to be applied are determined by the "sourcing sequence" for the parameter. That is, a rule might state

    If inventory__use__correlation = 'yes'
    then there is .5 evidence that strategy = 'convenience'.

In this case, if the system were back chaining and trying to determine a value for strategy, this rule might be used. Thus if "inventory__use__correlation" were not known to the system, it would attempt to derive its value. To do this, the system would consult the "sourcing sequence" for the parameter. The sourcing sequence might be

    Rule Consequent
    User Will Input From The Terminal

In this case, there are only two methods provided for finding the parameter's value, and the system would try determining that value first from other rules, and if that failed, it would ask the user for a value. The concept of a sourcing sequence is very powerful in directing the action of the inference engine. This approach is echoed in the GURU system in the form of the "find" instructions for a parameter.

In the process of inferencing, therefore, it is possible, when seeking a value for a parameter, to stop the backward- or forward-chaining activity and temporarily execute a procedural routine. However, this routine must be written outside the

ESE environment and "linked" to the system. This process is greatly simplified in the case where the parameter's value can be found in an SQL or DB2 data base. ESE allows the user to define queries within the ESE system which will be passed directly to the relational data base. The result from the query becomes the parameter's value.

Inferencing itself is conducted in either a forward- or backward-chaining fashion. The developer is able to direct this activity through the control text of an FCB. The instruction DETERMINE invokes backward chaining. For example, the control text of an FCB in the Promotion Advisor includes the instruction

DETERMINE f3__Device.

This directs the system to use backward chaining to find a value for strategy in that FCB.

When using backward chaining, however, ESE is under considerably more developer control than M.1. Consider the situation in which the system is backward chaining for "strategy." In M.1, the inference engine will simply check rules in the order in which they appear in the knowledge base. In ESE, the user can tell the inference engine how to choose among rules that could all conclude a value for the parameter being sought; that is, in the Promotion Advisor knowledge base, several rules conclude with "then strategy = ". ESE can be instructed to consider these rules in different sequences, depending on how they are to be ordered. ESE can order the rules in the following ways:

1. *By certainty factors.* In this case, the rules that conclude a value for the sought after parameter with the highest certainty factors are considered first.

2. *By unknown premises.* Here, relevant rules are arranged in such a way that those with the fewest number of unknown values in the premises are considered first.

3. *Most true premises first.*

4. *"Out of focus last."* This directs the inference engine first to consider rules in the present FCB, then to look at already processed and in-process FCBs, and finally to FCBs that have not yet been accessed.

There are some other methods of control for rule processing in the backward-chaining mode as well, but they require more in-depth explanation than is appropriate in this review.

If forward chaining is desired for the value of a parameter, the control text of an FCB would state

DISCOVER parameter.

Just as in the backward-chaining approach to inferencing, extensive controls can be applied when considering rules in a forward-chaining mode. The same methods for arranging rules for consideration that are available in backward chaining are available in forward chaining. These controls are powerful extensions to knowledge systems development. They allow the developer to modify not only the direction of the search process but also to "tune" the process to gain greater efficiencies.

In dealing with uncertainty, ESE allows for two types of inferencing rules— those with an "IF" premise and those with a "FIF" premise. The distinctions between them are in the way in which the certainty factor of the conclusion of a rule is affected by a certainty factor of the premise. In an "IF" form, the certainty factor of the premise has no impact on the certainty factor of the conclusion. For example, consider the following rule:

IF USE__CORRELATION = 'YES' THEN STRATEGY = 'CONVENIENCE'

If USE__CORRELATION were known to equal to 'YES' with a certainty factor of 80, or a certainty factor of 60, or a certainty factor of 90, it would make no difference. The conclusion that STRATEGY = 'CONVENIENCE' would still be made with a certainty factor of 100. However, if the rule were in the "FIF," or "Fuzzy IF," form:

FIF USE__CORRELATION = 'YES' THEN STRATEGY = 'CONVENIENCE'

the certainty factor of the premise would affect the certainty factor of the conclusion in the manner employed by M.1. That is, it is converted to a decimal number and multiplied by the certainty factor of the conclusion.

INTEGRATION AND NONINFERENTIAL PROCESSING

One of the strengths of the ESE system is its ability not only to run on business information processing machines, but also to give the developer access to externally stored data and external information processing power. This is accomplished through the ESE external interface. ESE provides three general methods to access outside information. The first is the "external data" instruction in a parameter's sourcing sequence. Using this option in the sourcing sequence, the developer provides a procedure name for the external routine. Any additional information such as file names or lists of arguments are provided in the external procedure's definition.

Other mechanisms for accessing the external world are provided by the control language instructions ACQUIRE and PROCESS. When the control text of an FCB encounters an ACQUIRE instruction, it invokes a defined procedure to access external data and use these data to assign values to a defined parameter. Since a parameter type in ESE can be a list, a list of values can be returned from the external source. Also, a list of different parameters can be the object of an ACQUIRE instruction. The PROCESS command is used to pass control from ESE to an external routine, but not for the purpose of importing data. Rather, this is the way in which ESE passes results of its processing to an external routine for external processing of those results.

ESE provides a set of general routines for passing data in and out of the knowledge systems environment. These routines perform a variety of import and export functions and reduce the burden on the developer of having to construct this kernel of functions from scratch. They provide "building blocks" for constructing application-specific interfaces to files and routines.

As important and powerful as these routines are, they do not replicate the ability to actually represent and process data in other forms. One could erroneously conclude that these importing and exporting interfaces allow ESE to treat external data management systems and procedural languages as subroutines. Although they add important extensions to knowledge systems processing, they do not provide such features as the representation of simple tabular data, or the ability to sort a list of numbers. However, it is possible to "bend" the system and accomplish some of these processing tasks through alternative uses of other functions and features. Although these "tricks" can be applied, they are not substitutes for a wide variety of representation and processing capabilities.

THE PROMOTION ADVISOR IN ESE

Because ESE is essentially "screen-oriented" in its consulting mode, each question presented to the user appears on a separate screen. To reproduce a complete consultation with the Promotion Advisor would take a number of somewhat repetitious pages. What is reproduced in Figure 8–2, therefore, is a screen taken from

```
              Focus: f2 data to strat (1)                      2
                                              |  PF1   Help      |
                                              |  PF2   Review    |
                                              |  PF3   End       |
                                              |  PF4   What      |
What is the rate of trial for this brand over |  PF5   Question  |
the past 12 months? In other words, of all    |  PF6   Unknown   |
purchases of this brand, what proportion are  |  PF7   Up        |
trial (rather than retrial or continuity)     |  PF8   Down      |
purchases?                                    |  PF9   Tab       |
                                              |  PF10  How       |
                                              |  PF11  Why       |
(Choose one of the following:)                |  PF12  Command   |
                                              |_____|
_____ low
_____ medium
_____ high


==>
```

Figure 8–2 Sample Screen from Expert Systems Consultation Environment: User Input

a consultation session with the Promotion Advisor in ESE. This screen format is used throughout the consultation.

The screen is arranged so that the question appears in one area, with the possible responses displayed in a list below. In choosing among the possible answers, users may simply place an "x" on the line in front of the appropriate answer. Or they may place a number between zero and one (e.g., .80) on the line to indicate a certainty factor. With expressions declared as "multivalued," users may indicate more than one selection from the list. In the case of input that is not to be taken from a set of possible answers, users may simply enter the character string or number the system needs.

To the right of the question and answer area are displayed the values of the "program function," or PF keys. The PF keys can be used for single keystroke access to several options when a question is asked. For example, the user may request that the system discuss "why" the information is being sought, or "what" the system is asking for. If the question is unclear, the developer may have provided a "long prompt" when creating the parameter, which would result in a second, often more detailed explanation of what is being asked.

The screen in Figure 8–2 is fairly typical of the sort of interface created in the ESE system. However, it is important to note that the developer has extensive control of the appearance of these screens and may alter their appearance at will. This ability is not extensively documented in the ESE manual, and may require some familiarity with the Graphic Data Display Manager screen description language to be fully exploited.

The structured listing of the Promotion Advisor knowledge base in the Appendix was produced entirely by the ESE system itself. Once the developer has gone through the screen-oriented creating and editing activity, the system will create a formatted, indexed listing of all the essential information in the knowledge base. This is accomplished through the insertion of SCRIPT text processing control codes in the knowledge base. SCRIPT is an IBM text processing system that uses the "imbedded command" approach to document construction. The developer simply requests "kbprint" on the command line of one of the editing screens. ESE creates a SCRIPT source file. At any time, the developer can leave ESE and request that the SCRIPT system process this file, producing the style of output found in the Appendix.

As the reader can see, for each of the major components of the system (e.g., rules, parameters, FCBs, etc.) there is a facility for the developer to add comments and notes. For example, when creating rules, the developer can add comments and justification text to the rule. When the documentation is printed, these types of information are printed along with the more common information like the text of the rule. The user has some control over just how wordy the printout will be and what areas of the system will be documented.

Reviewing the documentation in the Appendix, the reader can see that the prototype Promotion Advisor was implemented using the Root and two additional FCBs. One of them is used to reason from the characteristics of the brands, performance of the brand in the market, and characteristics of the market to derive systems recommendations for promotion strategies. The second FCB reasons from the strategies the user agrees to in order to arrive at final recommendations for specific promotion devices. For the FCB described on the first page of the listing (see page 186), the goals, parameters, and rule names "owned" by that FCB are listed. Following this, the "control text" for the FCB is presented. This directs the action of the FCB and instructs it first to determine its goals (strategy) then to move on and establish the next FCB, which will determine appropriate promotion devices.

The listing of rules in the documentation begins with the first rule, RULE0001 (see page 189). The text of the rule is presented, as is the rule type. In this case, it is an inference rule, which means it is used by the chaining inference process. Other rule types control other aspects of knowledge base processing, such as "monitor" rules. It is not appropriate to go into details to explain these differences in this discussion; however, it should be noted that the system provides highly structured documentation in considerable detail. Information is also provided about the links between this rule and the rest of the system. This is presented in the sections labeled "owning FCBs," "I ref it list," and "It ref me list."

On page 211, the first documentation of parameters begins. This first page describes the parameter brand loyalty. It can take on the character string values of "low," "medium," and "high." In seeking a value for this parameter, the system follows the steps described in the sourcing sequence for this parameter. In this case, the system will first try to derive a value from examining rules. If this fails, then the user will be asked for input, using the prompt, and possibly the long prompt. If this fails, the system will take a default value, if one is provided. Other data regarding this parameter are also included in this listing.

Finally, on page 227, a description of the screen format used for the user interface is provided. This offers some insight into the screen description language to control the system's interaction with the user.

The process of developing this prototype Promotion Advisor in ESE was quite different from using M.1, but similar to GURU. The effort required to "get something up and running" was greater than in M.1, but similar to GURU. The small knowledge system reported in the Appendix is too simple at this stage to take much advantage of the strengths of ESE. Instead, it may make the system appear awkward because of the ratio of "system-related effort" to "application-specific effort" in this small example.

The strengths of ESE come into play when the expansion of the prototype Promotion Advisor is considered. The system's strengths for the development of large, rule-based systems are considerable. The Promotion Advisor could be expanded by adding many more factors that lead to the identification of promotion strategies. These sources of information about the characteristics of the brand, the performance of the brand in its market, and the nature of the market itself could be efficiently organized in the format of FCBs. The larger the rule base becomes, the more welcome the structured approach to knowledge representation. ESE has a methodology for organizing and managing the structure of knowledge that should be appropriate for very large applications.

ESE has a great deal to offer in a "team-oriented" systems development environment, where the team has both systems and applications area specialists. The applications area specialists can understand the knowledge representation schemes of rule-based knowledge systems and work closely with systems professionals in developing and presenting knowledge in an appropriate form for encoding in ESE. The structure of FCBs, although complex at the implementation level, is comprehensible as a method of compartmentalizing and focusing knowledge. In short, ESE can provide an environment around which these two groups can meet. Each group can understand enough about the other to work synergistically. The tool can provide a mechanism for focusing the effort on the model itself, as it provides a structure and language that spans and unifies the strengths of the individual team members. This is important because, unlike M.1, it is unlikely that ESE will be used to its full capability by individual systems developers, with a single perspective on the applications area.

Another characteristic of the tool that lends itself well to mid- to large-scale systems is its documentation facility. It is likely that substantial applications will be developed in ESE that need to be updated and maintained. From a larger organizational perspective, this constitutes the task of knowledge management. If systems are to be dynamic and have any longevity, they must be understandable and modifiable. The self-documenting facility of ESE is most valuable in providing a representation of the system's overall structure and individual components. The creation and editing screens provide the facility to add comments and justification. These simplify the task of documentation, which becomes increasingly important as the project grows.

All the considerations above point to the fact that ESE was designed to fit into the mainframe, systems-oriented environment. It is a package well suited for this style of application. Whereas small, quick-prototyping systems can outperform a system like ESE when it comes to rapid testing of ideas, these tools are simply aimed at different types of development tasks.

Another important set of functions and features are reflected in the developer's flexibility in implementing a system at the level of rules, rule processing, and parameter characteristics. It would seem that a great deal less "bending" of the system would be required to achieve a working system than with more focused applications development tools.

However, under circumstances where the knowledge system needs to repeatedly access and process data to complete its task, the import and export facilities may prove to be a bottleneck in systems development and performance. In terms of *interfaces*, the facilities are well conceived and implemented. A problem arises, however, when interfaces are not the appropriate solution.

Consider a manager who needs to reason about numbers arranged in a table. In a simple example, imagine a tabular arrangement of data in which the columns represent different reporting periods, such as quarters, and the rows represent various items in the firm's line of products. The numbers in the table may represent some measure of performance like dollar sales. Finally, the data reflect national figures, aggregated from 60 regional sales offices. In examining the report, the manager spots some irregularity in the percentage change from one time period to another. This number is an "exception" to the expected value. Once this irregularity has been "spotted," the job is to "trace" it and try to identify its source. In this way it can be understood, which may give rise to some approach to either solving the problem or capturing the opportunity that this number represents.

In this search, a number of questions arise:

• Is this "problem" also found at the regional level? If so, in what regions? If it is found in specific regions, what characteristics might those regions have in common that may explain the pattern?

• Is this problem specific to this producer, or is it also found in the performance of competitors, and the market in general?

• Is the problem simply a result of the type of measure used? Do other performance measures, such as case volume, or market share, show a similar pattern?

• Have there been changes in some other key, causal variables, such as advertising expenditures, or the size of the sales force?

In conducting such a search, there are significant, frequent, and repetitive needs to access and analyze information. A problem like this is difficult to solve with the interface approach to noninferential processing. Many management problems are of this type—*iterative* reviews of data, with each iteration being driven by previous examinations. It is not possible to state in advance just what information will be required. These needs are created anew at each turn of the search and analysis process. This type of problem requires much more in the way of integrated methods for representing and processing information.

However, the ability of ESE to access the mainframe world of existing files and processing is an extremely powerful feature. This promises to move knowledge systems from stand-alone curiosities into the mainstream of applications development tools, alongside data base management systems, procedural programming, and the like. While providing this opportunity for integration, when ESE is explored as a stand-alone system, it provides a welcome level of sophisticated developer support through its structured, form-oriented systems entry, and thorough consistency checking. In this mode, it is a tool that delivers on the promise of development shells by being quite suitable for use by individuals without training in the more complex underlying concepts of knowledge systems programming techniques. Finally, the ability to construct and document FCBs as a technique for managing complex knowledge systems at a more abstract level should provide support for extending the power of rule-based systems.

9

Forces Affecting the Future of Knowledge Systems in Business

The tools described in the previous chapters were selected because they appear to illustrate points along the continuums of ease-of-use, flexibility, power, and integration of function. There are many other knowledge systems development tools on the market and more are being introduced regularly. Some of these systems represent a different constellation of features and functions, may provide highly similar features at different prices, or may be suitable for operating with different underlying computer systems. The market for business-oriented knowledge systems development tools is still young and not well defined. In these early stages, requirements are not well known, and market niches have not had an opportunity to develop. As experience grows, the marketplace will become more critical and tool developers will become more responsive. In the world of software development, it is often said that customers do not know what they want until they see it, and this may well be a dominant factor until end-users and applications developers have acquired experience with a variety of tools.

The packages reviewed in some detail here share some common factors in their design philosophies, however. They are

1. Aimed primarily at individuals who have no formal training in the field of artificial intelligence in general, and knowledge systems in particular.
2. Designed to run on existing business-oriented computing hardware and operating systems.
3. Rule-based, with a stronger emphasis on backward than forward chaining. Among currently available systems, few are exclusively forward chaining. Those that offer forward chaining seem to do so in addition to backward chaining. Several systems on the market are exclusively backward-chaining inference engines.

These systems represent the first look at a potentially expansive array of knowledge-oriented technologies. As discussed earlier, they have been adapted from their counterparts in research and development laboratories for use by a new audience. Their success will very likely create a new market for a variety of similar technologies that are as yet untested in the business applications arena.

Prices for systems currently range from thousands to fewer than one hundred dollars. This price range does not always correspond with the traditional mainframe vs. personal computer distinction, or with the capabilities of the tools. Presently, systems with comparable features and functions are being offered with price ratios exceeding 50 to 1. This, again, is a function of the emerging quality of the market, and the consumer's lack of experience in assessing the value of various features.

Another factor influencing this market is the "exploration" phase of many corporate enterprises relative to this technology. There are, in many organizations, groups labeled "emerging technologies," "advanced technologies," "strategic information systems," and so on. Their charge is to examine forefront technologies and evaluate their potential for application. Groups like these are often well budgeted, and will purchase "samples" of many individual systems to carry out comparative assessments. Under these conditions, some software suppliers are experiencing sales generated by these "exploratory" purchases. When experience is gained, and the consumers of these systems shift toward the purchase of systems for true applications development, a shakeout and redefinition of requirements is likely to follow, and market niches will develop.

As has been argued throughout this book, the ground is fertile for the rapid development and integration of knowledge systems for the support of management activity. This results from the relatively short history of business computing. In the span of approximately two decades the role of computing in business has moved in a series of stages through transaction processing, information systems, management information systems, decision support systems, and strategic information systems. There has been a powerful interaction among the following factors:

1. *Price/performance of computing technology.* This is a well-understood phenomenon that has led to increasingly powerful tools at more and more attractive prices. The most recent impact of the price/performance curve has been the appearance of extremely powerful workstations for management support.

2. *Increasing sophistication of applications development software tools.* In a very short time, orders of magnitude improvements have been made in the effort required to develop and maintain complex systems.

3. *Experience curve for management.* As cited above, often users do not know what they want until they see it in tangible form. Current generations of management information systems and decision support systems have provided users with the experience necessary to envision more and more sophisticated applications. In many situations, these visions involve the desire to use these technologies to gain a significant competitive advantage, in addition to increased efficiencies and general managerial effectiveness.

Rather than an alien or tangential technology, knowledge systems seem to represent a logical extension of the use of computing in support of complex decision making and reasoning under conditions of uncertainty. Whereas previous applications of technology have been suitable to automate record keeping and decisions that are more or less algorithmic, the current interest in systems to support increasingly unstructured decision making fits well with the promise of knowledge systems. Along this trajectory, knowledge systems that can be integrated or "coupled" with existing support systems can offer a significant new opportunity.

Many options are available to an organization in terms of how it chooses to respond to the availability of this technology. For some, the opportunities are vast, and competitive forces intense. Circumstances like these may call for rapid assessment, training, prototyping, and systems development. For others, the emergence of knowledge systems technology represents an opportunity to gain efficiencies and otherwise support noncritical aspects of their operations. Under these conditions, purchasing packaged applications developed by software suppliers for their industry, much as one might purchase an order entry system, may be all that is justified.

Figure 9–1 presents three general sources of risk involved with the development of knowledge systems. This model describes a three-dimensional space defined by

1. The degree to which the organization must undergo any significant structural accommodation or assimilation of this technology to achieve its potential benefit
2. The degree to which the applications require solving of significant underlying technological support problems
3. The extent to which there is uncertainty surrounding the suitability of the application to knowledge systems development tools

As an application moves further from the point of origin along these dimensions, the certainty of success diminishes. These factors must be considered when evaluating potential applications areas, and weighed against the perceived benefits of the application.

THE NEED FOR ORGANIZATIONAL ACCOMMODATION/ ASSIMILATION

Indeed, many hold the view that much of the structure of organizations exists because of the organization's need to maintain, structure, and provide information for decision making. This view has given rise to the concept of the "knowledge worker" and to "knowledge management." From this perspective, new information technologies have a strong interaction with organizational structures. Some organizations may be structured in such a way that the opportunity presented by new information processing technologies cannot be well assimilated, owing to the organization's inability to accommodate the change. Such organizations were established in ways that make them efficient in terms of older information processing technologies, but inefficient in the context of new technologies. To the extent that new information processing technologies represent opportunities to gain a competitive advantage, adaptivity in the organization may be a critical factor in determining future success. The study of innovation and technological change has

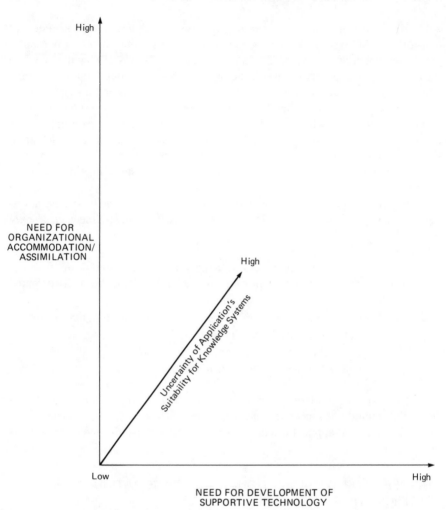

Figure 9-1 Some Determinants of Risk in Knowledge Systems
Applications Development

emerged to help us better understand this phenomenon. With this view in mind, there are some industries and lines of business for which organizational assimilation of knowledge systems technologies and the constellation of related advanced information technologies will be at least as important as having an "understanding" of or expertise with the technology itself.

THE NEED TO DEVELOP SUPPORTIVE TECHNOLOGY

Much of the long-range benefit from knowledge systems will come from their integration with other systems and tools. When considered in isolation, they do provide a significant opportunity to apply computer support to human decision making; however, they have the potential to greatly leverage the investment already being made in other computing systems. The pressure that knowledge systems development places on supportive computing technologies is an extension of many forces already at play.

The desktop computer appears to be the tool of choice for many managerial applications. As processing power increases, the number of computing cycles running on the desktop will continue to increase, with the role of centralized computers shifting to that of organizing and transmitting data for local processing. The growing amount of relevant data and the desirability of powerful personal computers places increasing emphasis on the quality of communications, operating systems, and high-capacity data management. For many knowledge systems applications to achieve significant impact, performance along these dimensions must be improved.

The degree to which a knowledge-based application depends on these capabilities places it in an increasingly risky position. The solutions to these problems are becoming more and more useful and affordable; but depending on their solution for a knowledge systems application adds new dimensions to the problem of assessing the probability of project success.

UNCERTAINTY OF THE APPLICATION'S SUITABILITY FOR KNOWLEDGE SYSTEMS

There is an important process that involves moving from the specific experience of solving a particular problem to a more generalized understanding of types of problems. In the early use of any technology there are numerous isolated attempts to apply it. From these individual efforts, a framework emerges for "classes" of problems and applications. For example, after several years of developing information systems, there is some agreement as to what types of applications are well suited for a "file management" as opposed to a "data management" approach. In the realm of knowledge systems, little in the way of analogous experience really exists.

Although many volumes describe the "general characteristics" of problems suitable for knowledge systems applications (this being one of them), this understanding is still fairly vague and not very predictive as to what specific challenges any one application will encounter. Many areas seem to be appropriate for knowledge systems modeling, but they are not a one-to-one match with previously successful attempts. They may encounter significant problems owing to some unforeseen, unique aspect of the application. Most of what is known about knowledge systems applications development in management is derived from experience with rule-based systems. As more complex and capable object-oriented and frame-based systems become commercially available, they will challenge the boundaries established by their forerunners. This evolution in tool sophistication compounds the problem of developing guidelines for the identification of applications areas. Until there is considerably more experience in creating business-oriented applications, there will be a risk factor associated with the novelty of systems development in many areas. This risk factor is also an important consideration when evaluating potential applications.

COMPETITIVE FORCES, THE ACCEPTANCE OF RISK, AND THE FUTURE OF KNOWLEDGE SYSTEMS

Recalling an earlier example from the area of marketing and brand management may make this point. One of the organizational features of most consumer goods manufacturers is a centralized, national, brand management group. This group is responsible for making decisions about introducing, advertising, and promoting individual brands of products. Over the past 60 years, this centralized organizational structure has been dominant. These groups typically engage in varying amounts of market research, evaluating the effectiveness of decisions regarding advertising and product promotion. As information technologies have evolved, many of these organizations have been "enhanced" by the addition of more sophisticated analysts and quantitative modeling specialists responsible for measurement, evaluation, and forecasting. The introduction of "uniform product code" scanning equipment at retail checkout counters, in combination with other new sources of relevant data, has significantly increased the quality and quantity of data available to brand management groups.

An apparently unrelated phenomenon that is also affecting these organizational units is the rapidly growing concept that "localized" or "regional" marketing has advantages over national marketing efforts. Marketing research has revealed that advertisements and product promotions have widely varying impacts in different regions and local markets. This view has led to a growing desire to make decisions about product advertising and promotion on a local or regional level.

The quantity and richness of the newly available sources of marketing data are well suited to measure, assess, and forecast at a local level, and are capable of supporting local decision making. However, there is a lack of trained marketing analysts and decision makers at the central brand group, and a complete absence of this expertise at the local level. It has been proposed that the availability of knowledge-based marketing systems, coupled with data management and analytical systems, could provide an opportunity to support more local decisions regarding product advertising and promotion, by making analytical and interpretive knowledge available in support of regional offices.

In this setting, the competitive forces are quite strong. The technology of knowledge systems may be well suited to this type of application, but it has not been applied to an analogous area before. However, whatever risks are associated with the use of knowledge systems in this type of application and the need to develop strong supporting technologies for data management and analysis are intensified by the need to restructure the organization in response to the potential opportunity. Actually implementing such a system involves significant reorganization of decision making and responsibility, and a redefinition of roles for many. The interaction of the information processing technology and the organizational structure is critical and nontechnological in nature.

Although this brief restatement of a previous example helps to point out some of the sources of risk inherent in technological adaptation, other classes of knowledge systems applications are characterized by their relatively low risk. These are located very close to the points of origin along the three dimensions in Figure 9-1. They constitute the "sitting ducks."

As an analogy, consider the familiar spreadsheet modeling support package, Lotus 1-2-3. Although this approach to modeling has been applied to managerial decision support via its "what if" simulation characteristics, it is also applicable as a very straightforward accounting package. When one considers the time spent maintaining accounting records by hand, and then assesses the impact of a workstation-based accounting tool like 1-2-3, the advantage is obvious. The role of the individual responsible for keeping accounting records and the organization surrounding that person are not significantly affected by the new tool, the need for developing supporting technology is very low, as it requires only a personal computer, and the match of the application to the characteristics is very high.

This is generally not the sort of application that results in a significant gain from the perspective of strategic business planning, but the risk is also very low. There are numerous analogous applications of knowledge systems technologies. These are, as described before, the "sitting ducks." An organization of any size could easily identify dozens or hundreds of small, stand-alone applications of knowledge systems that require little risk and offer some benefit. The significant impact of knowledge systems is not likely to be found in these applications, however.

From a longer-range perspective, there are very real incentives for many to engage in "pushing the limits" along these dimensions of risk, and capturing the opportunities that they seek, as well as those that they consequently discover. The technology of knowledge-based computer systems and the sophistication of supporting technologies will undergo marked change from the influence of these forces. However, to more fully realize the promise of these developments, it will be necessary to better understand the organizational and competitive environments in which they will be applied, as well as the underlying technology itself. This understanding will, to a large extent, be the function of experience, and will be possessed in increasing share by those who actively seek the opportunity to explore and learn.

Appendix
Knowledge Bases for the Promotion Advisor

Written in M.1, GURU, and Expert System Environment

THE PROMOTION ADVISOR KNOWLEDGE BASE IN M.1

```
/*
```

```
 _____
|                                                             |
|    This is a prototype system designed to be used by a brand|
| manager in charge of marketing a packaged product.          |
|                                                             |
|    The manager answers questions which help specify the product's|
| current performance.  Based on the performance data, the system|
| concludes one or more suitable marketing strategies.        |
|                                                             |
|    The user may choose to accept the system's suggested strategies,|
| or substitute his own.  The system then suggests one or more specific|
| promotion devices for the product.                          |
|                                                             |
|_____|
```

```
*/
```

```
/**********************************************************/
/*                      GOALS                           */
/**********************************************************/
```

```
goal = device.

initialdata = [sys_strat,strategy].


legalvals(sys_strat)=[trial, retrial, convenience, continuity].
multivalued(sys_strat).
legalvals(strategy) = [trial, retrial, convenience, continuity].
multivalued(strategy).
multivalued(device).
```

```
/********************************************************/
/*                  DATA FROM MARKETER                 */
/********************************************************/


/* OW (OVERWHELMING) -------------------------------------*/

rule1:
        if ow = yes
           then
              sys_strat = trial cf 50.

        question(ow) =
           [nl,nl,nl,nl,nl,nl,
               nl,'----------------------------------------------------',
               nl,'| Would you say that preference for this brand |',
               nl,'| is overwhelming among those consumers who    |',
               nl,'| have tried it?                               |',
               nl,'----------------------------------------------------',nl].

        legalvals(ow) = [yes,no].
        automaticmenu(ow).
        enumeratedanswers(ow).

        explanation(rule1) =
           [nl,'Your answer will help determine what',
            nl,'promotion strategy to use.',nl,
            nl,'Based on blind taste tests (or the like) or',
            nl,'based on purchase history, is it clear that',
            nl,'consumers consistently prefer this brand to',
            nl,'others in the category?',nl].
/*-----------------------------------------------------------*/


/* SHARE (MARKET SHARE) -----------------------------------*/

rule2:
        if share = yes
           then
              sys_strat = retrial cf 50.

        question(share) =
           [nl,nl,'----------------------------------------------------',
               nl,'| Would you say that market share is developing |',
               nl,'| normally for this brand?                      |',
               nl,'----------------------------------------------------',nl].

        legalvals(share) = [yes,no].
        automaticmenu(share).
        enumeratedanswers(share).

        explanation(rule2) =
           [nl,'Your answer will help determine what',
            nl,'promotion strategy to use.',nl,
            nl,'Is this brand performing as expected with',
            nl,'respect to market share?',nl].
/*-----------------------------------------------------------*/
```

```
/* PAST_12 (PAST 12 MONTH TRIAL RATE) --------------------*/

rule3:
        if past_12 = medium
            then
                sys_strat = continuity cf 80.

        question(past_12) =
            [nl,nl,'----------------------------------------------------',
                nl,'| Would you say that the past 12 month trial rate |',
                nl,'| for this brand is high, medium or low?          |',
                nl,'----------------------------------------------------',nl].

        legalvals(past_12) = [high,medium,low].
        automaticmenu(past_12).
        enumeratedanswers(past_12).

        explanation(rule3) =
            [nl,'Your answer will help determine what',
             nl,'promotion strategy to use.',nl,
             nl,'What is the rate of trial for this brand over',
             nl,'the past 12 months?  In other words, of all',
             nl,'purchases of this brand, what proportion are',
             nl,'trial (rather than retrial or continuity)',
             nl,'purchases?',nl].
/*-----------------------------------------------------------*/



/* PAST_12 (PAST 12 MONTH TRIAL RATE) --------------------*/

rule4:
        if past_12 = low
            then
                sys_strat = trial cf 80.
/*-----------------------------------------------------------*/



/* LOYALTY ------------------------------------------------*/

rule5:
        if loyalty = low
            then
                sys_strat = convenience cf 50.

        question(loyalty) =
            [nl,nl,'----------------------------------------------------',
                nl,'| Is this a brand with high consumer loyalty? |',
                nl,'----------------------------------------------------',nl].

        legalvals(loyalty) = [yes,no].
        automaticmenu(loyalty).
        enumeratedanswers(loyalty).

        explanation(rule5) =
            [nl,'Your answer will help determine what',
             nl,'promotion strategy to use.',nl,
```

```
        nl,'How strong is this brand''s consumer franchise?',
        nl,'Are people generally repeat purchasers or is',
        nl,'there alot of switching among brands in this',
        nl,'category?',nl].
/*------------------------------------------------------------*/



/* GROWTH --------------------------------------------------*/

rule6:
        if growth = growing
           then
               sys_strat = trial cf 50.

        question(growth) =
           [nl,nl,'---------------------------------------------------',
               nl,'| Would you describe the market for this brand |',
               nl,'|as growing, stable or declining?              |',
               nl,'---------------------------------------------------',nl].

        legalvals(growth) = [growing,stable,declining].
        automaticmenu(growth).
        enumeratedanswers(growth).

        explanation(rule6) =
           [nl,'Your answer will help determine what',
            nl,'promotion strategy to use.',nl,
            nl,'How would you describe the growth rate for this',
            nl,'product category?',nl].
/*------------------------------------------------------------*/



/* SIX_TO_ONE (SIX MONTH TO ONE MONTH) ------------------*/

rule7:
        if six_to_one = yes
           then
               sys_strat = retrial cf 80.

        question(six_to_one) =
           [nl,nl,'-----------------------------------------------------',
               nl,'| Would you describe the numbers of consumers who  |',
               nl,'| have used this brand in the past month as lower  |',
               nl,'| than the number who used it over the past six    |',
               nl,'| months?                                          |',
               nl,'-----------------------------------------------------',
               nl].

        legalvals(six_to_one) = [yes,no].
        automaticmenu(six_to_one).
        enumeratedanswers(six_to_one).

        explanation(rule7) =
           [nl,'Your answer will help determine what',
            nl,'promotion strategy to use.',nl,
            nl,'Is the number of consumers who have used this',
```

```
        nl,'brand in the last month alot lower than the',
        nl,'number who have used it over the last six months?',nl].
/*----------------------------------------------------------*/



/* SHARE_OF_CON_P (SHARE CONSECUTIVE PURCHASES) ----------*/

rule8:
        if share_of_con_p = low
           then
              sys_strat = continuity cf 50.

        question(share_of_con_p) =
           [nl,nl,'------------------------------------------------',
               nl,'| How would you compare the percent of your     |',
               nl,'| customers who are totally brand loyal versus  |',
               nl,'| the percent for your competitors?            |',
               nl,'------------------------------------------------',nl].

        legalvals(share_of_con_p) = [low,medium,high].
        automaticmenu(share_of_con_p).
        enumeratedanswers(share_of_con_p).

        explanation(rule8) =
           [nl,'Your answer will help determine what',
            nl,'promotion strategy to use.',nl,
            nl,'How would you compare the percent of our',
            nl,'customers who are totally brand loyal versus',
            nl,'the percent for our competitors?',nl].
/*----------------------------------------------------------*/



/* (LOCK_UP) ----------------------------------------------*/

rule9:
        if lock_up = yes
           then
              sys_strat = convenience cf 50.

        question(lock_up) =
           [nl,nl,'------------------------------------------',
               nl,'| Is this product one for which multiple |',
               nl,'| purchasing keeps consumers out of the  |',
               nl,'| market?                                |',
               nl,'------------------------------------------',nl].

        legalvals(lock_up) = [yes,no].
        automaticmenu(lock_up).
        enumeratedanswers(lock_up).

        explanation(rule9) =
           [nl,'Your answer will help determine what',
            nl,'promotion strategy to use.',nl,
            nl,'If consumers load up on this product will it',
            nl,'remove them from the market for a long enough',
            nl,'time to give us a competitive edge?  Can we',
```

```
            nl,'preempt competitor''s sales by loading up the',
            nl,'consumer?',nl].
/*----------------------------------------------------------*/



/* USE_CORR (INVENTORY/USER CORRELATION) ----------------*/

rule10:
        if use_corr = yes
            then
                sys_strat = convenience cf 50.

        question(use_corr) =
            [nl,nl,'------------------------------------------------',
                nl,'| Is this a brand for which consumer inventory |',
                nl,'| is correlated with user consumption?         |',
                nl,'------------------------------------------------',nl].

        legalvals(use_corr) = [yes,no].
        automaticmenu(use_corr).
        enumeratedanswers(use_corr).

        explanation(rule10) =
            [nl,'Your answer will help determine what',
                nl,'promotion strategy to use.',nl,
                nl,'Does the consumption rate for this product',
                nl,'increase when consumers have alot of it in',
                nl,'their pantries?  Will consumers use more',
                nl,'if they have more on hand?',nl].
/*----------------------------------------------------------*/



/* CON_PURCH (CONSECUTIVE PURCHASES) --------------------*/

rule11:
        if con_purch = yes
            then
                sys_strat = retrial cf 50.

        question(con_purch) =
            [nl,nl,'------------------------------------------------',
                nl,'| Is it true that a consumer must use this     |',
                nl,'| brand several times in order to appreciate   |',
                nl,'| this brand''s benefits?                       |',
                nl,'------------------------------------------------',nl].

        legalvals(con_purch) = [yes,no].
        automaticmenu(con_purch).
        enumeratedanswers(con_purch).

        explanation(rule11) =
            [nl,'Your answer will help determine what',
                nl,'promotion strategy to use.',nl,
                nl,'Is this a brand whose benefits aren''t obvious',
                nl,'after only one use?  Does it take a consumer',
```

```
                 nl,'several trials before s/he can say s/he prefers',
                 nl,'this brand over another?',nl].
/*---------------------------------------------------------*/


/*********************************************************/
/*         REVIEW SYSTEM STRATEGY W/USER              */
/*********************************************************/

/*  Review with the user the strategy that the system recommends.
    If the user doesn't like the system's recommendations, let the
    user select one or more strategies to use in finding suitable
    marketing devices.
*/

/*---------------------------------------------------------*/

rule12:
        if
               display([nl,nl,nl,nl,nl,nl,
                        'The strategies the system recommends are:',
                        nl,nl])
           and do(show sys_strat)
           and user_agrees = yes
           and sys_strat = A
        then
               strategy = A.

        question(user_agrees) =
           [nl,nl,'------------------------------------',
                nl,'| Do you agree with this strategy? |',
                nl,'------------------------------------',nl].

        legalvals(user_agrees) = [yes,no].
        automaticmenu(user_agrees).
        enumeratedanswers(user_agrees).

        explanation(rule12) =
           [nl,'If you agree with this strategy the system will',
                nl,'proceed directly to finding a suitable marketing',
                nl,'device for your product.  If you disagree you',
                nl,'will be asked to select the strategy(ies) you',
                nl,'prefer and the system will use your selections',
                nl,'to find a device.',nl].

/*---------------------------------------------------------*/

rule13:
        if user_agrees = no
           and user_strat = B
           then
               strategy = B.

        question(user_strat) =
           [nl,nl,'------------------------------------------',
                nl,'| Select the strategy(ies) you prefer    |',
                nl,'| from the list below.  You may include  |',
                nl,'| certainty factors.                     |',
                nl,'------------------------------------------',nl].
```

```
        legalvals(user_strat) = [trial,retrial,continuity,convenience].
        automaticmenu(user_strat).
        enumeratedanswers(user_strat).

        explanation(rule13) =
           [nl,'You may select one or more of the strategies listed.',
            nl,'Then the system will proceed to find suitable marketing',
            nl,'devices using your strategies.  The strategies you',
            nl,'select replace the strategies the system recommended.',
            nl].
/*----------------------------------------------------------*/



/* WHENFOUND STRATEGY ------------------------------------*/

whenfound(strategy) =
   display([nl,nl,nl,nl,nl,nl,nl,nl,nl,nl,nl,nl,
           nl,nl,nl,nl,nl,nl,tab(12),
           '**  The system is now seeking marketing device.  **',
           nl,nl,nl,nl,nl,nl,nl,nl]).
/*----------------------------------------------------------*/




/********************************************************/
/*          SYSTEM FINDS MARKETING DEVICE              */
/********************************************************/


/* TRIAL -------------------------------------------*/

rule14:
        if strategy = trial
           then
        device = sampling cf 100 and
        device = trial_size cf 100 and
        device = own_brand_coupon cf 100 and
        device = pack_premiums cf 80 and
        device = free_mail_in_low_proof_premiums cf 80 and
        device = high_value_single_unit_refunds cf 80 and
        device = group_refunds cf 80 and
        device = high_value_smaller_sizes_price_pack cf 80 and
        device = refund_coupons cf 60 and
        device = container_pack_premiums cf 60 and
        device = generic_refunds cf 60 and
        device = bonus_pack cf 60 and
        device = feature_display_allowances cf 60 and
        device = contests cf 60 and
        device = promotion_advertising cf 60 and
        device = in_pack_games cf 60 and
        device = progressive_refunds cf 40 and
        device = off_invoice_allowances cf 40 and
        device = cross_ruff_coupons cf 0 and
        device = free_mail_in_premium_high_proof_required cf 0 and
        device = self_liquidating_premium cf 0 and
        device = continuity_catalog_premiums cf 0 and
```

```
        device = high_value_multiple_unit_refunds cf 0 and
        device = low_value_refunds cf 0 and
        device = normal_low_value_price_pack cf 0 and
        device = high_value_multiple_unit_price_pack cf 0 and
        device = sweepstakes cf 0.
/*---------------------------------------------------------*/



/* RETRIAL ------------------------------------------------*/

rule15:
        if strategy = retrial
            then
        device = sampling cf 80 and
        device = trial_size cf 100 and
        device = own_brand_coupon cf 100 and
        device = pack_premiums cf 80 and
        device = free_mail_in_low_proof_premiums cf 80 and
        device = high_value_single_unit_refunds cf 80 and
        device = group_refunds cf 80 and
        device = high_value_smaller_sizes_price_pack cf 80 and
        device = refund_coupons cf 60 and
        device = container_pack_premiums cf 60 and
        device = generic_refunds cf 20 and
        device = bonus_pack cf 60 and
        device = feature_display_allowances cf 60 and
        device = contests cf 60 and
        device = promotion_advertising cf 60 and
        device = in_pack_games cf 60 and
        device = progressive_refunds cf 20 and
        device = off_invoice_allowances cf 20 and
        device = cross_ruff_coupons cf 0 and
        device = free_mail_in_premium_high_proof_required cf 0 and
        device = self_liquidating_premium cf 0 and
        device = continuity_catalog_premiums cf 0 and
        device = high_value_multiple_unit_refunds cf 80 and
        device = low_value_refunds cf 0 and
        device = normal_low_value_price_pack cf 0 and
        device = high_value_multiple_unit_price_pack cf 0 and
        device = sweepstakes cf 0.
/*---------------------------------------------------------*/



/* CONTINUITY ---------------------------------------------*/

rule16:
        if strategy = continuity
            then
        device = sampling cf 0 and
        device = trial_size cf 0 and
        device = own_brand_coupon cf 60 and
        device = pack_premiums cf 60 and
        device = free_mail_in_low_proof_premiums cf 0 and
        device = high_value_single_unit_refunds cf 20 and
        device = group_refunds cf 20 and
        device = high_value_smaller_sizes_price_pack cf 80 and
```

```
        device = refund_coupons cf 100 and
        device = container_pack_premiums cf 100 and
        device = generic_refunds cf 60 and
        device = bonus_pack cf 80 and
        device = feature_display_allowances cf 60 and
        device = contests cf 0 and
        device = promotion_advertising cf 60 and
        device = in_pack_games cf 60 and
        device = progressive_refunds cf 60 and
        device = off_invoice_allowances cf 20 and
        device = cross_ruff_coupons cf 0 and
        device = free_mail_in_premium_high_proof_required cf 80 and
        device = self_liquidating_premium cf 0 and
        device = continuity_catalog_premiums cf 100 and
        device = high_value_multiple_unit_refunds cf 0 and
        device = low_value_refunds cf 20 and
        device = normal_low_value_price_pack cf 80 and
        device = high_value_multiple_unit_price_pack cf 60 and
        device = sweepstakes cf 0.
/*----------------------------------------------------------*/



/* CONVENIENCE ---------------------------------------------*/
rule17:
        if strategy = convenience
           then
        device = sampling cf 0 and
        device = trial_size cf 0 and
        device = own_brand_coupon cf 60 and
        device = pack_premiums cf 60 and
        device = free_mail_in_low_proof_premiums cf 0 and
        device = high_value_single_unit_refunds cf 0 and
        device = group_refunds cf 0 and
        device = high_value_smaller_sizes_price_pack cf 0 and
        device = refund_coupons cf 80 and
        device = container_pack_premiums cf 100 and
        device = generic_refunds cf 60 and
        device = bonus_pack cf 100 and
        device = feature_display_allowances cf 60 and
        device = contests cf 0 and
        device = promotion_advertising cf 60 and
        device = in_pack_games cf 0 and
        device = progressive_refunds cf 80 and
        device = off_invoice_allowances cf 20 and
        device = cross_ruff_coupons cf 0 and
        device = free_mail_in_premium_high_proof_required cf 100 and
        device = self_liquidating_premium cf 0 and
        device = continuity_catalog_premiums cf 60 and
        device = high_value_multiple_unit_refunds cf 80 and
        device = low_value_refunds cf 0 and
        device = normal_low_value_price_pack cf 0 and
        device = high_value_multiple_unit_price_pack cf 0 and
        device = sweepstakes cf 0.
/*----------------------------------------------------------*/
```

```
/**********************************************************/
/*                    CONFIGURATION                      */
/**********************************************************/

configuration(prompt) =
    'Input response here: >'.

configuration(banner) =
    [nl,nl,nl,nl,nl,
     tab(14),
     'This is a prototype expert system to help a marketing',nl,tab(14),
     'manager promote his product.  The marketer provides',nl,tab(14),
     'a profile of the product''s current market position',nl,tab(14),
     'and the system then suggests a marketing strategy',nl,tab(14),
     'and a marketing device.',nl,nl,tab(14),
     'To begin the consultation type go. at the prompt.',nl,tab(14)].


/* END */
```

THE SIMPLIFIED PROMOTION ADVISOR KNOWLEDGE
BASE IN M.1

```
goal = device.

initialdata = [sys_strat,strategy].

multivalued(sys_strat).

multivalued(strategy).

multivalued(device).

if ow = yes
then sys_strat = trial cf 50.

if share = yes
then sys_strat = retrial cf 50.

if past_12 = medium
then sys_strat = continuity cf 80.

if past_12 = low
then sys_strat = trial cf 80.

if loyalty = low
then sys_strat = convenience cf 50.

if growth = growing
then sys_strat = trial cf 50.

if six_to_one = yes
then sys_strat = retrial cf 80.

if share_of_con_p = low
then sys_strat = continuity cf 50.

if lock_up = yes
then sys_strat = convenience cf 50.

if use_corr = yes
then sys_strat = convenience cf 50.

if con_purch = yes
then sys_strat = retrial cf 50.

if display([nl,nl,nl,nl,nl,nl,
            'The strategies the system recommends are:',
            nl,nl])
        and do(show sys_strat)
        and user_agrees = yes
        and sys_strat = A
then strategy = A.

if user_agrees = no
        and user_strat = B
then strategy = B.
```

```
whenfound(strategy) =
    display([nl,nl,nl,nl,nl,nl,nl,nl,nl,nl,nl,nl,
             nl,nl,nl,nl,nl,nl,tab(12),
             '** The system is now seeking marketing device.  **',

if strategy = trial
then    device = sampling cf 100 and
        device = trial_size cf 100 and
        device = own_brand_coupon cf 100 and
        device = pack_premiums cf 80 and
        device = free_mail_in_low_proof_premiums cf 80 and
        device = high_value_single_unit_refunds cf 80 and
        device = group_refunds cf 80 and
        device = high_value_smaller_sizes_price_pack cf 80 and
        device = refund_coupons cf 60 and
        device = container_pack_premiums cf 60 and
        device = generic_refunds cf 60 and
        device = bonus_pack cf 60 and
        device = feature_display_allowances cf 60 and
        device = contests cf 60 and
        device = promotion_advertising cf 60 and
        device = in_pack_games cf 60 and
        device = progressive_refunds cf 40 and
        device = off_invoice_allowances cf 40 and
        device = cross_ruff_coupons cf 0 and
        device = free_mail_in_premium_high_proof_required cf 0 and
        device = self_liquidating_premium cf 0 and
        device = continuity_catalog_premiums cf 0 and
        device = high_value_multiple_unit_refunds cf 0 and
        device = low_value_refunds cf 0 and
        device = normal_low_value_price_pack cf 0 and
        device = high_value_multiple_unit_price_pack cf 0 and
        device = sweepstakes cf 0.

if strategy = retrial
 then   device = sampling cf 80 and
        device = trial_size cf 100 and
        device = own_brand_coupon cf 100 and
        device = pack_premiums cf 80 and
        device = free_mail_in_low_proof_premiums cf 80 and
        device = high_value_single_unit_refunds cf 80 and
        device = group_refunds cf 80 and
        device = high_value_smaller_sizes_price_pack cf 80 and
        device = refund_coupons cf 60 and
        device = container_pack_premiums cf 60 and
        device = generic_refunds cf 20 and
        device = bonus_pack cf 60 and
        device = feature_display_allowances cf 60 and
        device = contests cf 60 and
        device = promotion_advertising cf 60 and
        device = in_pack_games cf 60 and
        device = progressive_refunds cf 20 and
        device = off_invoice_allowances cf 20 and
        device = cross_ruff_coupons cf 0 and
        device = free_mail_in_premium_high_proof_required cf 0 and
        device = self_liquidating_premium cf 0 and
        device = continuity_catalog_premiums cf 0 and
        device = high_value_multiple_unit_refunds cf 80 and
        device = low_value_refunds cf 0 and
        device = normal_low_value_price_pack cf 0 and
        device = high_value_multiple_unit_price_pack cf 0 and
        device = sweepstakes cf 0.
```

```
if strategy = continuity
then    device = sampling cf 0 and
        device = trial_size cf 0 and
        device = own_brand_coupon cf 60 and
        device = pack_premiums cf 60 and
        device = free_mail_in_low_proof_premiums cf 0 and
        device = high_value_single_unit_refunds cf 20 and
        device = group_refunds cf 20 and
        device = high_value_smaller_sizes_price_pack cf 80 and
        device = refund_coupons cf 100 and
        device = container_pack_premiums cf 100 and
        device = generic_refunds cf 60 and
        device = bonus_pack cf 80 and
        device = feature_display_allowances cf 60 and
        device = contests cf 0 and
        device = promotion_advertising cf 60 and
        device = in_pack_games cf 60 and
        device = progressive_refunds cf 60 and
        device = off_invoice_allowances cf 20 and
        device = cross_ruff_coupons cf 0 and
        device = free_mail_in_premium_high_proof_required cf 80 and
        device = self_liquidating_premium cf 0 and
        device = continuity_catalog_premiums cf 100 and
        device = high_value_multiple_unit_refunds cf 0 and
        device = low_value_refunds cf 20 and
        device = normal_low_value_price_pack cf 80 and
        device = high_value_multiple_unit_price_pack cf 60 and
        device = sweepstakes cf 0.

if strategy = convenience
then    device = sampling cf 0 and
        device = trial_size cf 0 and
        device = own_brand_coupon cf 60 and
        device = pack_premiums cf 60 and
        device = free_mail_in_low_proof_premiums cf 0 and
        device = high_value_single_unit_refunds cf 0 and
        device = group_refunds cf 0 and
        device = high_value_smaller_sizes_price_pack cf 0 and
        device = refund_coupons cf 80 and
        device = container_pack_premiums cf 100 and
        device = generic_refunds cf 60 and
        device = bonus_pack cf 100 and
        device = feature_display_allowances cf 60 and
        device = contests cf 0 and
        device = promotion_advertising cf 60 and
        device = in_pack_games cf 0 and
        device = progressive_refunds cf 80 and
        device = off_invoice_allowances cf 20 and
        device = cross_ruff_coupons cf 0 and
        device = free_mail_in_premium_high_proof_required cf 100 and
        device = self_liquidating_premium cf 0 and
        device = continuity_catalog_premiums cf 60 and
        device = high_value_multiple_unit_refunds cf 80 and
        device = low_value_refunds cf 0 and
        device = normal_low_value_price_pack cf 0 and
        device = high_value_multiple_unit_price_pack cf 0 and
        device = sweepstakes cf 0.
```

THE PROMOTION ADVISOR KNOWLEDGE BASE IN GURU

```
GOAL: device

WINDOW:
          ROW: 5
          COLUMN: 6
          DEPTH: 10
          WIDTH: 60
          FOGC: Green
          BAGC: White

INITIAL:
          ow = unknown
          share = unknown
          past12 = unknown
          loyalty = unknown
          growth = unknown
          six2one = unknown
          shareofconp = unknown
          lockup = unknown
          usecorr = unknown
          sysstrat = unknown
          conpurch = unknown
          agrees = unknown
          device = unknown
          strategy = unknown
          e.lstr = 80
          e.numv = 30
          e.ofuz = 30
          e.ocf = true
          e.rigr = "A"
          e.icf = true
          #cf = "\13\10\10Input a CF, or Press Return for CF = 100: "

DO:
          #cf = " with certainty factor"
          clear
          output "The devices the system recommends for promoting the
          output "brand under consideration in this session are:"
          output
          output device


RULE: RULE1
          IF: ow = "yes"
          THEN: sysstrat +="trial" cf 50
          REASON: Your answer will help determine what
                  Promotion strategy to use.
                  Based upon blind taste tests (or the like) or
                  based on purchase history, is it clear that
                  customers consistently prefer this brand to
                  others in the category?

RULE: RULE2
          IF: share = "yes"
          THEN: sysstrat +="retrial" cf 50
          REASON: Your answer will help determine what
```

promotion strategy to use.
Is this brand performing as expected with
respect to market share?

RULE: RULE3
    IF: past12 = "medium"
    THEN: sysstrat +="continuity" cf 50
    REASON: Your answer will help determine what
        promotion strategy to use.
        What is the rate of trial for this brand over
        the past 12 months? Is other words, of all
        purchases of this brand, what proportion are
        trial (rather than retrial or continuity)
        purchases?

RULE: RULE4
    IF: past12 ="low"
    THEN: sysstrat +="trial" cf 80

RULE: RULE5
    IF: loyalty = "low"
    THEN: sysstrat +="convenience" cf 50
    REASON: Your answer will help determine what
        promotion strategy to use.
        How strong is this brand's consumer franchise?
        Are people generally repeat purchasers of is
        there a lot of switching among brands in this
        category?

RULE: RULE6
    IF: growth = "growing"
    THEN: sysstrat +="trial" cf 50
    REASON: Your answer will help determine what
        promotion strategy to use.
        How would you describe the growth rate for this
        product category?

RULE: RULE7
    IF: six2one = "yes"
    THEN: sysstrat +="retrial" cf 80
    REASON: Your answer will help determine what
        promotion strategy to use.
        Is the number of consumers who have used this
        brand in the last month a lot lower than the
        number who have used it over the last six months?

RULE: RULE8
    IF: shareofconp = "low"
    THEN: sysstrat +="continuity" cf 50
    REASON: Your answer will help determine what
        promotion strategy to use.
        How would you compare the percent of your
        customers who are totally brand loyal versus
        the percent for your competitors?

RULE: RULE9
    IF: lockup = "yes"
    THEN: sysstrat +="convenience" cf 50

            REASON: Your answer will help determine what
                    promotion strategy to use.
                    If consumers load up on this product, will it
                    remove them from the market for a long enough
                    time to give you a competitive edge? Can you
                    preempt competitor's sales by loading up the
                    consumer?

RULE: RULE10
        IF: usecorr = "yes"
        THEN: sysstrat +="convenience" cf 50
        REASON: Your answer will help determine what
                promotion strategy to use.
                Does the consumption rate for this product
                increase when consumers have a lot of it in
                their pantries? Will consumers us more
                if they have more on hand?

RULE: RULE11
        IF: conpurch = "yes"
        THEN: sysstrat +="retrial" cf 50
        REASON: Your answer will help determine what
                promotion strategy to use.
                Is this a brand whose benefits aren't obvious
                after only one use? Does it take a consumer
                several trials before s/he can say s/he prefers
                this brand over another?

RULE: RULE12
        IF: known("sysstrat") and
                agrees = "yes"
        THEN: strategy = sysstrat
        REASON: If the user agrees with the system's recommendations,
                then the system will go ahead with these strategies
                in determining the appropriate promotion devices.

RULE: RULE13
        IF: strategy = "trial"
        THEN: device += {"sampling" cf 100\
                "trial size" cf 100\
                "own brand coupon" cf 100\
                "pack premiums" cf 80\
                "free mail in low proof premiums" cf 80\
                "high value single unit refunds" cf 80\
                "group refunds" cf 80\
                "high value smaller sizes price pack" cf 80\
                "refund coupons" cf 60\
                "container pack premiums" cf 60\
                "generic refunds" cf 60\
                "bonus pack" cf 60\
                "feature display allowances" cf 60\
                "contests" cf 60\
                "promotion advertising" cf 60\
                "in pack games" cf 60\
                "progressive refunds" cf 40\
                "off invoice allowances" cf 40}
        COMMENT: This rule and the ones that follow determine
                appropriate devices when the system has

identified the appropriate promotion strategies
in consultation with the user.

RULE: RULE14
     IF: strategy = "retrial"
     THEN: device += ("sampling" cf 80,\
                        "trial size" cf 100,\
                        "own brand coupon" cf 100,\
                        "pack premiums" cf 80,\
                        "free mail in low proof premiums" cf 80,\
                        "high value single unit refunds" cf 80,\
                        "group refunds" cf 80,\
                        "high value smaller sizes price pack" cf 80,\
                        "refund coupons" cf 60,\
                        "container pack premiums" cf 60,\
                        "generic refunds" cf 20,\
                        "bonus pack" cf 60,\
                        "feature display allowances" cf 60,\
                        "contests" cf 60,\
                        "promotion advertising" cf 60,\
                        "in pack games" cf 60,\
                        "progressive refunds" cf 20)

RULE: RULE15
     IF: strategy = "continuity"
     THEN: device += ("own brand coupon" cf 60,\
                        "pack premiums" cf 60,\
                        "high value single unit refunds" cf 20,\
                        "group refunds" cf 20,\
                        "high value smaller sizes price pack" cf 80,\
                        "refund coupons" cf 100,\
                        "container pack premiums" cf 100,\
                        "generic refunds" cf 60,\
                        "bonus pack" cf 80,\
                        "feature display allowances" cf 60,\
                        "promotion advertising" cf 60,\
                        "in pack games" cf 60,\
                        "progressive refunds" cf 60,\
                        "off invoice allowances" cf 20,\
                        "free mail in premium high proof required" cf 80,\
                        "continuity catalog premiums" cf 100,\
                        "low value refunds" cf 20,\
                        "normal low value price pack" cf 80,\
                        "high value multiple unit price pack" cf 60)

RULE: RULE16
     IF: strategy = "convenience"
     THEN: device += ("own brand coupon" cf 60,\
                        "pack premiums" cf 60,\
                        "refund coupons" cf 80,\
                        "container pack premiums" cf 100,\
                        "generic refunds" cf 60,\
                        "bonus pack" cf 100,\
                        "feature display allowances" cf 60,\
                        "promotion advertising" cf 60,\
                        "progressive refunds" cf 80,\
                        "off invoice allowances" cf 20,\
                        "free mail in premium high proof required" cf 100,\

```
                    "continuity catalog premiums" cf 60,\
                    "high value multiple unit refunds" cf 80)

VAR: OW
  FIND: clear
  output  "Would  you  say  that  preference  for  this  brand  is\
          overwhelming"
  output "among those consumers who have tried it?"
  input ow str using "lll" with "Please answer yes or no."
  LABEL: Overwhelming Product Preference

VAR: SHARE
  FIND: clear
  output "Would you say that market share is developing
  output "normally for this brand?"
  input share str using "lll" with "Please answer yes or no."
  LABEL: Market Share

VAR: PAST12
  FIND: clear
  output "Would you say that the past 12 month trial rate for this brand"
  output "is high, medium, or low?"
  input past12 str using "llllll"
  LABEL: Past 12 Month Trial Rate

VAR: LOYALTY
  FIND: clear
  output "Is this a brand with high consumer loyalty?"
  input loyalty str using "lll" with "Please answer yes or no."
  LABEL: Brand Loyalty

VAR: GROWTH
  FIND: clear
  output "Would you describe the market for this brand as growing,stable,"
  input growth str using "lllllllll" with "or declining?"
  LABEL: Market Growth

VAR: SIX2ONE
  FIND: clear
  output "Would you describe the numbers  of  consumers  who  have used this"
  output  "brand  in  the  past month as lower than the number who
          used it"
  input six2one str using "lll" with "over the  past  six  months?\
          Please answer yes or no."
  LABEL: Ratio of Trial Rate This Month to that Six Months Ago

VAR: SHAREOFCONP
  FIND: clear
  output  "How would you compare the percent of your customers who\
          are totally"
  output "brand loyal versus the percent for your competitors?"
  input shareofconp str using "llllll" with "Please  answer  high,\
          medium, or low."
  LABEL: Share of Consecutive Purchases

VAR: LOCKUP
  FIND: clear
  output  "Is this product one for which multiple purchasing keeps consumers"
```

```
    input lockup str using "111" with "out  of   the   market?  Please\
            answer yes or no."
    LABEL: Consumer Lock Up

VAR: USECORR
    FIND: clear
    output "Is this product one for which multiple purchasing keeps consumers"
    output "out of the market?"
    input usecorr str using "111" with "Please answer yes or no."
    LABEL: The Correlation of Brand Use with Consumer Inventory

VAR: CONPURCH
    FIND: clear
    output "Is it true that a consumer must use this  brand  several times in"
    output "order to appreciate its benefits?"
    input conpurch str using "111" with "Please answer yes or no"
    LABEL: Requirement for Consecutive Purchasing

VAR: AGREES
    FIND: clear
    output"The strategy, or strategies, the system recommends are:"
    output
    #cf = " with certainty factor "
    output sysstrat
    output
    output "Do you agree?"
    e.icf = false
    input agrees str using "111" with "Please answer yes or no."
    e.icf = true
    #cf = "\10\10\13Input a CF, or press return for CF = 100 "
    LABEL: User agreement with system recommendations regarding strategies

VAR: STRATEGY
    LIMIT: 4
    WHEN: 1
    FIND: clear
    e.ifuz = 4
    output "Please  type  in the strategies you want to employ, and the"
    output "certainty factors for each below."
    output
    output "You may choose any or all of the following set:"
    output
    output"trial\13\retrial\13convenience\13continuity\10\13"
```

THE PROMOTION ADVISOR KNOWLEDGE BASE IN EXPERT SYSTEM ENVIRONMENT

Knowledge Base Index

CONTROL BLOCK: F2__DATA__TO__STRAT	186
CONTROL BLOCK: F3__STRAT__TO__DEVICE	188
RULE: RULE0001	189
RULE: RULE0002	190
RULE: RULE0003	191
RULE: RULE0004	192
RULE: RULE0005	193
RULE: RULE0006	195
RULE: RULE0007	197
RULE: RULE0008	199
RULE: RULE0009	201
RULE: RULE0010	202
RULE: RULE0011	203
RULE: RULE0012	204
RULE: RULE0013	205
RULE: RULE0014	206
RULE: RULE0015	207
RULE: RULE0016	208
RULE: RULE0017	209
RULE: RULE0018	210
PARAMETER: F2__BRAND__LOYALTY	211
PARAMETER: F2__CON__PURCH__REQUIRED	212
PARAMETER: F2__MARKET__GROWTH	213
PARAMETER: F2__OW__PRODUCT__PREF	214
PARAMETER: F2__PAST__12__MO__TRIAL	215
PARAMETER: F2__PRODUCT__LOCK__UP	216
PARAMETER: F2__SHARE__DEVELOPMENT__OK	217
PARAMETER: F2__SHARE__OF__CON__PURCH	218
PARAMETER: F2__STRATEGY	219
PARAMETER: F2__USE__INVENT__CORR	220
PARAMETER: F2__6__TO__1__MO__USE__RAT__LOW	221
PARAMETER: F3__DEVICE	222
PARAMETER: F3__SYS__STRATEGY	224
PARAMETER: F3__USR__STRATEGY	225
PARAMETER: F3__USR__TO__SET__STRATEGY	226
SCREEN: SCR__SYS__STRAT	227

```
CONTROL BLOCK:  F2_DATA_TO_STRAT

Goals              PARAMETER:F2_STRATEGY

Parameters         PARAMETER:F2_BRAND_LOYALTY
                   PARAMETER:F2_CON_PURCH_REQUIRED
                   PARAMETER:F2_OW_PRODUCT_PREF
                   PARAMETER:F2_PAST_12_MO_TRIAL
                   PARAMETER:F2_PRODUCT_LOCK_UP
                   PARAMETER:F2_SHARE_DEVELOPMENT_OK
                   PARAMETER:F2_SHARE_OF_CON_PURCH
                   PARAMETER:F2_STRATEGY
                   PARAMETER:F2_USE_INVENT_CORR
                   PARAMETER:F2_6_TO_1_MO_USE_RAT_LOW
                   PARAMETER:F2_MARKET_GROWTH

Rules              RULE:RULE0001
                   RULE:RULE0002
                   RULE:RULE0003
                   RULE:RULE0004
                   RULE:RULE0012
                   RULE:RULE0013
                   RULE:RULE0014
                   RULE:RULE0015
                   RULE:RULE0016
                   RULE:RULE0017
                   RULE:RULE0018

Control text
                   determine goals;
                   establish f3_strat_to_device

Announce           :CE ON
                   FUQUA SCHOOL OF BUSINESS
                   MARKETING WORKBENCH PROJECT
                   :SP 2
                   IBM EXPERT SYSTEM ENVIRONMENT
                   :SP 2
                   Sample Session:
                   :SP 1
                   Selection of BRAND STRATEGY/PROMOTION DEVICE
                   :SP 1
                   (Rules broken down to single-clause premises)

Max instances      1

Parent             ROOT


Dyn Rule Order     FALSE

I ref it list      RULE:RULE0018-FCBToRules
                   RULE:RULE0017-FCBToRules
                   RULE:RULE0016-FCBToRules
                   RULE:RULE0015-FCBToRules
                   RULE:RULE0014-FCBToRules
                   RULE:RULE0013-FCBToRules
                   RULE:RULE0012-FCBToRules
                   RULE:RULE0004-FCBToRules
                   RULE:RULE0003-FCBToRules
                   RULE:RULE0002-FCBToRules
```

```
                    RULE:RULE0001-FCBToRules
                    PARAMETER:F2_MARKET_GROWTH-FCBToParams
                    PARAMETER:F2_6_TO_1_MO_USE_RAT_LOW-FCBToParams
                    PARAMETER:F2_USE_INVENT_CORR-FCBToParams
                    PARAMETER:F2_STRATEGY-FCBToParams
                    PARAMETER:F2_SHARE_OF_CON_PURCH-FCBToParams
                    PARAMETER:F2_SHARE_DEVELOPMENT_OK-FCBToParams
                    PARAMETER:F2_PRODUCT_LOCK_UP-FCBToParams
                    PARAMETER:F2_PAST_12_MO_TRIAL-FCBToParams
                    PARAMETER:F2_OW_PRODUCT_PREF-FCBToParams
                    PARAMETER:F2_CON_PURCH_REQUIRED-FCBToParams
                    PARAMETER:F2_BRAND_LOYALTY-FCBToParams
                    PARAMETER:F2_STRATEGY-FCBToGoals
                    FCB:F3_STRAT_TO_DEVICE-ParenttoDesc

It ref me list     FCB:F3_STRAT_TO_DEVICE-DesctoParent

Descendants        F3_STRAT_TO_DEVICE
```

CONTROL BLOCK: F3_STRAT_TO_DEVICE

Parameters   PARAMETER:F3_DEVICE
                    PARAMETER:F3_SYS_STRATEGY
                    PARAMETER:F3_USR_STRATEGY
                    PARAMETER:F3_USR_TO_SET_STRATEGY

Rules   RULE:RULE0005
                    RULE:RULE0006
                    RULE:RULE0007
                    RULE:RULE0008
                    RULE:RULE0009
                    RULE:RULE0010
                    RULE:RULE0011

Control text   ASK F3_Usr_to_Set_Strategy;
                    Determine F3_Usr_Strategy;
                    Determine f3_Device;
                    Display F3_Sys_Strategy
                    -- If Known
                    -- Header;
                    Display (F2_strategy, F3_Device)
                    -- Header;

Max instances   1

Parent   F2_DATA_TO_STRAT

Dyn Rule Order   FALSE

I ref it list   RULE:RULE0011-FCBToRules
                    RULE:RULE0010-FCBToRules
                    RULE:RULE0009-FCBToRules
                    RULE:RULE0008-FCBToRules
                    RULE:RULE0007-FCBToRules
                    RULE:RULE0006-FCBToRules
                    RULE:RULE0005-FCBToRules
                    PARAMETER:F3_USR_TO_SET_STRATEGY-FCBToParams
                    PARAMETER:F3_USR_STRATEGY-FCBToParams
                    PARAMETER:F3_SYS_STRATEGY-FCBToParams
                    PARAMETER:F3_DEVICE-FCBToParams
                    FCB:F2_DATA_TO_STRAT-DesctoParent

It ref me list   FCB:F2_DATA_TO_STRAT-ParenttoDesc

```
RULE: RULE0001

Rule text        FIF f2_ow_product_pref is true
                    THEN there is .5 evidence that
                       f2_strategy= 'trial'

Owning FCBs      x:FCB:F2_DATA_TO_STRAT
                 :FCB:F3_STRAT_TO_DEVICE

Rule type          Inference


I ref it list    PARAMETER:F2_STRATEGY-LHSPaInThen
                 PARAMETER:F2_OW_PRODUCT_PREF-TestPaInPrem

It ref me list   FCB:F2_DATA_TO_STRAT-FCBToRules
```

RULE: RULE0002

Rule text   FIF f2_share_development_ok is true
                       THEN there is .5 evidence that
                           f2_strategy = 'retrial'

Owning FCBs   x:FCB:F2_DATA_TO_STRAT
                   :FCB:F3_STRAT_TO_DEVICE

Rule type   Inference

I ref it list   PARAMETER:F2_STRATEGY-LHSPaInThen
                   PARAMETER:F2_SHARE_DEVELOPMENT_OK-TestPaInPrem

It ref me list   FCB:F2_DATA_TO_STRAT-FCBToRules

```
RULE: RULE0003

Rule text        FIF f2_past_12_mo_trial is 'medium'
                   THEN there is .8 evidence that
                     f2_strategy = 'continuity'

Owning FCBs      x:FCB:F2_DATA_TO_STRAT
                 :FCB:F3_STRAT_TO_DEVICE

Rule type        Inference


I ref it list    PARAMETER:F2_STRATEGY-LHSPaInThen
                 PARAMETER:F2_PAST_12_MO_TRIAL-TestPaInPrem

It ref me list   FCB:F2_DATA_TO_STRAT-FCBToRules
```

```
RULE: RULE0004

Rule text        FIF f2_brand_loyalty is 'low'
                    THEN there is .5 evidence that
                        f2_strategy = 'convenience'

Owning FCBs      x:FCB:F2_DATA_TO_STRAT
                 :FCB:F3_STRAT_TO_DEVICE

Rule type        Inference


I ref it list    PARAMETER:F2_STRATEGY-LHSPaInThen
                 PARAMETER:F2_BRAND_LOYALTY-TestPaInPrem

It ref me list   FCB:F2_DATA_TO_STRAT-FCBToRules
```

RULE: RULE0005

Rule text
```
fif f2_strategy is 'trial'
then
there is 1.0 evidence that f3_device = 'sampling',
there is 1.0 evidence that f3_device = 'trial size',
there is 1.0 evidence that f3_device = 'own brand cou
ns',
there is 0.8 evidence that f3_device =
'pack premiums',
there is 0.8 evidence that f3_device =
'free mail in, low proof required premiums',
there is 0.8 evidence that f3_device =
'high value/ single unit refunds',
there is 0.8 evidence that f3_device =
'group refunds',
there is 0.8 evidence that f3_device =
'high value/smaller sizes price pack',
there is 0.6 evidence that f3_device =
'refund coupons',
there is 0.6 evidence that f3_device =
'container pack premiums',
there is 0.6 evidence that f3_device =
'generic refunds',
there is 0.6 evidence that f3_device =
'bonus pack',
there is 0.6 evidence that f3_device =
'feature/display allowances',
there is 0.6 evidence that f3_device =
'contests',
there is 0.6 evidence that f3_device =
'promotion advertising',
there is 0.6 evidence that f3_device =
'in-pack games',
there is 0.4 evidence that f3_device =
'progressive refunds',
there is 0.4 evidence that f3_device =
'off-invoice allowances',
there is 0.0 evidence that f3_device =
'cross-ruff coupon',
there is 0.0 evidence that f3_device =
'free mail-in premium with high proof required',
there is 0.0 evidence that f3_device =
'self-liquidating premium',
there is 0.0 evidence that f3_device =
'continuity catalog premiums',
there is 0.0 evidence that f3_device =
'high value/multiple unit refunds',
there is 0.0 evidence that f3_device =
'low value refunds',
there is 0.0 evidence that f3_device =
'normal/low-value price pack',
there is 0.0 evidence that f3_device =
'high value/multiple unit price pack',
there is 0.0 evidence that f3_device =
'sweepstakes'
```

Owning FCBs
```
:FCB:F2_DATA_TO_STRAT
x:FCB:F3_STRAT_TO_DEVICE
```

Rule type   Inference

```
I ref it list    PARAMETER:F3_DEVICE-LHSPaInThen
                 PARAMETER:F3_DEVICE-LHSPaInThen
                 PARAMETER:F3_DEVICE-LHSPaInThen
                 PARAMETER:F3_DEVICE-LHSPaInThen
                 PARAMETER:F3_DEVICE-LHSPaInThen
                 PARAMETER:F3_DEVICE-LHSPaInThen
                 PARAMETER:F3_DEVICE-LHSPaInThen
                 PARAMETER:F3_DEVICE-LHSPaInThen
                 PARAMETER:F3_DEVICE-LHSPaInThen
                 PARAMETER:F3_DEVICE-LHSPaInThen
                 PARAMETER:F3_DEVICE-LHSPaInThen
                 PARAMETER:F3_DEVICE-LHSPaInThen
                 PARAMETER:F3_DEVICE-LHSPaInThen
                 PARAMETER:F3_DEVICE-LHSPaInThen
                 PARAMETER:F3_DEVICE-LHSPaInThen
                 PARAMETER:F3_DEVICE-LHSPaInThen
                 PARAMETER:F3_DEVICE-LHSPaInThen
                 PARAMETER:F3_DEVICE-LHSPaInThen
                 PARAMETER:F3_DEVICE-LHSPaInThen
                 PARAMETER:F3_DEVICE-LHSPaInThen
                 PARAMETER:F3_DEVICE-LHSPaInThen
                 PARAMETER:F3_DEVICE-LHSPaInThen
                 PARAMETER:F3_DEVICE-LHSPaInThen
                 PARAMETER:F3_DEVICE-LHSPaInThen
                 PARAMETER:F3_DEVICE-LHSPaInThen
                 PARAMETER:F3_DEVICE-LHSPaInThen
                 PARAMETER:F2_STRATEGY-TestPaInPrem

It ref me list   FCB:F3_STRAT_TO_DEVICE-FCBToRules
```

RULE: RULE0006

Rule text   FIF F2_strategy is 'Retrial' THEN
                    there is .8 evidence that
                       f3_device = 'Sampling',
                    there is 1.0 evidence that
                       f3_device = 'Trial Size',
                    there is 1.0 evidence that
                       f3_device = 'Own-Brand Coupons',
                    there is 0.0 evidence that
                       f3_device = 'Cross Ruff Carrier Coupons',
                    there is .6 evidence that
                       f3_device = 'Refund Coupons',
                    there is .8 evidence that
                       f3_device = 'Pack Premiums',
                    there is .6 evidence that
                       f3_device = 'Container Pack Premiums',
                    there is .8 evidence that
                       f3_device = 'Free Mail-in Premiums (low-proof req)
                    there is 0.0 evidence that
                       f3_device = 'Free Mail-in Premiums (hi-proof req)'
                    there is 0.0 evidence that
                       f3_device = 'Self-liquidating Premiums',
                    there is 0.0 evidence that
                       f3_device = 'Continuity Catalog Premiums',
                    there is .8 evidence that
                       f3_device = 'Hi Value/Single Unit Refunds',
                    there is 0.0 evidence that
                       f3_device = 'Hi Value/Multiple Unit Refunds',
                    there is .2 evidence that
                       f3_device = 'Progressive Refunds',
                    there is .8 evidence that
                       f3_device = 'Group Refunds',
                    there is .2 evidence that
                       f3_device = 'Generic Refunds',
                    there is 0.0 evidence that
                       f3_device = 'Low Value Refunds',
                    there is .6 evidence that
                       f3_device = 'Bonus Pack',
                    there is .8 evidence that
                       f3_device = 'Price Pack (Hi Value/Smaller Sizes)',
                    there is 0.0 evidence that
                       f3_device = 'Price Pack (Normal/Low Values)',
                    there is 0.0 evidence that
                       f3_device = 'Price Pack (Hi Value/Multiple Units)'
                    there is .2 evidence that
                       f3_device = 'Off Invoice Allowances',
                    there is .6 evidence that
                       f3_device = 'Feature/Display Allowances',
                    there is .6 evidence that
                       f3_device = 'Contests',
                    there is .6 evidence that
                       f3_device = 'Promotion Advertising',
                    there is 0.0 evidence that
                       f3_device = 'Sweepstakes',
                    there is .6 evidence that
                       f3_device = 'In-pack Games'

Owning FCBs   :FCB:F2_DATA_TO_STRAT
                     x:FCB:F3_STRAT_TO_DEVICE

Rule type   Inference

I ref it list   PARAMETER:F3_DEVICE-LHSPaInThen
                 PARAMETER:F3_DEVICE-LHSPaInThen
                 PARAMETER:F3_DEVICE-LHSPaInThen
                 PARAMETER:F3_DEVICE-LHSPaInThen
                 PARAMETER:F3_DEVICE-LHSPaInThen
                 PARAMETER:F3_DEVICE-LHSPaInThen
                 PARAMETER:F3_DEVICE-LHSPaInThen
                 PARAMETER:F3_DEVICE-LHSPaInThen
                 PARAMETER:F3_DEVICE-LHSPaInThen
                 PARAMETER:F3_DEVICE-LHSPaInThen
                 PARAMETER:F3_DEVICE-LHSPaInThen
                 PARAMETER:F3_DEVICE-LHSPaInThen
                 PARAMETER:F3_DEVICE-LHSPaInThen
                 PARAMETER:F3_DEVICE-LHSPaInThen
                 PARAMETER:F3_DEVICE-LHSPaInThen
                 PARAMETER:F3_DEVICE-LHSPaInThen
                 PARAMETER:F3_DEVICE-LHSPaInThen
                 PARAMETER:F3_DEVICE-LHSPaInThen
                 PARAMETER:F3_DEVICE-LHSPaInThen
                 PARAMETER:F3_DEVICE-LHSPaInThen
                 PARAMETER:F3_DEVICE-LHSPaInThen
                 PARAMETER:F3_DEVICE-LHSPaInThen
                 PARAMETER:F3_DEVICE-LHSPaInThen
                 PARAMETER:F3_DEVICE-LHSPaInThen
                 PARAMETER:F3_DEVICE-LHSPaInThen
                 PARAMETER:F2_STRATEGY-TestPaInPrem

It ref me list   FCB:F3_STRAT_TO_DEVICE-FCBToRules

RULE: RULE0007

Rule text   FIF F2_strategy is 'Continuity' THEN
                   there is 0.0 evidence that
                       f3_device = 'Sampling',
                   there is 0.0 evidence that
                       f3_device = 'Trial Size',
                   there is .6 evidence that
                       f3_device = 'Own-Brand Coupons',
                   there is 0.0 evidence that
                       f3_device = 'Cross Ruff Carrier Coupons',
                   there is 1.0 evidence that
                       f3_device = 'Refund Coupons',
                   there is .6 evidence that
                       f3_device = 'Pack Premiums',
                   there is 1.0 evidence that
                       f3_device = 'Container Pack Premiums',
                   there is 0.0 evidence that
                       f3_device = 'Free Mail-in Premiums (low-proof req)
                   there is .8 evidence that
                       f3_device = 'Free Mail-in Premiums (hi-proof req)'
                   there is 0.0 evidence that
                       f3_device = 'Self-liquidating Premiums',
                   there is 1.0 evidence that
                       f3_device = 'Continuity Catalog Premiums',
                   there is .2 evidence that
                       f3_device = 'Hi Value/Single Unit Refunds',
                   there is .8 evidence that
                       f3_device = 'Hi Value/Multiple Unit Refunds',
                   there is .6 evidence that
                       f3_device = 'Progressive Refunds',
                   there is .2 evidence that
                       f3_device = 'Group Refunds',
                   there is .6 evidence that
                       f3_device = 'Generic Refunds',
                   there is .2 evidence that
                       f3_device = 'Low Value Refunds',
                   there is .8 evidence that
                       f3_device = 'Bonus Pack',
                   there is 0.0 evidence that
                       f3_device = 'Price Pack (Hi Value/Smaller Sizes)',
                   there is .8 evidence that
                       f3_device = 'Price Pack (Normal/Low Values)',
                   there is .6 evidence that
                       f3_device = 'Price Pack (Hi Value/Multiple Units)'
                   there is .2 evidence that
                       f3_device = 'Off Invoice Allowances',
                   there is .6 evidence that
                       f3_device = 'Feature/Display Allowances',
                   there is 0.0 evidence that
                       f3_device = 'Contests',
                   there is .6 evidence that
                       f3_device = 'Promotion Advertising',
                   there is 0.0 evidence that
                       f3_device = 'Sweepstakes',
                   there is .6 evidence that
                       f3_device = 'In-pack Games'

Owning FCBs   :FCB:F2_DATA_TO_STRAT
                   x:FCB:F3_STRAT_TO_DEVICE

Rule type   Inference

I ref it list   PARAMETER:F3_DEVICE-LHSPaInThen
                   PARAMETER:F3_DEVICE-LHSPaInThen
                   PARAMETER:F3_DEVICE-LHSPaInThen
                   PARAMETER:F3_DEVICE-LHSPaInThen
                   PARAMETER:F3_DEVICE-LHSPaInThen
                   PARAMETER:F3_DEVICE-LHSPaInThen
                   PARAMETER:F3_DEVICE-LHSPaInThen
                   PARAMETER:F3_DEVICE-LHSPaInThen
                   PARAMETER:F3_DEVICE-LHSPaInThen
                   PARAMETER:F3_DEVICE-LHSPaInThen
                   PARAMETER:F3_DEVICE-LHSPaInThen
                   PARAMETER:F3_DEVICE-LHSPaInThen
                   PARAMETER:F3_DEVICE-LHSPaInThen
                   PARAMETER:F3_DEVICE-LHSPaInThen
                   PARAMETER:F3_DEVICE-LHSPaInThen
                   PARAMETER:F3_DEVICE-LHSPaInThen
                   PARAMETER:F3_DEVICE-LHSPaInThen
                   PARAMETER:F3_DEVICE-LHSPaInThen
                   PARAMETER:F3_DEVICE-LHSPaInThen
                   PARAMETER:F3_DEVICE-LHSPaInThen
                   PARAMETER:F3_DEVICE-LHSPaInThen
                   PARAMETER:F3_DEVICE-LHSPaInThen
                   PARAMETER:F3_DEVICE-LHSPaInThen
                   PARAMETER:F3_DEVICE-LHSPaInThen
                   PARAMETER:F3_DEVICE-LHSPaInThen
                   PARAMETER:F3_DEVICE-LHSPaInThen
                   PARAMETER:F2_STRATEGY-TestPaInPrem

It ref me list   FCB:F3_STRAT_TO_DEVICE-FCBToRules

RULE: RULE0008

```
Rule text              FIF F2_strategy is 'Convenience' THEN
              there is 0.0 evidence that
              f3_device = 'Sampling',
              there is 0.0 evidence that
              f3_device = 'Trial Size',
              there is  .6 evidence that
              f3_device = 'Own-Brand Coupons',
              there is 0.0 evidence that
              f3_device = 'Cross Ruff Carrier Coupons',
              there is  .8 evidence that
              f3_device = 'Refund Coupons',
              there is  .6 evidence that
              f3_device = 'Pack Premiums',
              there is 1.0 evidence that
              f3_device = 'Container Pack Premiums',
              there is 0.0 evidence that
              f3_device = 'Free Mail-in Premiums (low-proof req)
              there is 1.0 evidence that
              f3_device = 'Free Mail-in Premiums (hi-proof req)'
              there is 0.0 evidence that
              f3_device = 'Self-liquidating Premiums',
              there is  .6 evidence that
              f3_device = 'Continuity Catalog Premiums',
              there is 0.0 evidence that
              f3_device = 'Hi Value/Single Unit Refunds',
              there is 1.0 evidence that
              f3_device = 'Hi Value/Multiple Unit Refunds',
              there is  .8 evidence that
              f3_device = 'Progressive Refunds',
              there is 0.0 evidence that

              f3_device = 'Group Refunds',
              there is  .6 evidence that
              f3_device = 'Generic Refunds',
              there is 0.0 evidence that
              f3_device = 'Low Value Refunds',
              there is 1.0 evidence that
              f3_device = 'Bonus Pack',
              there is 0.0 evidence that
              f3_device = 'Price Pack (Hi Value/Smaller Sizes)',
              there is 0.0 evidence that
              f3_device = 'Price Pack (Normal/Low Values)',
              there is  .8 evidence that
              f3_device = 'Price Pack (Hi Value/Multiple Units)'
              there is  .2 evidence that
              f3_device = 'Off Invoice Allowances',
              there is  .6 evidence that
              f3_device = 'Feature/Display Allowances',
              there is 0.0 evidence that
              f3_device = 'Contests',
              there is  .6 evidence that
              f3_device = 'Promotion Advertising',
              there is 0.0 evidence that
              f3_device = 'Sweepstakes',
              f3_device = 'In-pack Games'

Owning FCBs    :FCB:F2_DATA_TO_STRAT
               x:FCB:F3_STRAT_TO_DEVICE
```

```
Rule type          Inference


I ref it list   PARAMETER:F3_DEVICE-LHSPaInThen
                PARAMETER:F3_DEVICE-LHSPaInThen
                PARAMETER:F3_DEVICE-LHSPaInThen
                PARAMETER:F3_DEVICE-LHSPaInThen
                PARAMETER:F3_DEVICE-LHSPaInThen
                PARAMETER:F3_DEVICE-LHSPaInThen
                PARAMETER:F3_DEVICE-LHSPaInThen
                PARAMETER:F3_DEVICE-LHSPaInThen
                PARAMETER:F3_DEVICE-LHSPaInThen
                PARAMETER:F3_DEVICE-LHSPaInThen
                PARAMETER:F3_DEVICE-LHSPaInThen
                PARAMETER:F3_DEVICE-LHSPaInThen
                PARAMETER:F3_DEVICE-LHSPaInThen
                PARAMETER:F3_DEVICE-LHSPaInThen
                PARAMETER:F3_DEVICE-LHSPaInThen
                PARAMETER:F3_DEVICE-LHSPaInThen
                PARAMETER:F3_DEVICE-LHSPaInThen
                PARAMETER:F3_DEVICE-LHSPaInThen
                PARAMETER:F3_DEVICE-LHSPaInThen
                PARAMETER:F3_DEVICE-LHSPaInThen
                PARAMETER:F3_DEVICE-LHSPaInThen
                PARAMETER:F3_DEVICE-LHSPaInThen
                PARAMETER:F3_DEVICE-LHSPaInThen
                PARAMETER:F3_DEVICE-LHSPaInThen
                PARAMETER:F3_DEVICE-LHSPaInThen
                PARAMETER:F3_DEVICE-LHSPaInThen
                PARAMETER:F3_DEVICE-LHSPaInThen
                PARAMETER:F2_STRATEGY-TestPaInPrem

It ref me list  FCB:F3_STRAT_TO_DEVICE-FCBToRules
```

```
RULE:  RULE0009

Rule text       IF F3_Usr_to_Set_Strategy is 'no'
                   THEN
                       Dont Consider F3_Usr_Strategy

Owning FCBs     :FCB:F2_DATA_TO_STRAT
                x:FCB:F3_STRAT_TO_DEVICE

Rule type        Single fire monitor

Comment         If the user wants to continue with the    :BR
                system's recommendations, then bypass     :BR
                processing that would save the system's   :BR
                recommendations in another parameter and  :BR
                would elicit new values for strategies    :BR
                from the user.


I ref it list   PARAMETER:F3_USR_STRATEGY-LHSPaInThen
                PARAMETER:F3_USR_TO_SET_STRATEGY-TestPaInPrem

It ref me list  FCB:F3_STRAT_TO_DEVICE-FCBToRules
```

RULE: RULE0010

Rule text   IF there is an F3_Usr_Strategy
                      THEN
                         F3_Sys_Strategy = F2_Strategy,
                         F2_Strategy   = F3_Usr_Strategy

Owning FCBs   :FCB:F2_DATA_TO_STRAT
                   x:FCB:F3_STRAT_TO_DEVICE

Rule type   Single fire monitor

Comment   If the user has elected to provide a strategy
                   instead of using the one(s) determined by the
                   system, then save the system's recommendations
                   in the parameter called F3_Sys_Strategy, and
                   move the user's new strategy into the parameter
                   the system will use, called F2_Strategy.

I ref it list   PARAMETER:F3_USR_STRATEGY-RHSPaInThen
                   PARAMETER:F2_STRATEGY-LHSPaInThen
                   PARAMETER:F2_STRATEGY-RHSPaInThen
                   PARAMETER:F3_SYS_STRATEGY-LHSPaInThen
                   PARAMETER:F3_USR_STRATEGY-TestPaInPrem

It ref me list   FCB:F3_STRAT_TO_DEVICE-FCBToRules

```
RULE: RULE0011

Rule text          IF  f3_Usr_to_Set_Strategy is 'no'
                       THEN
                           Dont Consider F3_Sys_Strategy

Owning FCBs        :FCB:F2_DATA_TO_STRAT
                   x:FCB:F3_STRAT_TO_DEVICE

Rule type          Single fire monitor


I ref it list      PARAMETER:F3_SYS_STRATEGY-LHSPaInThen
                   PARAMETER:F3_USR_TO_SET_STRATEGY-TestPaInPrem

It ref me list     FCB:F3_STRAT_TO_DEVICE-FCBToRules
```

```
RULE: RULE0012

Rule text        FIF f2_past_12_mo_trial is 'low'
                    THEN there is .8 evidence that
                       f2_strategy= 'trial'

Owning FCBs      x:FCB:F2_DATA_TO_STRAT
                 :FCB:F3_STRAT_TO_DEVICE

Rule type        Inference


I ref it list    PARAMETER:F2_STRATEGY-LHSPaInThen
                 PARAMETER:F2_PAST_12_MO_TRIAL-TestPaInPrem

It ref me list   FCB:F2_DATA_TO_STRAT-FCBToRules
```

```
RULE: RULE0013

Rule text        FIF f2_market_growth is 'growing'
                   THEN  there is .5 evidence that
                        f2_strategy = 'trial'

Owning FCBs      x:FCB:F2_DATA_TO_STRAT
                 :FCB:F3_STRAT_TO_DEVICE

Rule type        Inference


I ref it list    PARAMETER:F2_STRATEGY-LHSPaInThen
                 PARAMETER:F2_MARKET_GROWTH-TestPaInPrem

It ref me list   FCB:F2_DATA_TO_STRAT-FCBToRules
```

```
RULE: RULE0014

Rule text        FIF  f2_6_to_1_mo_use_rat_low is true
                   THEN  there is .8 evidence that
                      f2_strategy = 'retrial'

Owning FCBs      x:FCB:F2_DATA_TO_STRAT
                  :FCB:F3_STRAT_TO_DEVICE

Rule type        Inference


I ref it list    PARAMETER:F2_STRATEGY-LHSPaInThen
                 PARAMETER:F2_6_TO_1_MO_USE_RAT_LOW-TestPaInPrem

It ref me list   FCB:F2_DATA_TO_STRAT-FCBToRules
```

```
RULE: RULE0015

Rule text        FIF f2_con_purch_required is true
                    THEN there is .5 evidence that
                      f2_strategy = 'retrial'

Owning FCBs      x:FCB:F2_DATA_TO_STRAT
                 :FCB:F3_STRAT_TO_DEVICE

Rule type        Inference


I ref it list    PARAMETER:F2_STRATEGY-LHSPaInThen
                 PARAMETER:F2_CON_PURCH_REQUIRED-TestPaInPrem

It ref me list   FCB:F2_DATA_TO_STRAT-FCBToRules
```

RULE: RULE0016

Rule text   FIF f2_share_of_con_purch is 'low'
                       THEN there is .5 evidence that
                           f2_strategy = 'continuity'

Owning FCBs   x:FCB:F2_DATA_TO_STRAT
                   :FCB:F3_STRAT_TO_DEVICE

Rule type   Inference

I ref it list   PARAMETER:F2_STRATEGY-LHSPaInThen
                   PARAMETER:F2_SHARE_OF_CON_PURCH-TestPaInPrem

It ref me list   FCB:F2_DATA_TO_STRAT-FCBToRules

RULE: RULE0017

```
Rule text        FIF f2_product_lock_up is true
                    THEN there is .5 evidence that
                        f2_strategy = 'convenience'

Owning FCBs      x:FCB:F2_DATA_TO_STRAT
                 :FCB:F3_STRAT_TO_DEVICE

Rule type          Inference


I ref it list    PARAMETER:F2_STRATEGY-LHSPaInThen
                 PARAMETER:F2_PRODUCT_LOCK_UP-TestPaInPrem

It ref me list   FCB:F2_DATA_TO_STRAT-FCBToRules
```

RULE: RULE0018

Rule text   FIF f2_use_invent_corr is true
                   THEN there is .5 evidence that
                   · f2_strategy = 'convenience'

Owning FCBs   x:FCB:F2_DATA_TO_STRAT
                 :FCB:F3_STRAT_TO_DEVICE

Rule type   Inference

I ref it list   PARAMETER:F2_STRATEGY-LHSPaInThen
                 PARAMETER:F2_USE_INVENT_CORR-TestPaInPrem

It ref me list   FCB:F2_DATA_TO_STRAT-FCBToRules

```
PARAMETER: F2_BRAND_LOYALTY

Constraint        taken from ('low','medium','high')

Sourcing seq.     Rule Consequent
                  User will input from terminal
                  Default will be taken

Prompt            How would you describe the level   :br
                  of brand loyalty for this brand?

Long Prompt       How strong is this brand's consumer franchise?   :br
                  Are people generally repeat purchasers or is     :br
                  there a lot of switching among brands in this    :br
                  category?

Owning FCBs       x:FCB:F2_DATA_TO_STRAT
                  :FCB:F3_STRAT_TO_DEVICE

Val can chg flg   FALSE

Print name        brand loyalty

It ref me list    FCB:F2_DATA_TO_STRAT-FCBToParams
                  RULE:RULE0004-TestPaInPrem
```

```
PARAMETER: F2_CON_PURCH_REQUIRED
```

Constraint   is a boolean

Sourcing seq.   Rule Consequent
                    User will input from terminal
                    Default will be taken

Prompt   Is it true that a consumer must use this   :br
                    brand several times in order to appreciate   :br
                    this brand's benefits?

Long Prompt   Is this a brand whose benefits aren't obvious   :br
                    after only one use? Does it take a consumer   :br
                    several trials before s/he can say s/he prefers :br
                    this brand over another?

Owning FCBs   x:FCB:F2_DATA_TO_STRAT
                    :FCB:F3_STRAT_TO_DEVICE

Val can chg flg   FALSE

Print name   repeat use required

It ref me list   FCB:F2_DATA_TO_STRAT-FCBToParams
                    RULE:RULE0015-TestPaInPrem
```
```

```
PARAMETER: F2_MARKET_GROWTH

Constraint        taken from ('declining','stagnant','growing')

Sourcing seq.     Rule Consequent
                  User will input from terminal
                  Default will be taken

Prompt            How would you describe the growth  :br
                  rate for this product category?


Owning FCBs       x:FCB:F2_DATA_TO_STRAT
                  :FCB:F3_STRAT_TO_DEVICE

Val can chg flg   FALSE

Print name        market growth

It ref me list    FCB:F2_DATA_TO_STRAT-FCBToParams
                  RULE:RULE0013-TestPaInPrem
```

PARAMETER: F2_OW_PRODUCT_PREF

Constraint   is a boolean

Sourcing seq.   Rule Consequent
                     User will input from terminal
                     Default will be taken

Prompt   Is consumer preference for this   :br
                  brand versus others overwhelming?

Long Prompt   Based on blind taste tests (or the like) or   :br
                  based on purchase history, is it clear that   :br
                  consumers consistently prefer this brand to   :br
                  others in the category?

Owning FCBs   x:FCB:F2_DATA_TO_STRAT
                  :FCB:F3_STRAT_TO_DEVICE

Val can chg flg FALSE

Print name   overwhelming preference for this brand

It ref me list   FCB:F2_DATA_TO_STRAT-FCBToParams
                  RULE:RULE0001-TestPaInPrem

PARAMETER: F2_PAST_12_MO_TRIAL

Constraint   taken from ("low","medium","high")

Sourcing seq.   Rule Consequent
                    User will input from terminal
                    Default will be taken

Prompt   Describe the past 12 month   :br
                    trial level for this brand.

Long Prompt   What is the rate of trial for this brand over :br
                    the past 12 months? In other words, of all   :br
                    purchases of this brand, what proportion are :br
                    trial (rather than retrial or continuity)   :br
                    purchases?

Owning FCBs   x:FCB:F2_DATA_TO_STRAT
                    :FCB:F3_STRAT_TO_DEVICE

Val can chg flg   FALSE

Print name   past 12 month trial rate

It ref me list   FCB:F2_DATA_TO_STRAT-FCBToParams
                    RULE:RULE0012-TestPaInPrem
                    RULE:RULE0003-TestPaInPrem

PARAMETER: F2_PRODUCT_LOCK_UP

Constraint   is a boolean

Sourcing seq.   Rule Consequent
                    User will input from terminal
                    Default will be taken

Prompt   Is the product one for which convenience :br
                  purchasing locks up users?

Long Prompt   If consumers load up on this product will it   :br
                  remove them from the market for a long enough   :br
                  time to give us a competitive edge? can we   :br
                  preempt competitors' sales by loading up the   :br
                  consumer?

Owning FCBs   x:FCB:F2_DATA_TO_STRAT
                  :FCB:F3_STRAT_TO_DEVICE

Val can chg flg FALSE

Print name   convenience purchasing locks up users

It ref me list   FCB:F2_DATA_TO_STRAT-FCBToParams
                  RULE:RULE0017-TestPaInPrem

```
PARAMETER: F2_SHARE_DEVELOPMENT_OK

Constraint       is a boolean

Sourcing seq.       Rule Consequent
                    User will input from terminal
                    Default will be taken

Prompt              Is this brand performing as expected      :br
                    with respect to market share?


Owning FCBs         x:FCB:F2_DATA_TO_STRAT
                    :FCB:F3_STRAT_TO_DEVICE

Val can chg flg FALSE

Print name          performance good with respect to market share

It ref me list   FCB:F2_DATA_TO_STRAT-FCBToParams
                 RULE:RULE0002-TestPaInPrem
```

PARAMETER: F2_SHARE_OF_CON_PURCH

Constraint   taken from ('low','medium','high')

Sourcing seq.   Rule Consequent
                    User will input from terminal
                    Default will be taken

Prompt   How would you compare the percentage of   :br
                    consumers who make consecutive purchases of   :br
                    this brand to the percentage who consecutively   :br
                    purchase one of our competitor's products?   :br

Long Prompt   How would you compare the percent of our   :br
                    customers who are totally brand loyal   :br
                    versus the percent for our competitors?

Owning FCBs   x:FCB:F2_DATA_TO_STRAT
                    :FCB:F3_STRAT_TO_DEVICE

Val can chg flg FALSE

Print name   share of consecutive purchases made compared to the c
                    petition

It ref me list   FCB:F2_DATA_TO_STRAT-FCBToParams
                 RULE:RULE0016-TestPaInPrem

```
PARAMETER: F2_STRATEGY

Constraint        taken from ('trial','retrial','continuity',
                  'convenience'); multivalued

Sourcing seq.     Rule Consequent
                  Default will be taken



Owning FCBs       x:FCB:F2_DATA_TO_STRAT
                  :FCB:F3_STRAT_TO_DEVICE

Val can chg flg TRUE

Print name        The strategy(ies) the system is using      :br
                  to find promotion devices

It ref me list    FCB:F2_DATA_TO_STRAT-FCBToParams
                  FCB:F2_DATA_TO_STRAT-FCBToGoals
                  SCREEN:SCR_SYS_STRAT-ScreenToParam
                  RULE:RULE0018-LHSPaInThen
                  RULE:RULE0017-LHSPaInThen
                  RULE:RULE0016-LHSPaInThen
                  RULE:RULE0015-LHSPaInThen
                  RULE:RULE0014-LHSPaInThen
                  RULE:RULE0013-LHSPaInThen
                  RULE:RULE0012-LHSPaInThen
                  RULE:RULE0010-LHSPaInThen
                  RULE:RULE0010-RHSPaInThen
                  RULE:RULE0008-TestPaInPrem
                  RULE:RULE0007-TestPaInPrem
                  RULE:RULE0006-TestPaInPrem
                  RULE:RULE0005-TestPaInPrem
                  RULE:RULE0004-LHSPaInThen
                  RULE:RULE0003-LHSPaInThen
                  RULE:RULE0002-LHSPaInThen
                  RULE:RULE0001-LHSPaInThen
```

PARAMETER: F2_USE_INVENT_CORR

Constraint   is a boolean

Sourcing seq.   Rule Consequent
                    User will input from terminal
                    Default will be taken

Prompt   Is this product one for which the usage   :br
                  level is positively correlated with the   :br
                  consumer's inventory level?

Long Prompt   Does the consumption rate for this product :br
                  increase when consumers have a lot of it in :br
                  their pantries? Will consumers use more if :br
                  they have more on hand?

Owning FCBs   x:FCB:F2_DATA_TO_STRAT
                  :FCB:F3_STRAT_TO_DEVICE

Val can chg flg FALSE

Print name   usage level correlated to inventory level

It ref me list   FCB:F2_DATA_TO_STRAT-FCBToParams
                  RULE:RULE0018-TestPaInPrem

PARAMETER: F2_6_TO_1_MO_USE_RAT_LOW

Constraint   is a boolean

Sourcing seq.   Rule Consequent
                    User will input from terminal
                    Default will be taken

Prompt   Is the ratio of six-month   :br
                    to one-month usage low?

Long Prompt   Is the number of consumers who have used   :br
                    this brand in the last month a lot lower   :br
                    than the number who have used it over the   :br
                    last six months?

Owning FCBs   x:FCB:F2_DATA_TO_STRAT
                    :FCB:F3_STRAT_TO_DEVICE

Val can chg flg FALSE

Print name   6 month to 1 month usage ratio is low

It ref me list FCB:F2_DATA_TO_STRAT-FCBToParams
                RULE:RULE0014-TestPaInPrem

```
PARAMETER: F3_DEVICE

Constraint        is a string;multivalued;

Sourcing seq.     Rule Consequent
                  Default will be taken



Owning FCBs       :FCB:F2_DATA_TO_STRAT
                  x:FCB:F3_STRAT_TO_DEVICE


Val can chg flg FALSE

Print name        :sp 2
                  The promotion devices recommended based :br
                  on the strategy(ies) used by the system :br


It ref me list    FCB:F3_STRAT_TO_DEVICE-FCBToParams
                  RULE:RULE0008-LHSPaInThen
                  RULE:RULE0008-LHSPaInThen
                  RULE:RULE0008-LHSPaInThen
                  RULE:RULE0008-LHSPaInThen
                  RULE:RULE0008-LHSPaInThen
                  RULE:RULE0008-LHSPaInThen
                  RULE:RULE0008-LHSPaInThen
                  RULE:RULE0008-LHSPaInThen
                  RULE:RULE0008-LHSPaInThen
                  RULE:RULE0008-LHSPaInThen
                  RULE:RULE0008-LHSPaInThen
                  RULE:RULE0008-LHSPaInThen
                  RULE:RULE0008-LHSPaInThen
                  RULE:RULE0008-LHSPaInThen
                  RULE:RULE0008-LHSPaInThen
                  RULE:RULE0008-LHSPaInThen
                  RULE:RULE0008-LHSPaInThen
                  RULE:RULE0008-LHSPaInThen
                  RULE:RULE0008-LHSPaInThen
                  RULE:RULE0008-LHSPaInThen
                  RULE:RULE0008-LHSPaInThen
                  RULE:RULE0008-LHSPaInThen
                  RULE:RULE0008-LHSPaInThen
                  RULE:RULE0008-LHSPaInThen
                  RULE:RULE0008-LHSPaInThen
                  RULE:RULE0008-LHSPaInThen
                  RULE:RULE0007-LHSPaInThen
                  RULE:RULE0007-LHSPaInThen
                  RULE:RULE0007-LHSPaInThen
                  RULE:RULE0007-LHSPaInThen
                  RULE:RULE0007-LHSPaInThen
                  RULE:RULE0007-LHSPaInThen
                  RULE:RULE0007-LHSPaInThen
                  RULE:RULE0007-LHSPaInThen
                  RULE:RULE0007-LHSPaInThen
                  RULE:RULE0007-LHSPaInThen
                  RULE:RULE0007-LHSPaInThen
                  RULE:RULE0007-LHSPaInThen
                  RULE:RULE0007-LHSPaInThen
                  RULE:RULE0007-LHSPaInThen
```

```
RULE:RULE0007-LHSPaInThen
RULE:RULE0007-LHSPaInThen
RULE:RULE0007-LHSPaInThen
RULE:RULE0007-LHSPaInThen
RULE:RULE0007-LHSPaInThen
RULE:RULE0007-LHSPaInThen
RULE:RULE0007-LHSPaInThen
RULE:RULE0007-LHSPaInThen
RULE:RULE0007-LHSPaInThen
RULE:RULE0007-LHSPaInThen
RULE:RULE0007-LHSPaInThen
RULE:RULE0007-LHSPaInThen
RULE:RULE0006-LHSPaInThen
RULE:RULE0006-LHSPaInThen
RULE:RULE0006-LHSPaInThen
RULE:RULE0006-LHSPaInThen
RULE:RULE0006-LHSPaInThen
RULE:RULE0006-LHSPaInThen
RULE:RULE0006-LHSPaInThen
RULE:RULE0006-LHSPaInThen
RULE:RULE0006-LHSPaInThen
RULE:RULE0006-LHSPaInThen
RULE:RULE0006-LHSPaInThen
RULE:RULE0006-LHSPaInThen
RULE:RULE0006-LHSPaInThen
RULE:RULE0006-LHSPaInThen
RULE:RULE0006-LHSPaInThen
RULE:RULE0006-LHSPaInThen
RULE:RULE0006-LHSPaInThen
RULE:RULE0006-LHSPaInThen
RULE:RULE0006-LHSPaInThen
RULE:RULE0006-LHSPaInThen
RULE:RULE0006-LHSPaInThen
RULE:RULE0006-LHSPaInThen
RULE:RULE0006-LHSPaInThen
RULE:RULE0006-LHSPaInThen
RULE:RULE0006-LHSPaInThen
RULE:RULE0006-LHSPaInThen
RULE:RULE0005-LHSPaInThen
RULE:RULE0005-LHSPaInThen
RULE:RULE0005-LHSPaInThen
RULE:RULE0005-LHSPaInThen
RULE:RULE0005-LHSPaInThen
RULE:RULE0005-LHSPaInThen
RULE:RULE0005-LHSPaInThen
RULE:RULE0005-LHSPaInThen
RULE:RULE0005-LHSPaInThen
RULE:RULE0005-LHSPaInThen
RULE:RULE0005-LHSPaInThen
RULE:RULE0005-LHSPaInThen
RULE:RULE0005-LHSPaInThen
RULE:RULE0005-LHSPaInThen
RULE:RULE0005-LHSPaInThen
RULE:RULE0005-LHSPaInThen
RULE:RULE0005-LHSPaInThen
RULE:RULE0005-LHSPaInThen
RULE:RULE0005-LHSPaInThen
RULE:RULE0005-LHSPaInThen
RULE:RULE0005-LHSPaInThen
RULE:RULE0005-LHSPaInThen
```

PARAMETER: F3_SYS_STRATEGY

Constraint   taken from ('trial', 'retrial', 'continuity',
                    'convenience'); multivalued

Sourcing seq.   Rule Consequent

Owning FCBs   :FCB:F2_DATA_TO_STRAT
                    x:FCB:F3_STRAT_TO_DEVICE

Val can chg flg FALSE

Print name   The strategies available are   :br :il +2
                    Trial   :br :il +2
                    Retrial   :br :il +2
                    Continuity   :br :il +2
                    Convenience
                    :sp 2
                    The stragegy(ies) the system recommended :br
                    (replaced by the user's strategy)

It ref me list   FCB:F3_STRAT_TO_DEVICE-FCBToParams
                    RULE:RULE0011-LHSPaInThen
                    RULE:RULE0010-LHSPaInThen

PARAMETER: F3_USR_STRATEGY

Constraint   taken from ('trial', 'retrial', 'continuity',
                    'convenience'); multivalued

Sourcing seq.   Rule Consequent
                    User will input from terminal
                    Default will be taken

Prompt   :IL +4
                      You have elected to select your own strategy :BR
                    instead of using the strategy suggested by   :BR
                    the system.   :BR
                    :IL +4
                      Select one or more strategies from the list :BR
                    below. You can provide confidence factors   :BR
                    for your selections.

Owning FCBs   :FCB:F2_DATA_TO_STRAT
                    x:FCB:F3_STRAT_TO_DEVICE

Val can chg flg FALSE

It ref me list   FCB:F3_STRAT_TO_DEVICE-FCBToParams
                    RULE:RULE0009-LHSPaInThen
                    RULE:RULE0010-RHSPaInThen
                    RULE:RULE0010-TestPaInPrem

PARAMETER: F3_USR_TO_SET_STRATEGY

Constraint   taken from ('yes','no')

Sourcing seq.   Rule Consequent
                     User will input from terminal
                     Default will be taken

Prompt   Do you want to change the strategy   :br
                     the system will use in determining   :br
                     promotion devices?

Long Prompt   You can let the system continue with the   :br
                     strategies it's determined so far by responding :br
                     "No". If you respond "Yes", you'll be prompted :br
                     to supply the strategies you want the system to :br
                     use as it looks for promotion devices for the   :br
                     brand.

Owning FCBs   :FCB:F2_DATA_TO_STRAT
                     x:FCB:F3_STRAT_TO_DEVICE

Screen   SCREEN:SCR_SYS_STRAT

Val can chg flg FALSE

I ref it list   SCREEN:SCR_SYS_STRAT-ParamToScreen

It ref me list   FCB:F3_STRAT_TO_DEVICE-FCBToParams
                     SCREEN:SCR_SYS_STRAT-ScreenToParam
                     SCREEN:SCR_SYS_STRAT-ScreenToParam
                     RULE:RULE0011-TestPaInPrem
                     RULE:RULE0009-TestPaInPrem

```
SCREEN: SCR_SYS_STRAT


I ref it list     PARAMETER:F3_USR_TO_SET_STRATEGY-ScreenToParam
                  PARAMETER:F3_USR_TO_SET_STRATEGY-ScreenToParam
                  PARAMETER:F2_STRATEGY-ScreenToParam

It ref me list    PARAMETER:F3_USR_TO_SET_STRATEGY-ParamToScreen

        :ce Focus: :*

    Recommended strategies:                                   |   PF1   H
                       |  PF2   R
    CCC |  AAAAAAAAAAAAAAAAAAAAAAAAAAAAAAAAAAAAAAAAAAAAAA     |   PF3   E
    CCC |  AAAAAAAAAAAAAAAAAAAAAAAAAAAAAAAAAAAAAAAAAAAAAA     |   PF4   W
    CCC |  AAAAAAAAAAAAAAAAAAAAAAAAAAAAAAAAAAAAAAAAAAAAAA     |   PF5   Q
    CCC |  AAAAAAAAAAAAAAAAAAAAAAAAAAAAAAAAAAAAAAAAAAAAAA     |   PF6   U
    CCC |  AAAAAAAAAAAAAAAAAAAAAAAAAAAAAAAAAAAAAAAAAAAAAA     |   PF7   U
                       |  PF8   D
                       |  PF9   T
    QQQQQQQQQQQQQQQQQQQQQQQQQQQQQQQQQQQQQQQQQQQQQQQQQQQQQQ     |   PF10  H
    QQQQQQQQQQQQQQQQQQQQQQQQQQQQQQQQQQQQQQQQQQQQQQQQQQQQQQ     |   PF11  W
    QQQQQQQQQQQQQQQQQQQQQQQQQQQQQQQQQQQQQQQQQQQQQQQQQQQQQQ     |   PF12  C
    QQQQQQQQQQQQQQQQQQQQQQQQQQQQQQQQQQQQQQQQQQQQQQQQQQQQQQ     |_____
    CCC AAAAAAAAAAAAAAAAAAAAAAAAAAAAAAAAAAAAAAAAAAAAAA
    CCC AAAAAAAAAAAAAAAAAAAAAAAAAAAAAAAAAAAAAAAAAAAAAA
    CCC AAAAAAAAAAAAAAAAAAAAAAAAAAAAAAAAAAAAAAAAAAAAAA


==>
```

Index

American Hospital Supply, 10–11
Apple Macintosh, 45
Applications programmers, 60
Applications, sample
　consumer packaged-goods marketing,
　　66–70
　financial statement analysis advisor, 70–
　　73
　load control advisor, 48, 61–66, 79–80,
　　82–83
Applications suitability, future trends,
　　159–60
Arrays, 109
Artificial intelligence (AI), 4, 17 (*See also*
　　Development tools, knowledge
　　systems)
　detractors/critics, 24
　tools, 3, 4–5
　workstations, 19, 20
ASCII format, 102, 103
Assembly language, 107, 109
Automated knowledge acquisition, 89–93
Automobile engine fault diagnosis, 87, 103

Backing out, expert, 83–84, 85
Backward chaining, 29–36, 38, 39, 81,
　　86, 155
　ESE, 144, 146
　GURU, 128–30
　M.1, 104–7, 118
Bandwidth, channel, 52
Booz, Allen, and Hamilton, 10
Borland, 102
Bottom-up (inductive) approaches, 23

Cash, James, 6
Channel bandwidth, 52
Chunks of knowledge, 25–26, 34, 36, 79
C language, 46, 100–101, 107, 109, 117,
　　122
Clashes, 91
CMS, 140
COBOL, 6, 13, 46
Common-sense knowledge, 24
Competitive advantage, 6–14, 59
　future trends, 160–61

Competitive forces model, 9–10, 20
　expanded, 11
Complexity, levels of, 86
Consumer packaged-goods marketing, 66–
　　70

Data Base 2 (DB2), 140, 145
Database management system, 51, 52
　systems integration, 134, 135
dBASE, 49
Decomposition, 81, 103, 122
Deductive approach, 23
Default decisions, 101, 104
Design cf. diagnosis, 36
Development environment
　ESE, 140–44
　GURU, 122–27
　M.1, 101–4
Development tools, knowledge systems,
　　15–39, 59, 80 (*See also* Expert
　　System Environment; GURU; M.1)
　available, nature and impact, 22–25
　backward chaining, 29–36, 38, 39
　choosing, 19–22
　ease of use vs. power, 89
　evaluation, 43–56
　　business cf. research environment, 44–
　　　47
　　data access, 47–50
　　development support environment, 53–
　　　56
　　hardware, 44–47
　　information representation, 50–53
　evolution from techniques, 17–19
　forward chaining, 29, 35–37
　frame-based systems, 37–39
　inference process, 29–33
　object-oriented systems, 37–39
　uncertainty, 33–35
Diagnosis cf. design, 36
Diagnostic systems, 29, 34
　engine fault, 87, 103
Digital Equipment Corporation (DEC)
　minicomputers, 44
　VAX systems, 122
　XCON, 35

Documentation
   ESE, 140, 150
   M.1, 101
Domain experts, 60
DOS, 109, 122, 132

Electrical utility, sample application, 48,
      61–66, 79–80, 82–83
EMYCIN, 29, 33, 100
Engine fault diagnosis, 87, 103
Environment variables, 127
Evaluation, development tools, 43–56
Experience curve, management, 156
Expert(s), 79, 80, 83
   backing out, 83–84, 85
   domain, 60
Expertise, 23
Expert System Environment (ESE), 97,
      103, 115, 117, 124, 125, 137–51
   ACQUIRE and PROCESS instructions,
      146
   backward chaining, 144, 146
   development environment, 140–44
   development (ESDE) cf. consultation
      (ESCE) environments, 141, 142
   documentation, 140, 150
   focus control blocks (FCBs), 140–46,
      148–49, 150
      root, 143, 148
   forward chaining, 144, 145, 146
   cf. GURU, 139, 140, 144, 149
   IF cf. FIF, 146
   inferencing and uncertainty, 144–46
   integration and noninferential
      processing, 146–47
   cf. M.1, 139, 141, 142, 145, 146, 149,
      150
   parameters, 144
   Promotion Advisor in, 139, 142, 144,
      145, 147–51, 185–227
   as standalone system, 151
   system bending, 147, 150, 151
   system-related cf. application-specific
      efforts, 149
   team-oriented development, 150
Expert systems, 4, 23, 24

File transfer, GURU, 132–33
Financial services, 21–22
   sample application, 70–73
First Class, 90–91
Focus control blocks (FCBs), ESE, 140–
      46, 148–49, 150
FORTRAN, 18, 44, 46
Forward chaining, 29, 35–37, 81, 155
   ESE, 144, 145, 146

Frame-based systems, 37–39, 88, 89, 159
Future trends, 153–61
   applications suitability, 159–60
   competitive forces, 160–61
   experience curve, management, 156
   increasing sophistication, 156, 159–60
   organizational accommodation/assimila-
      tion, need for, 157–58
   prices, 155–56
   risk, 157, 158, 160–61
   supportive technology, need for, 158–59

Generally Accepted Accounting Principles
      (GAAP), 70
Goals, 29–32, 112, 113
Graphic Data Display Manager (IBM),
      140, 148
GURU, 97, 115, 119–35, 139
   backward chaining and uncertainty, 128–
      30
   classify procedure, 131
   data storage in, 131–32, 134
   development environment, 122–27
   DO:, GOAL:, INITIAL:, and RULE:
      labels, 133
   DOS commands in, 132
   cf. ESE, 139, 140, 144, 149
   external routines, 132
   file transfer, 132–33
   Find clause, 134
   help, context-sensitive, 126
   integration and noninferential
      processing, 130–33
   cf. M.1, 121, 123, 124, 128, 129, 130
   Promotion Advisor in, 127, 132, 133–
      35, 178–84
   rigor, 129
   rule sets, parts, 124
   as standalone system, 135
   text processor, 134
   windows, 124–26

Hardware, 44–47
   purchase, 5–6
Holistic approach, 78, 81–85

IBM, 97, 102, 139–40 (See also Expert
      System Environment)
   PC series, 100, 109, 122
   training, 123
IF...THEN rules, 25, 38, 92
Implementation, system, 5
Inconsistencies, 91
Inductive approach, 23
Inference engine, definition, 32–33

Inferencing, 29–33
  ESE, 144–46
  GURU, 128–30
  M.1, 104–7, 118
Information as corporate asset, 3 (*See also* Knowledge)
Information systems
  lack of leadership, 13
  management, alignment, 60
Information technology, strategic competitive advantage, 6–14, 22
In-store point-of-sale product-scanning equipment, 66–67
Integrated cf. integratable systems, 70, 73
Integration and noninferential processing
  ESE, 146–47
  GURU, 130–33
  M.1, 107–9
Interfaces, 150
Inventory and use correlation, 26
Iterative data reviews, 151

Knowledge
  as capital good, 93
  chunks, 25–26, 34, 36, 79
  common-sense, 24
  as corporate asset, 3
  decomposition, 81, 103, 122
  management, 3
  ownership of, 60
  relevant, 34
  separation from reasoning, 25–29
Knowledge base
  rule-based. (*See* Rule-based systems)
  top-level cf. lower level, 103
Knowledge engineering, 26, 75–93
  automated knowledge acquisition, 89–93
  holistic approach, 78, 81–85
  knowledge representation, 85–89
  cf. traditional system development, 77–78
Knowledge engineers, 60
Knowledge management, 93, 157
KNOWLEDGE MANAGER (K MAN), 121
Knowledge representation, 85–89
Knowledge systems, 4, 72 (*See also* Development tools, knowledge systems)
Knowledge workers, 157

LINK, 109
LISP, 19–20, 44, 45, 46, 52, 53
LISP machines, 19, 45
Load control advisor, utility, 48, 61–66, 79–80, 82–83

Local area networks (LANs), 13
Lotus 1-2-3, 18, 27, 28, 49, 54, 101, 102, 103, 104, 126, 161 (*See also* Spreadsheets)
Lower-level knowledge bases, 103

M.1, 26, 28, 97, 100–118, 139
  BOTH and EITHER statements, 106
  development environment, 101–4
  documentation, 101
  DONTASK function, 104
  cf. ESE, 139, 141, 142, 145, 146, 149, 150
  expressions, 144
  external routines, 107, 109, 117
  cf. GURU, 121, 123, 124, 128, 129, 130
  inferencing and uncertainty, 104–7, 118
  INITIALDATA function, 104
  integration and noninferential processing, 107–9
  Promotion Advisor in, 109–17, 165–75
    simplified knowledge base, 176–78
  system bending, 107, 108, 118
Macintosh, Apple, 45
Mainframe-oriented systems, 55–56
Maintenance, system, 5
Marketing, localized/regional, 160
The Marketing Workbench (McCann), 66
Market research, 160
McCann, John, 66
Memory, semantic network model, 37
Menus, pop-up/pull-down, 45
Meta-Facts, 113, 114, 115
Micro Data Base Systems (MDBS), 97, 123, 139, 140 (*See also* GURU)
Microsoft, 102
MIS groups, 60, 63, 64, 72, 134
Mouse, 45
MS-DOS, 109, 122, 132
Multiple regression, 92
MVS, 140
MYCIN, 29, 33

Noninferential processing
  ESE, 146–47
  GURU, 130–33
  M.1, 107–9
Novell Netware 286, 122

Object-oriented systems, 88, 89, 159
  development tools, 37–39
  cf. rule-based systems, 38
Organizational accommodation/assimilation, need for, 157–58
Ownership of knowledge, 60

PARC facility, Xerox, 45
Pascal, 46, 140
PC-DOS, 109, 122, 132
Personal computers, 8–9, 53–55
  corporate environment, 47
  development tools, 80
  interfaces, 45
Point-of-sale product-scanning equipment,
    66–67
Porter, Michael, 9
Prices, future trends, 155–56
PRISM, 139
Product-scanners, 66–67
Project leader, corporate, 5
PROLOG, 19–20, 100
Promotion Advisor, sample application,
    97–100
  ESE, 139, 142, 144, 145, 147–51, 185–
    227
  GURU, 127, 132, 133–35, 179–84
  M.1, 165–75
    simplified knowledge base, 176–78
Proof of concept, 81, 83, 84
Prototyping, rapid, 81

Query mode, 91

R1 (DEC), 35
Rapid prototyping, 81
Reasoning cf. knowledge, 25–29
Reductionist approach, 78, 81, 85
Regression, multiple, 92
Relevance
  knowledge, 34
  rules, 30–31
Research cf. business environments, 44–47
Robotics, 20–22
Rule-based systems, 26–28, 81, 83, 88,
    89, 155, 159
  cf. object-oriented systems, 38
  relevance, 30–31
  structured, 88, 89
  unstructured, 88, 89
Rule-induction systems, 80, 89–93
Rule sets, 127
  GURU, 124

S.1, 100
SCRIPT text processor (IBM), 140
Semantic network model, human, 37
Simulation modeling, 18
Software, purchase, 5–6
Spreadsheets, 51, 52, 53, 54–55, 86 (*See
    also* Lotus 1-2-3)
  systems integration, 134, 135
Standalone design, 59, 135, 151

Stanford University, 100, 139
Strategic competitive advantage, 6–14, 22
Structural Query Language (SQL), 13, 49,
    140, 145
Structured selection, 29, 34, 64
System
  implementation, 5
  knowledge, 72
  maintenance, 5
System bending
  ESE, 147, 150, 151
  M.1, 107, 108, 118
Systems development
  mainframe-oriented, 55–56
  team-oriented, 150
  traditional, cf. knowledge engineering,
    77–78
Systems engineering, reductionist
    approach, 78, 81, 85

Team-oriented development, 150
Teknowledge Inc., 97, 101, 118, 139, 140
    (*See also* M.1)
  training, 123
Three era model, 6, 7–8, 59
Tools, 3, 4–5 (*See also* Development
    tools, knowledge systems)
Top-down development, 23, 78, 81
Top-level cf. lower-level knowledge bases,
    103
Tracing function, 103
Truth maintenance, 38

Uncertainty, 33–35
  ESE, 144–46
  GURU, 128–30
  M.1, 104–7, 118
Uniform Price Code, 67
UNIX, 122
Utility, electrical, sample application, 48,
    61–66, 79–80, 82–83
Utility variables, 127

Value-added stream, 10–11, 12
VisiCalc, 18
Vision processing systems, 20–22
VM operating system, 140

What if analysis, 71, 161
Windows, 45, 124–26
Word processing, 51, 53, 54–55, 101
Work group computing, 72
Workstations, AI, 19, 20

XCON (DEC), 35
Xerox PARC, 45